The Economics of Organizational Choice

The Economics of
Organizational Choice

Workers, Jobs, Labor Markets, and Implicit Contracting

Marvin E. Rozen

Ann Arbor

THE UNIVERSITY OF MICHIGAN PRESS

1994   1993   1992   1991   4   3   2   1

Library of Congress Cataloging-in-Publication Data

Rozen, Marvin E.
    The economics of organizational choice : workers, jobs, labor
markets, and implicit contracting / Marvin E. Rozen.
        p.   cm.
    Includes bibliographical references and index.
    ISBN 0-472-10278-8 (alk. paper)
    1. Industrial organization.   2. Industrial management—Employee
participation.   3. Employee motivation.   4. Labor market.
I. Title.
HD31.R787   1991
302.3′5—dc20   91-28042
                                                                CIP
                        73696

British Lib.   ...ng in Publication Data

Rozen, Marvin E.
    The economics of organizational choice : workers,
    jobs, labor markets, and implicit contracting.
    I. Title
    658.4

    ISBN 0472102788

Distributed in the United Kingdom and Europe by
Manchester University Press, Oxford Road,
Manchester M13 9PL, UK

For Frieda and our children:
Yona and Paul, Leah, Sarah, Miriam,
Josh and Hoa, and Elihu

Preface

Justifying one's work in a preface, although not uncommon, is usually a tactical mistake. It appears too defensive; after all, a book should speak for itself and stand or fall on its own merits. Yet in this case, perhaps the book's unorthodoxy condones such an approach. (For some very broad parallels, see the prefaces in Keynes 1936; Scitovsky 1976; and Frank 1985.) The book goes against the grain of much professional work in economics; it tries to stake out a position in that treacherous middle ground between those works concentrating on formal and tight logical exercises in high economic theory and those focusing on econometric and statistical inquiry; and it challenges some of economists' most ancient and deeply held shibboleths and verities.

It argues that organizations are important for efficient resource allocation; that organizational choice, far from being predetermined and constrained to fall within narrow boundaries, is a very open and lively issue and reflects fundamental differences in views on jobs, workers, and the milieu in which they interact; that many developments within the discipline, when synthesized and properly interpreted, point toward the growth of more cooperative and participative organizational forms; and that, virtually unimaginably, something akin to a "free lunch" may be the sturdy twin of such organizational reform. In short, once the view is accepted, as increasingly seems to be happening, that getting potentially highly productive workers to do what they can and should do is not simply a matter of paying the right wage and monitoring performance, but a more complicated and formidable undertaking, then organizational forms geared to that objective—what the book terms *implicit contracting plus*—become a natural focus of attention.

Vigorous objections to these arguments will be raised. First, is such a radical departure necessary, why fight against the success of traditional approaches, why not stick with the familiar and tractable, why take Stigler's "mighty leap" into such unknown territory? Second, it will be suggested that there is nothing really new in this approach, the specific points are well known, have indeed been often made by others, and the exercise is really caricaturing the state of received theory; conveniently, a straw man. Third, it is not simply heretical but, more pointedly, just plain wrong; its logic is not bound by any adherence to maximizing behavior, its implications do not square with observation, and its factual basis is slender and precarious. Finally, it does not lead anywhere, neither generating new and testable hypotheses nor setting an agenda for alternative research programs; it would have the profession embark on chasing will-of-the-wisps.

Such criticisms are not completely misdirected; they mark potential dangers, warn against slipshod assertion, caution to proceed extremely carefully. But they can also be effectively rebutted. To argue with success is the precondition for doing better, and in any case, economists can hardly point to an unblemished record of invincibility at either the theoretical or practical level. Exploring the implications of organizational choice is not a mighty leap into the unknown; it simply extrudes the consequences of changing views of workers, jobs, and their milieu. Similarly, novelty is not the defining prize; rather, the objective is to draw upon the diverse contributions of others and, through synthesis and rearrangement, present a fundamentally different view of relatively familiar material. Nor is it desirable or, given the nature of the profession, possible to claim infallibility and possession of absolute truth. I have tried to make my arguments soundly and reasonably explicative; naturally, others may, and will, disagree. Clearly, vigorous competitors cannot be excluded from the marketplace of ideas. It would be a strange economist who is blind to the virtues of competition, so the ruling spirit is the more contenders, the merrier and the more ultimately productive the outcome. Exclusivity is not sought, and I am comforted by my heresies usually finding themselves in very good company and resonating nicely with the work of many other economists.

Finally, I simply disagree that the paths followed are likely to lead nowhere; above all, economists must more straightforwardly confront the complexities of human behavior and motivation and the influence of institutional circumstance, rather than make do with one-dimensional maximizers placed within an antiseptic and artificial world. Or, as I suggest in the book, economics and "economisticism" must part company. If there were not, prospectively, an attractive payoff from exploring issues of organizational choice and the motivational considerations behind them, the subject would hardly be the focus of such rapt and extensive attention. Profound changes in job and worker qualities and in the firm's defining environment, efficient production frontiers, the influence of organizational form and motivational variability on productivity, the role of conflict and contestation in determining organizational choice, the sources of differing innovation propensities, the interest in flexible manufacturing and service systems, cross-sectional differences in firm performance within a country, and comparative studies across national boundaries—these constitute a research agenda guaranteed to keep economists busy for a long time.

It is thus in a spirit of reconciliation that I make a case for the importance and sweep of organizational choice. Tension among alternative explanations, dismissing none, building upon many, incorporating what seems most useful, rejecting the idea that perfection has already arrived—all such operational guidelines are relevant. Economics is like an oyster that needs a splendid kind of irritation occurring within to eventually produce exquisite and universally admired pearls of accomplished wisdom. When all is said and done, where is the economist completely and truly content with the state of our discipline? This book attempts to do its part in furthering this necessary process of improvement.

I must acknowledge my indebtedness to my colleagues, Irwin Feller, Gerry Glyde, Ray Lombra, Jan Prybyla, Mark Roberts, and Jim Rodgers, who were kind enough to read various parts of this book and give me their valuable comments. Colin Day and a reader for the University of Michigan Press also provided some very useful insights. They are all, of course, not responsible for the book's contents. So too, my wife, Frieda, provided some very helpful suggestions. And finally, I would like to thank the University of Michigan Press for permission to incorporate some material that draws upon my chapter in Weiermair and Perlman 1990 and to acknowledge my indebtedness to Barbara Cohen for compiling the index.

Contents

CHAPTER 1

Introduction

For economists, the worst of times can paradoxically be the best of times. The more troubled the real world, the greater the opportunities for useful practical advice; the more unsettled and controversial the world of economic theory, the greater the potential for innovative analytical advance. Like the duties of physicians confronted with a major epidemic, agendas become well defined and urgent. Do labor markets function efficiently? Is the internal organization of firms appropriate? What vision of the theory of the firm can best tie labor markets and work organization together, and how can such a vision be incorporated within the ever-changing tableaux of economic growth and structural adjustment? Can firms' organizational arrangements contribute toward achieving the macroeconomic goals of full employment and a stable price level and assisting the economy to respond more smoothly and promptly to the inevitable transformational imperatives posed by a more integrated and rapidly adjusting world economy?

These musings are prompted by recent developments in both worlds. In the real world, economic troubles have persisted for almost two decades; the seventies were marked by an inflationary binge, oil price shocks, and lagging productivity growth; the eighties have been characterized by relatively slow growth, moderately high unemployment, persistent Third World debt problems, international imbalance among industrial countries, and unresolved doubts about achieving macroeconomic stability and smooth processes of economic transformation. Many of these issues continue into the nineties, and the record does not instill confidence regarding the future.

Similarly, theoretical disarray is much in evidence: the neo-Keynesian synthesis is being shunted aside by the new classical resurgence—the advent of "real business cycles" threatens to reduce macroeconomics to a minor offshoot of general microeconomic theory, and microeconomics itself is being relentlessly pushed by some into a never-never world of perfect markets and superrational maximizing behavior. Although economists have never been noted for singing in unison, today's cacophony outdoes our reputation.

Accordingly, this book is concerned with broad and basic themes relating to how work is organized and the consequent implications for the structural forms and behavioral modalities of the firm. There has been both an explosion of interest by economists in these matters and, as adumbrated above, the usual spate of sharp disagreements and divergent positions. Such divisions cut across many categories: theoretical and abstract versus practical and concrete, traditional versus unorthodox, austerely formal versus suggestively impressionistic, rigidly deterministic versus substantial wiggle room, laissez-faire versus interventionist, or a narrowly economic versus a more widely ranging outlook.

With regard to such polarities, this book approaches organizational choice issues more from the direction of the second-indicated in each case than the first. In so doing, it argues against a rigid, deterministic, superrational conception of the firm and a parallel view of markets functioning as instantaneous clearing mechanisms. It suggests, rather, that once the richness and complexity associated with the combination of potentially very productive human beings, idiosyncratic and essentially nonmonitorable jobs, and circumscribed and imperfect labor markets and matching processes becomes more widely appreciated, then the firm's traditional organizational form will be seen to have serious flaws. Incentive structures matter much more, and their content embraces wider considerations than a simple money wage that will invariably call forth a standard quantum of effort. Being trustful, cooperative, honest, and forthcoming, sustaining high levels of effort, initiative, and intensity, developing and fully deploying one's firm-specific human capital—all are very relevant. Motivating workers along such lines will be necessary to achieve the best that workers can do in jobs that they largely control.

The organizational structure to which such considerations point is likely to be a variant of what I term *implicit contracting plus*, IC+, wherein the employment relationship is defined as the long-run interests of the parties being best served by developing an ambience of trust and cooperation. In other words, the narrow confines of a simple, cut-and-dried, quid pro quo exchange of work for pay are too restrictive to tap the full potential for high-level performance when both work and workers are so multifaceted and labor markets so imperfect. Consequently, organizational innovation implies that most elusive of all prizes, something akin to a "free lunch," as fairly modest changes in work arrangements can lead to quite substantial gains in output and productivity. Thus, Blinder (1990, 13) has suggested, "It appears that changing the way workers are *treated* may boost productivity more than changing the way they are *paid*, although profit sharing or employee stock ownership combined with worker participation may be the best system of all" (italics in original). As I will demonstrate, such views are neither hopelessly naive nor unimaginable, but they do confront the great obstacle of rearranging the balance of power within the firm, and that is never easy.

I am not unmindful of the many hurdles lying in wait for those suggesting such radical departures from the more traditional paths economists tread. Since the presumption of agents trying to do the very best they can for themselves lies at the center of an economist's universe, how can outcomes be improved upon—except where well-known conditions, like externalities, generate market failure? Despairing of where the silly-clever relentless logic of unrestrained maximizing is taking our discipline, Paul Samuelson (1989, 97) has prophetically intoned: "The refutation of unrealistic paradigms will come from prosaic scientific researches, and even from investigations carried on by rational expectationists themselves. It is not elder statesmen's wisdoms that kills off a young whippersnapper's foolishness, but rather another whippersnapper's regression data." Although the old-fashioned character of my arguments will be offputting to many, the division of labor still has its uses, and others may wish to dress up my thoughts in more modern techniques.

I am under no illusion that all work and all workers are cut from the same cloth, and I am aware that the argument extends only to a well-defined (but large and important) subgroup and is not universally applicable. Yet I would also insist that their numbers are increasing. Further, since my argument suggests a positive role for public policy, that position may seem retrograde in a day and age when many assume that the pursuit of narrow private interest will inevitably and fatally infect any public endeavor, no matter what its professed purpose may be. Suffice it to say that I believe there is still room for fashioning the intelligent use of public measures to achieve collective goals or, as in the title of a book by Charles Schultze (1977), for "the public use of private interest."

Finally, I must point out that the red thread running through most of the more traditionally minded new approaches to the theory of the firm is the belief that economic agents, in the natural pursuit of their self-interest, continuously and meticulously weigh the costs of being caught doing wrong against the potential gain from their violation of commonly accepted social norms and moral injunctions. Only self-interest can prevent cheating and dishonesty; hence, prospective loss therefrom must always dominate the possibility of gain. Organizational choice, in this view, becomes largely focused on inhibiting shirking, ensuring compliance, extracting the fulfillment of agreements, and compelling observance in a Hobbesian-like world in which cunning and crafty agents are forever seeking their own narrow and selfish aggrandizement. How to respond to this endemic moral hazard must then be at the very core of thinking about economic organization.

Such an unremittingly and unrelievedly harsh view of human beings (not faceless economic agents) and the nature of the work relationship cannot, I believe, be the proper foundation for a general theory of organizations. Certainly self-interest matters, honesty and forthcomingness are not in infinitely elastic supply, and human beings are not saints. But it is one thing to take such considerations into account in thinking about organizational structure; it is something very different to make them the completely controlling factor in organizational design. Implicit contracting plus tries to redress this tilt by suggesting that the employment relationship rests upon a more complicated range of interactions than merely preventing cheating and that unleashing the full creative powers of human beings as productive agents should be the true object of organizational choice.

Plan of the Book

As this brief introduction indicates, new views of the nature of the firm and their application to major economic issues raise far-reaching and substantive questions that require analysis and explanation in detail. Accordingly, the plan of the book is as follows. Chapter 2 will introduce the concept of IC+, briefly compare it with its neoclassical competition, and raise some issues concerning this rivalry. Chapter 3 will focus on the external labor market and the short-comings and anomalies revealed in the labor allocation process. Chapter 4 will discuss the operation of the internal labor market as it seeks to respond to those deficiencies, and how various characteristics of the employment rela-tionship bear upon the firm's potential efficiency and productivity. Chapter 5 will tie these considerations together to make the case for an enriched version of implicit contracting, and chapter 6 will explore, in detail, the neoclassical critique of implicit contracting and the counterresponse. Chapter 7 will dis-cuss the labor-managed firm and its relationship to implicit contracting. Chap-ter 8 will spell out, in greater detail, the implications of these various con-siderations for the future shape of work organization. Chapter 9 will contain a concluding summary of the book's argument and a brief evaluation of its relevance to some important current economic issues.

CHAPTER 2

Implicit Contracting, Free Lunches, and the Theory of the Firm

Disharmony among economists is often a reprise of an old and continuing argument between true believers, who have great faith in the market's powers to work virtual miracles, and those skeptics who doubt its magical qualities for almost painlessly creating near bliss out of chaos. Robert Solow (1980, 1–2) has elegantly stated this issue:

> There is a long standing tension in economics between belief in the advantages of the market mechanism and awareness of its imperfections. Ever since Adam Smith, economists have been distinguished from lesser mortals by their understanding of and—I think one has to say—their admiration for the efficiency, anonymity, and subtlety of decentralized competitive markets as an instrument for the allocation of resources and the imputation of income. . . . Simultaneously, however, there is an important current in economics that focuses on the flaws in the price system, the ways that real markets fail because they lack some of the characteristics that make idealized markets so attractive. . . . There is a large element of Rohrschach test in the way each of us responds to this tension. Some of us see the Smithian virtues as a needle in the haystack, as an island of measure zero in a sea of imperfections. Others see all the potential sources of market failure as so many fleas on the thick hide of an ox, requiring only an occasional flick of the tail to be brushed away. A hopeless eclectic without any strength of character, like me, has a terrible time of it.

Solow's strictures, and the great practical difficulties and heightened theoretical controversy mentioned in chapter 1, are a proper background for an inquiry into how changing views about what happens in labor markets and on the job can lead to substantive revisions in the theory of the firm. At issue are diametrically opposed notions about the organization of the firm, embracing not only fundamental questions of economics but also directly practical applications of great current importance. On the one hand, a new line of thought, exemplified by an enriched concept of implicit contracting (what I call IC+), is developing that emphasizes the firm's internal organization—

5

especially the complicated relationships among skilled and experienced work-groups, incentive structures, and workplace behavior—as the critical element determining its ultimate performance. On the other hand, along more tradi-tional, neoclassical lines, more sophisticated views of external market circum-stances and agent rationality in decision making (what I shall call NC+) are finding renewed support and strength among many economists as the all-powerful directing influence on firm behavior. For both, organizational choice seems to matter a great deal.[1]

Implicit Contracting and Neoclassical Views of the Firm

The implicit contracting view stresses the overriding importance of skilled workgroups and the shared continuity of their on-the-job experience for achieving high-level firm performance. The firm is viewed as an organic entity whose constituent members have attained, through long years of work-ing together, a considerable accumulation of firm-specific human capital and a highly refined sense of teamwork and group dependence. Productivity in the workplace depends upon their effort supply and willingness to fully utilize these capabilities for working together. Such performance cannot be com-manded or ensured through vigilant watchfulness. Rather, it must be induced by an incentive structure that recognizes this dependence upon workers' con-tributions. Nor can the prospective sanctions stemming from market pressures be relied upon to compel workers to always do their best. Generally speaking, considerable slippage in the links connecting specific on-the-job activities to ultimate market outcomes inhibits the speedy and direct transmission of such pressures.

As with all contracts, the elements of reciprocal offer and acceptance are present: firms offer to provide something of value to workers—say, the prom-ise of more stable income growth or, more generally, equitable and beneficial treatment—in return for something of value to them—say, a lower wage bill or workers accepting the obligation to be forthcoming and put out their best effort. The implicit feature of such contracts is that the behaviors and con-tingencies covered cannot be fully specifiable a priori since they are neither easily described nor verified. They are subjectively perceived by all parties,

---

1. For some representative samples of the new approach, see Putterman 1986b; Dow 1987; Yarbrough and Yarbrough 1988; Aoki 1988a, 1988b, 1990. For the more traditionally based approach see Alchian and Demsetz 1972; Jensen and Meckling 1979; Williamson 1985; Milgrom and Roberts 1988; and Carmichael 1989 and 1990. Some have called the latter the New Eco-nomics of Personnel, or NEP (Jacoby and Mitchell 1990). A recent symposium.(Mitchell and Zaidi 1990a) explores many of these same themes, and particularly Jacoby's article therein, is very close to my position, both in substance and spirit. Finally, several chapters in a recent Brookings volume (Blinder 1990) that takes up the closely related aspect of pay systems and productivity outcomes also support, in many respects, my general argument.

and this quality leads to a self-enforcing mechanism as each party adheres to the understanding as long as its expectations concerning the other party are broadly being realized. A substantive breach by any party will probably trigger a like response from the other. These mutual understandings must be implicit, since a worker cannot successfully sue a firm for breaching non-specific obligations or indefinite undertakings any more than a firm can legally compel workers to invariably do their best. Actualizing sophisticated and complicated quid pro quos must be volitional; each party must believe that honoring implicit agreements is the best way of furthering its interests.

In addition, most jobs are not a simple collection of rote and easily assignable activities, and relying on supervision and sophisticated monitoring technology is unlikely to be cost effective. Workers, in brief, must be "turned on," for the firm's success depends upon their initiative and intelligence. There are no substitutes or shortcuts; a newly recruited, identical collection of workers, without comparable experience in working together, would not be as productive. As many managerialist theorists have long contended, work-groups perform best when they internalize the firm's goals. The practical consequences of implicit contracting would then be to devolve authority, foster peripheral initiatives, decentralize decision making, and encourage more participative and cooperative actions by workgroups. All parties in the firm would be joined in an implicit contract that says that if each treats the others correctly, then all will do their best. From that simple basis, improvement in levels of performance can reasonably be expected.

It should be noted, however, that both implicit contracting concepts and the allied notions, inter alia, of participation, consultation, joint decision making, cooperation, gain sharing, and employee ownership will inevitably be, to a greater or lesser degree, ambiguous and imprecise: partly because the exact nature of these relationships in any specific case is more a matter of rough empirical judgment than of formal specification, and partly because distinctions among them will differ, or even be glossed over, across analysts. This is a formidable problem; different studies will use the same words to describe different phenomena, causing great confusion, hindering comparability, and limiting generalization.

Further, the precise content and mechanisms of such arrangements are obviously more important than formal categorization. Judgments concerning the severity of these difficulties vary. Some would argue the absence of formal precision is a fatal flaw; others would be challenged to find reasonable functional equivalents for conceptually purer categories. My own bias in this matter is that, as the old saw goes, it is better to be vaguely right than precisely wrong, but I am aware that might be a minority view within the profession.

Many years ago, however, D. H. Robertson (1952, 49) in characterizing the "English process of jollying along" expressed at least part of the implicit contract idea most pungently: "encouragements which are not quite promises, frowns which are not quite prohibitions, understandings which are not quite agreements." In any case, as the text indicates, I will be using a generalized notion of implicit contracting that is sufficiently broad to cover the widest spectrum and most subtle array of understandings, arrangements, undertakings, and agreements that firm members can devise. The more subtle, intangible, and complicated the behaviors, the greater the reliance must be on such implicit relationships. As with trying to nail down other areas of infinitely varied human behavior, such description can hardly claim the status of an existence proof, but it is, nonetheless, helpful in fixing the phenomena under discussion more clearly and vividly in our minds.

The neoclassical position rejects these arguments for implicit contracting. Theoretically, it cannot accept what it views as a cavalier dismissal and disregard of the market's reach and potency. There is too much wiggle room in the implicit contracting formulation, depriving economic theory of its anchor in rational maximizing behavior. An immense variety of plausible explanations could then be entertained, no one of which would be demonstrably superior; such outcome variability and the economics of "anything goes" and "it all depends" do not seem very promising. Furthermore, neoclassical theorists believe their explanations of observables are sufficiently complete and accurate to make other approaches superfluous; whatever outcomes occur can be accounted for within the neoclassical framework. Implicit contracting is not only misguided, it is not even needed.

Empirically, neoclassicists point to trends concerning firm behavior and performance that run directly counter to the logic and predictions of implicit contracting. Mergers and acquisitions have boomed and an unprecedented wave of corporate restructuring has occurred; such developments scarcely give pride of place to associational continuity. Similarly, firms are demanding and receiving concessions from their workers, imposing stricter work regimes on them, and, in general, showing little inclination to devolve real authority. Such observations suggest that implicit contracting is more a gleam in the eyes of its creators, an artful construction, perhaps, but certainly not reality.

The neoclassical resurgence stresses that firms must be mean and lean. Not, of course, as pejorative injunctions, but as matter-of-fact descriptions of survival imperatives in an increasingly competitive world. The market is, as always, a stern disciplinarian, quickly handing out its punishments and rewards. Firms respond with alacrity or go under. These pressures become diffused to all parts of the firm in a Darwinian survival process, ensuring that only the fittest remain.

The firm must, accordingly, be mean in the behavioral sense of tough-minded, no-nonsense, top-down testing and evaluation, done continuously to weed out nonperformers and the less adept; slipshod practices and bad habits from palmier days must be ruthlessly excised to stay competitive. Likewise, the firm must be lean in the architectural sense of a streamlined and restructured organization that sheds and adds functions, contracts and expands activities, acquires and is acquired by other firms—all in harmony with the market's diktat. The firm has to be unsentimentally calculating and must never evade hard choices. The future is always now. This continuing structural reorganization may seem to levy cruel and unfortunate suffering on some, but the longer the delay, the worse the ultimate hurt. Radical surgery is never anyone's idea of fun and games, but must be done when necessary.

As is readily apparent, these two views are based on sharply divergent positions on many different questions: How well do markets work? What motivates workers? Will firms always establish optimal organizational arrangements? Do firms change mostly through a process of internal renewal and regeneration or through radical surgery induced by external market pressures? In response to ceaseless economic change, should firms quickly and completely shut down adversely affected activities or subcontract them, rather than reshape their in-house capabilities? Is the process of adjustment more dependent upon workplace performance than upon decisions made in the executive suite and boardroom, and what are the connections between the two? What is the proper time-horizon over which the firm should evaluate its options? To what extent are workers robots automatically executing commands from above, or quasi-principals possessing initiatory capabilities and an inalienable zone of discretion over compliance? How important are pecuniary incentives relative to relationships of trust and willing cooperation? What are the respective merits of authoritarian versus participatory management styles? Do firms act solely out of efficiency considerations, or does maintaining existing power and authority relations dominate their decisions? How situationally sensitive must the firm's organizational form and behavioral modalities (and economists' notions of rationality and maximizing behavior) be? The possibility of very different responses to these various facets of the firm's structure and functioning accurately reflects the deep gulf between opposing views.[2]

What makes these questions theoretically significant is that many of them raise the "free lunch" implications of implicit contracting—the possibility that great gains in output and welfare are available, at trivial resource costs, because specific organizational choices can result in superior worker performance. In other words, the presumption that actual situations tend to be the equilibrium outcomes of maximizing behavior, inevitably exhausting all possible sources of net gain, does not hold true. Outcomes depend upon organizational specification, and the belief that somehow the most appropriate organizational choice will be made as the direct consequence of rational, maximizing behavior by economic agents is not warranted. For several different and powerful reasons that will subsequently be discussed fully, the equivalent of getting a free lunch is not idle speculation but a realistic option. That

---

2. For another broadly comparable analysis which conceptually contrasts the Japanese firm with the neoclassical firm and its emerging descendants, see Aoki 1988a and, especially, 1990.

is where implicit contracting leads and why the neoclassical view regards it with great suspicion. Neoclassicists believe that agents always strive, within contextual constraints, to do the best they possibly can and, hence, equilibrium outcomes cannot be improved upon; the world is, however, not so Panglossian and actual outcomes do not exemplify the reification of those economistic beliefs.[3]

Real-World Considerations

What constitutes the most efficient organization of the firm is not only a question of fundamental importance itself, but also an extremely pertinent one for dealing with two of our most persistent and troublesome economic ills: achieving both high levels of employment and price stability, and making the process of economic transformation less wrenching and painful. Neoclassicists are inclined to minimize such concerns since the presumption that markets work well implies that the former is a minor and transitional problem and not a matter for serious policy consideration (except to ensure the fulfillment of the requisite institutional arrangements for freely functioning markets). Likewise, achieving the latter is the basis for the argument for allowing markets to operate freely in the first place. No other mechanism can accomplish the required reallocation of resources as efficiently or as fairly as the unimpeded workings of market forces.

Implicit contracting, alternatively, views these issues as more difficult to resolve, and the ability to contribute to their resolution as one of its strong points; market forces work better within the supportive framework of implicit contracting. With regard to macrostabilization, the case for implicit contracting is based upon responding to the distributional pressures arising in a high-employment economy, partly through achieving a more rapid rise in income and partly through lessening the inherent conflicts over its sharing. Implicit contracting should lead to greater productivity gains, greater receptivity to incomes policies based on restraint and accommodation, improved job conditions and satisfaction easing pressure for wage increases, and a generally more cooperative and conciliatory attitude to macroeconomic issues as the

---

3. By economistic, or perhaps better still economisticism, I mean presuming the omnipotence of pure economic forces to somehow grind out, no matter what (but with well-known qualifications for externalities, public goods, and the like), an optimal outcome—a competitive-equilibrium allocation equivalent—that is unmodified in any way by the realities of social and institutional counterpressures. Such outcomes are generated even if one or more adjustment variables are unresponsive since, it is argued, other more flexible elements can always take up the slack. Compensating differentials are a perfect example. More crudely put, this presumption simply means no wiggle room. Not only does such narrow determinism not permit noneconomic factors and discretionary actions by individuals to play any role, but also chance, history, custom, and luck are largely banished from the adjustment mechanism. For a general critique along these lines, see Nelson and Winter 1982; Rozen 1985; Dickens et al. 1989; for a defense of the traditional position, see Reder 1989; McCloskey 1990.

natural result of those same qualities being stressed at the microlevel. In combination, these trends should greatly improve our macroeconomic performance.

Economic transformation is similarly made smoother by improved productivity outcomes, and by having a longer time-perspective and an augmented sense of social interdependence that translates into a greater willingness to compromise and be flexible. Trust, the essential component of implicit contracts, can calm some very rough passages. As Joan Robinson (1951, 189) once said, "The hidden hand will always do its work, but it may work by strangulation."[4] Precisely because markets work so crudely and painfully, and the required behavioral variation by economic agents can be extensively drawn out and resisted, an intervening and mediating structure, the firm, can cushion and facilitate those hard and difficult adjustments. The implicit contracting approach offers a supporting, not strangulating, hand when it will be most needed and useful.

One factor that has a pervasive impact and greatly complicates choosing between opposing views is that accepting the implicit contracting idea entails a reconsideration of the internal distribution of control within the firm. If workers become so functionally more important, then the firm's governance arrangements must surely be accordingly revised. Perhaps an analogy with the Berle-Means argument concerning corporate control might be helpful. As will be recalled, they argued that diffuse ownership of the large corporation meant that actual control shifted to the firm's managers. Implicit contracting extends this argument one further step, because the logical consequence of attributing collective functional importance to workers would be to strengthen their claim to an augmented share of control within the firm. But any such development must also recognize that, so far, the impact of these new entrants into the market for corporate control has been limited, because they can only bid strongly as a collectivity and their aspirations have not included control. Collective solidarity, however, can become heightened and aspirations can change. Hence, what implicit contracting does is potentially raise the stakes for the parties. Once the functional importance of workers is accepted, then the answer to the question of what is it that workers want can range very widely. And of course, the more far-reaching those goals, the greater the apprehension of existing decision makers. Thus, implicit contracting poses fundamental issues of power sharing and control, which will greatly affect the parties' strategic choices.

Can real-world observation settle these controversies over which form of work organization is superior and best suited for dealing with our major economic problems? Does irrefutable evidence exist in favor of one or the

---

4. Also note the following passage: ". . . [I]t is necessary to recognize that the classical mechanism does not exclude starvation from the mechanism by which equilibrium tends to be established" (Robinson 1951, 189).

other of such opposed views? If implicit contracting is the wave of the future, is it becoming more ubiquitous and has its growth acquired an irreversible momentum? And if implicit contracting is painted in such glowing terms, should not some obvious demonstrations of its amazing potency and growing presence be apparent? Alas, quick confirmation of these matters is elusive. The world of practice mirrors the world of theory; conclusive and absolute proof is not easily found. Instead, a more complicated and varied picture emerges that, although offering no final and definitive answers to the broad questions posed, is nevertheless instructive and suggestive.[5]

On the one hand, the general ideas embodied in implicit contracting have significant practical expressions and counterparts. Indeed, they even have movement status; they have received wide publicity, have institutional support of various sorts in public and academic life, and have acquired sufficient popular appeal to have become a rallying cry for a wide spectrum of political leaders. After all, who could find fault with a doctrine that stresses the virtues of trust and cooperation; as long as it remains a vague and general exhortation, it sounds like an idea whose time has come. And its concrete manifestations are apparent: Quality-of-Worklife and Employee Involvement Programs, a rich harvest of labor-management cooperation schemes, large percentage increases in employee stock ownership arrangements (although this trend is largely motivated by tax-savings and antitakeover reasons), wistful and envious glances at the way Japanese firms are supposed to function, and the rapid rise in managerial styles emphasizing a more participative approach— all are straws in the wind indicating differences from more authoritarian approaches to work organization. By these lights, the economic logic of implicit contracting seems to enjoy considerable practical support.

But on the other hand, if one probes deeper, offsetting factors are apparent. Failure and reversions have also been widely noted; intragroup and intergroup conflicts have been frequent and hard to overcome; the ratio of PR noise to actual content change has been high; where cooperation implies significant power rearrangement, the going has been treacherous; and organizational changes have frequently been made under very inauspicious circumstances, sometimes as acts of desperation and last resort, as when a failing enterprise

---

5. For some generally supportive evidence for this position, see the recent and comprehensive surveys of empirical work on the consequences of more cooperative and participative forms of work organization by Mitchell, Lewin, and Lawler (1990), Weitzman and Kruse (1990), and Conte and Svejnar (1990) in Blinder 1990. In addition, but more tangentially, surveys of the empirical literature on X-efficiency (Frantz 1988), frontier production functions (Schmidt 1986), and the impact of unions on productivity (Freeman and Medoff 1984; Addison and Hirsch 1989) touch upon some of the questions at issue, and are illustrative of similar problems of interpretation and measurement. Finally, scattered throughout the industrial organization literature are various attempts to track the effect of this or that variation in organizational or structural characteristics (small firm/large firm, franchising status, entry conditions, etc.) on consequential firm performance, and these studies, too, may be relevant.

turns to its workers to bail it out. It is thus one thing to stress the potential gains from implicit contracting and quite something else to overcome all the barriers to its actualization. Certainly circumstances, history, and chance might be expected to leave their powerful imprint on what is possible in any given situation, and mixed outcomes, rather than uniformity, should not be surprising.

Whatever the verdict on implicit contracting itself, the fact that events and trends relating to real-world firm behavior and structure—the mean-lean syndrome—seem to be inconsistent with it cannot be ignored. Some are even thereby ready to reject implicit contracting in toto. But that would be injudicious, because such contrary indications need to be interpreted more carefully. First, whenever power is at stake, its voluntary transfer is a rare event; those already in authority have an overwhelming incentive to preclude the shifts implied by implicit contracting. Second, the time frame is important; the process aspects of change cannot be forgotten, and what eventually emerges can be very different from that which currently obtains. Third, I am not arguing for universality; diversity in organizational forms can quite happily coexist, given the underlying variation in all the relevant circumstances. Finally, many dismissals of implicit contracting reflect an attitude of generalized incredulity; it is viewed as an unwarranted encroachment on traditional governance arrangements, too unsympathetic to and too radical a departure from orthodox theory, too wedded to unproven beliefs, and too naive about the capabilities of ordinary workers. Holders of such views will quickly accept countertrends as confirming its demise.

Another consideration in evaluating the status of implicit contracting would be the attitudes of workers' representative institutions toward it. If, indeed, workers are now recognized as being functionally more important, it is surely very strange that their main instruments for collective expression, the trade unions, are not in the forefront of any movement to transfer greater power and responsibility to workers. Are unions asleep at the switch, or is implicit contracting a will-of-the-wisp that should not be pursued? This area, too, needs to be explained.[6]

Everything so far discussed establishes that controversy abounds and that closure and finality are absent; indeed, as Solow's remarks suggested, this is

---

6. A recent indication, though, of a greater, but still circumscribed, union interest should be noted. The AFL-CIO is backing the establishment of an Employee Partnership Fund to help workers buy factories in danger of shutting down (*New York Times*, 20 February 1990). The Fund itself will be financed by private investors but have trade unionists as advisers. The Fund will operate only on "sound investment" principles: "only plants with clear potential to survive would be involved; the worker-owners would be denied any say in running the operation for at least several years, and the workers would be expected to accept wage cuts, agree to long-term contracts and possibly make other concessions to enhance the plant's prospects for survival." In turn, those agreements would be the basis for going to outside lenders to leverage the buyout.

an ancient quarrel among economists, and it would be presumptuous to believe that its ultimate resolution is at hand. In fact, some may ask what is to be gained by again analyzing these old and perhaps stale issues? As I hope to show in the following pages, two basic reasons can justify the exercise. First, the possibilities for greater consensus and agreement are by no means dim. For one thing, the simultaneous indication of several different strands of evidence may be more convincing when taken together than any single element standing alone. For another, the analytical concept of nesting, wherein seemingly radically opposed conclusions simply reflect strategic parameters of a broadly similar model taking on sharply different values, may be very relevant.

Second, in my view, an enriched implicit contracting approach has many convincing and relatively novel arguments in its favor, and these have not yet received sufficient exposure. In any case, in line with a recent suggestion by two eminent theorists, it should also prove useful to present an approach that "is in striking contrast to the situation in the economics of organization, where the vast bulk of the research has primarily been deductive theorizing and where too often the questions that the latest paper seeks to answer arise not from consideration of puzzling aspects of observed practice or from present trends in business organization, but from the desire to extend the analysis in an earlier paper that, in turn, may have been only tenuously connected to observation" (Milgrom and Roberts 1988, 450).

Equally striking is the extent to which the approach taken by most economists is so different from practitioners seeking to achieve concrete improvements in the performance of actual firms. For instance, in the recent book by the MIT Commission on Industrial Productivity (Dertouzas et al. 1989), the range of issues covered—integrated product development, appropriate time-horizons, fostering linkages and cooperative arrangements among many contributory agents, more closely connecting pure and applied research, and the need to overcome outdated business strategies, or, in the Commission's words, ". . .the weaknesses we discovered concern the way people cooperate, manage, and organize themselves, as well as the way they use technology, learn a new job, and interact with government" (42)—are not those usually stressed in the economics literature.[7] Is the presumption that

---

7. Compare Nalbantian's (1987, 24) similar remarks:

From what I have gleaned from the testimony of practitioners, the major sources of efficiency earnings available to the firm are in changes in the organization of work, in cooperative efforts to uncover and eliminate organizational impediments to productivity, and in facilitating the introduction of new processes and techniques that permit more efficient use of labor and capital resources. Ultimately, these efficiency earnings are attributable to specific behaviors of employees and can thus be conceived as inputs to production. The inputs associated with information sharing, innovation, monitoring activity, coordination, and decision making will tend to have more impact on group performance indicators than on individual ones.

people are doing, within contextual constraints, the best they possibly can somehow so inbred that it inexorably leads to not being overly concerned about whether, in fact, that is the case, and why if not so, and what can be done about that? Equilibrium and optimality are certainly analytically useful, but both Walras and Pangloss have their limitations as practical guides.

CHAPTER 3

External Labor Market Anomalies: Wages, Matchups, and Job Quality

In recent years, a rich, extensive, and highly detailed literature has emerged concerning what actually happens in labor markets and on the job. This research has covered a wide array of labor market topics, pushed beyond traditional boundaries, and led to exciting new ideas concerning the theory of the firm. These developments will be the subject of this and subsequent chapters. In this chapter, two specific anomalous sets of observations, mostly external to the firm and relating to wage determination and certain aspects of labor market operation, raise particularly intriguing and challenging puzzles for economic analysis and will be intensively scrutinized. Chapter 4 will focus on similar complexities relating to circumstances within the firm that have profound organizational choice implications. Chapters 5, 6, and 7 will discuss alternative approaches to the problems of interpretation and analysis in the theory of the firm raised by these external and internal labor market revisions.

As Nordhaus (1984, 420) has observed, if the speed of adjustment in perfect markets approaches that of light, it is 55 miles per hour for the labor market. Although it has long been recognized that the external labor market cannot be viewed as having the almost instantaneous adjustment properties of, say, a continuously equilibrating auction market, such caveats have traditionally been blithely disregarded. An ideally functioning mechanism has been generally assumed in which wages would very flexibly respond to whatever supply/demand dispositions prevailed, and in the process adjust to whatever other, mostly invariant, job attributes dictated as an offsetting compensating differential. The outcome of equal hedonic wages so established creates a pattern of interfirm, interindustry, and interoccupational compensation wherein equivalent workers would receive equal pay across such boundaries, and that pay would be directly and closely related, at the margin, to their relative productivity. Further, traditional theorizing also presumed that labor markets would always speedily clear, as appropriate wage movements would eliminate excess supply or demand; that jobs and workers would be, on a more or less continuous basis, suitably matched; and that the process itself approximated a system of free and voluntary exchange among relatively equal economic agents. Thus, in this idealized version of how labor markets function, little could go wrong in either wage determination or job-worker matching, and sooner rather than later, equilibrium in the sense of no possible further net improvements would be achieved.

Increasingly, however, these traditional notions have come under fire. With regard to wage determination, the following three anomalous propositions have emerged that challenge traditional views: (a) the link between wages and productivity is neither rigid nor automatic; (b) compensating differentials cannot be presumed to be invariably and completely offsetting to equalize hedonic wages; and (c) equally qualified workers do not receive equal pay for broadly similar work.[1] With regard to labor market functioning, a similar trio of propositions that break with conventional analysis is put forward: (a) many labor markets do not clear but are subject to considerable job rationing; (b) jobs and workers are not perfectly matched, and in particular, workers can be generally overqualified; and (c) labor market transactions should be viewed in a more complicated relational and conflictual context, rather than as examples of pure voluntary exchange among putative equals.[2] The major focus in this chapter will be on these kinds of external labor market issues, and a subsequent chapter will look inside the firm at comparable issues regarding internal labor markets. Taken together, these far-reaching reformulations set the stage for major revisions in the theory of the firm, which will be discussed in the following chapters.

The labor market puzzles implied by these issues seem simple and straightforward, but their resolution leads to uncharted and unfamiliar terrain: How can wages and productivity not be like Siamese twins? Why cannot wage and on-the-job adjustments equalize the overall attractiveness of work opportunities? How can different wages persist for equally qualified workers? What prevents labor markets from clearing and allows queues for some jobs and chronic shortages for others to persist? Why cannot the labor market operate smoothly and quickly to correctly match jobs and workers? What are the consequences of conflictual relationships and disparities in relative transactor strength for wages and working conditions?

Traditionally, movements in relative money wages have been assumed to play the major role in resolving such labor market questions. Wage changes are supposed to faithfully reflect relative productivities, offset all other aspects of the job, ensure that equally qualified workers are identically compensated, effectively eliminate excess supply or demand, be instrumental in properly

---

1. For (a) see Thurow 1975; Hodgson 1982; Nolan and Brown 1983; Frank 1984; Schultze 1985; Bishop 1987; Leonard 1987; Hutchens (1989); for (b) see Lucas 1977; Smith 1979; Viscusi 1979; Brown 1980; Duncan and Stafford 1980; Oi 1983; Triplett 1983; for (c) see Dickens and Katz 1987; Krueger and Summers 1988; Brown and Medoff 1989; Gibbons and Katz 1989; Helwege 1989; Katz and Summers 1989. For a general review, see Groschen 1988.

2. For (a) see Hall and Lazear 1984; Pemberton 1985; Stiglitz 1987; Akerlof, Rose, and Yellen 1988; Greenwald and Stiglitz 1988; Osterman 1988; for (b) see Rozen 1982; Arnott and Stiglitz 1985; Dickens and Lang 1985; Akerlof, Rose, and Yellen 1988; for (c) see Edwards 1979; Bowles 1985; Bowles and Gintis (1988 and 1990).

matching jobs and workers, and be the major bone of contention between labor and capital. What is changing is that, increasingly and as exemplified in the burgeoning literature, explanations stressing the role of current money wages have been supplemented and supplanted by views of labor markets and work organization emphasizing the strategic importance and role of nonwage working conditions and worker heterogeneity and of more active intervention by firms and workers in answering these kinds of questions.

Considerations relating to nonwage working conditions can, collectively, be called job quality. Job quality is concerned with the content of work in all its dimensions; in its most general formulation, it is the summation, excluding pay, of all the various attributes and characteristics defining the work environment: the nature of specific tasks and duties, the adequacy of supportive resources, supervisory arrangements, employment security, career prospects, general work ambience, and any other related aspects salient to workers. Pay is excluded because of its presumptive compensatory and equilibrating function, although, as already indicated, whether that function is in fact accomplished is doubtful. Likewise, worker heterogeneity refers to differences— often insufficiently captured by our usual measures and sometimes even dismissed as irrelevant and unimportant—in worker capabilities, attitudes, and motivations. Similarly, firm and worker activism is displayed in the much greater scope for intervention, in the variety and richness of their instrumentalities used in affecting outcomes, and in the importance of their interaction and strategic interplay. Though these labor market anomalies have arisen in a more or less uncoordinated way (even independently of each other) when considered together, they reveal similar and recurrent themes concerning what drives labor markets and the organization of work. Indeed, that such diverse questions lead to such similar responses reinforces the notion that a fertile new area for inquiry is opening up.

Focusing on the significance of job quality and worker heterogeneity, and greater firm and worker intervention, in labor market equilibrating processes will show why equilibration is so much more complicated and intricate. In particular, at least five considerations figure importantly: (*a*) adjusting job quality is a complex and multidimensional activity, thus making it inherently more difficult to achieve equilibrium outcomes; (*b*) likewise, worker heterogeneity has an important and hard to trace labor market impact; (*c*) job quality affects worker motivation, and thus cannot be viewed solely as something to be offset by wage movements; (*d*) unlike simpler approaches, neither jobs nor workers are considered so fixed and unchanging that matching is only a once-for-all sorting process, but instead their potential and actual variability over time requires more continuous labor market adjustment processes; and (*e*) the workplace is contested terrain, a battleground where conflict inherent in the employment relationship finds expression as firms and workers actively seek an advantage. In the equilibrating process, the current money wage counts for less, job quality and worker heterogeneity for more, and the modes and instrumentalities of firm and worker intervention are critical in accounting for observed outcomes. This message obviously has profound implications for how work should be organized and how labor markets operate best.

Wage Determination

The Wage-Productivity Nexus

Consider first, with regard to the cluster of issues surrounding wage determination, the links between wages and productivity. No one is suggesting the absence of any linkage whatsoever; rather and more subtly, no rigid and automatic relationship exists. Most simply, both wages and worker productivity depend on a great many other factors. The importance of the intermediary function of the firm in eliciting favorable productivity responses cannot be overlooked. The labor contract is open-ended, and both the quids and the quos can be extremely complicated. When viewed from the perspective of the employment relationship, the wage is an exceedingly more difficult concept than standard theory's effort bargain that entails a specific money payment for a fixed and easily verified quantum of well-defined effort and productivity in the workplace. Most of all, this perspective reflects the wage's multifunctionality: it serves many purposes, seeks to achieve multiple objectives, and accordingly, at the margin, must equate a rich variety of trade-offs.[3]

In addition to being a payment for normal effort, the wage must properly compensate the worker-financed investment necessary to produce the general and firm-specific human capital embodied in the worker. It may, in its efficiency variant, be the key to unlocking the sources of greater motivational intensity. It may embody an insurance charge-off, in recognition of another party bearing the risk of income fluctuations that would otherwise fall upon the worker. Its movements may be likewise damped precisely because firms want to decouple it, as a productivity-enhancing measure, from transient shifts affecting the firm's position. It can incorporate a flexibility premium as firms, anticipating the necessity for future changes currently unforeseeable, stockpile and pay for more adaptable and redeployable workers. It may reflect the dynamics and costs of search as workers vary their notion of an acceptance wage and, less frequently, employers adjust their offer wage. It can be heavily

---

3. ". . . an important body of empirical research is built around the assumption that, at any point in time, a person's wage indicates the person's productivity. Included here is the extensive literature on the human capital earnings function, as well as work on labor demand, market discrimination, and compensating differentials. That assumption has become controversial in recent years in part because implicit contract theories predict that compensation will be redistributed over the period of the contract. If a person's spot wage has little to do with spot productivity, but rather is an instrument of a complex insurance or deferred compensation scheme, then a reassessment of the empirical research may be necessary" (Hutchens 1989, 49).

influenced by pay relativities created by orbits of coercive comparisons within both internal and external peer reference groups. It can contain a lottery element, as workers with imperfect mobility place their bets on future careers and levels of earnings. Its level may only make sense in relation to all other conditions of work to which it may be adjusted to equalize, in equilibrium, the attractiveness with similar employments. To deter shirking, the wage may be set so high relative to alternative job opportunities that a substantial earnings loss would be the just deserts of anyone whose termination for being caught soldiering on the job would compel entry into that alternative labor market. Contrarily, the wage can be set at an initially low level but rising more sharply with time on the job so that the prospect of higher future earnings deters shirking today and will even encourage much diligence and striving among junior workers, as the generous and glittering compensation of senior staff is dangled before them. If a firm wants to reduce costly turnover and enjoy the luxury of selecting from a large queue of high-quality applicants, a premium wage will work wonders. If the firm is confronted by a strong and disciplined collective organization of workers or the threat thereof and has little chance of escaping such strait-jacketing circumstances, the wage will have to mirror the bargaining facts of life. Finally, if the wage must be responsive to the organizational rent-derived claim for a participatory share as a condition for the full deployment of worker talent and energy, then some form of residual sharing will constitute part of the workers' wage.

What has thus seemed, and usually been regarded as, a sharply defined and exact payment for a specific productivity quantum from labor services rendered has instead turned into a complicated compensation package put together for a bewildering variety of reasons and seeking to achieve diverse objectives. Some bear an obviously close relationship to productivity factors, but this functional multiplicity must leave its mark on the wage-setting process and makes it unlikely that so complex and conditional a set of circumstances can generate a simple, direct, and uniquely interpretable representation. In what proportion any given wage will be a return on capital, search reward, employer-stabilized magnitude, flexibility premium, lottery prize, risk-discount factor, effort elicitor, shirking deterrent, aspirational prod, relativity-dominated sum, equalizing differential, worker-selection device, bargained extra, and participative residual as well as payment for a standard quantum of effort is unlikely to be an instantly available computation. Rather, any specific wage and the pattern of wages, across jobs and over time, must reflect the interplay of these various considerations, and analysis must account for a more complicated set of forces. We have, unhappily, a surfeit of potential explanations for wage behavior from which pure productivity elements cannot be isolated and extracted. Wage multifunctionality would strongly suggest a careful review of specific circumstances to discover which considerations are paramount in any particular case. Simplistic explanations, like the wage-effort bargain, are of limited value, and wage behavior can only be interpreted in the context of the dimensional space of the employment relationship as applied in a particular circumstance.

This line of thought supports an interactionist approach between the firm and the worker because the wage now becomes the firm's instrumentality to use in generating a desired outcome through a more complicated causal pattern. In other words, the wage is part of a complex and interactive strategic game; rather than necessarily being the sole product of unmitigated and overwhelming market forces, wage patterns and movements will also reflect strategic interplay. By focusing on how wages are decisively influenced by purposive interactions between firms and workers, new explanations become possible and new insights emerge.[4]

For instance, as stressed in efficiency wage notions, the concept of a unique equilibrium wage crumbles if worker productivity is itself dependent upon how the firm treats its workers. Likewise, an excess supply of workers does not necessarily indicate labor market disequilibrium if maintaining high applicant quality is of major importance for the firm. Similarly, if jobs are looked upon as lifetime careers, then the decision makers' perspective will be vastly different than if they were in an auction market; the current wage offers only a partial view through a very narrow window, not the total picture. And general tendencies to decouple—the efforts to smooth real income change and allow for productivity trends—wage movements from the shocks of short-lasting economic transients are readily explicable from a career, rather than auction-market, perspective. The fact, moreover, that both high-wage and low-initial-wage schemes for deterring shirking are contradictorily argued suggests the need to proceed with caution in this area. The interactionist approach to wage behavior thus has greater richness and denser texture than traditional explanations. There are more options, more decisions, more strategic choices, and the usual explanatory variables are more conditionally weighted by the impact of specific circumstances; above all, unidimensional accounts, even those relying on such a relevant and critical factor as productivity, must be heavily discounted. If this is to be disparagingly labeled as "ad hoccery", that is not too high a price to pay for a closer approximation to a genuine explanation for wage behavior.

---

4. Compare the following summation by Nolan and Brown (1983, 284):

We have argued that over the last decade a concerted attempt by British employers to reassert control over the performance of work and the process of wage determination has given rise to a number of changes. These have tended to facilitate the development of firm-specific pay policies, expressed in the labor market in the form of intraoccupational wage dispersion. Employers have attempted to restructure their payment systems in order to minimize the tensions and disruption associated with unanticipated changes in the internal wage structure. This has tended to reduce their ability to respond to changing conditions in the external labor market. At the same time, the dispersion of wage offers to a large extent reflects the different tactics pursued by employers in their efforts to achieve greater cooperation and productivity within the firm.

Compensating Differentials

Once the complexities of wage determination are apparent, the remaining two anomalous aspects no longer seem so puzzling. First, consider compensating differentials. Ever since Adam Smith, economists have been aware that competition in the labor market sets relative wages, among homogeneous groups of workers and in the long run, to reflect the differential evaluation of job quality elements. In traditional equilibrium analysis, differences in job quality, as reflected in workers' evaluations thereof, are completely offset by pay differentials; labor market equilibrium entails on-the-job, hedonic wage equality. Money wages are supposed to vary to the extent required to compensate a homogeneous work force for all other, liked and disliked, aspects of the job; the less desirable those aspects, the higher the wage. But accepting this as a reasonable and commonsense theoretical implication and actually establishing such an outcome as empirical fact have not tracked parallel courses. Recently, this divergence between theoretical presumption and its factual affirmation has been strikingly presented in two different general investigations of the issue.

Brown (1980), in a sophisticated econometric inquiry, estimated an earnings function, using job and worker characteristics as regressors. After correcting for measurement error, omitted variables, and misspecification, he finds that, ". . .the coefficients of job characteristics that might be expected to generate equalizing differences were often wrong-signed or insignificant" (131). That is, desirable job characteristics were not associated with a lower wage. Brown hypothesizes that these negative results might arise because of an inability to account for wage effects arising from individuals utilizing their positive human capital or natural ability differentials to "buy" better job conditions rather than higher wages. In other words, job quality was sufficiently improved, presumptively in response to strong preferences of workers, to reverse the posited inverse wage–working conditions relationship. Although such results do not theoretically invalidate compensating differential notions—since wages could still be lower than they would have been if the disagreeable conditions had not been ameliorated—they do raise some questions. Similarly, Smith (1979) is very pessimistic about validating the presence of equalizing differentials because of the pervasive influence of worker heterogeneity: "Testing the theory of compensating differentials requires *a priori* specification of disagreeable job characteristics, but worker tastes are so heterogeneous that such *a priori* specification is usually treacherous" (343).

Other, more limited studies show equally confounding results. Some (Fogel 1979) also find, contrary to presumption, distinctly positive associations between wage differentials and desirable job quality. Others (Duncan and Stafford 1980) find that union wage premiums are also associated with better working conditions. Some survey research (Dunn 1977; Best 1978) suggests the persistence of disequilibrium conditions in the sense of unfulfilled advantageous trade-offs between wages and job quality whereby potential improvements in working conditions have a higher shadow wage than the existing wage rate, that is, a dollar's worth of expenditure on job quality would yield greater worker satisfaction than a dollar's worth of wage gain. Even in the most unambiguous case—the increased risk of fatal injury—estimates of offsetting wage differentials, from nine different studies, vary by a factor of 15 for a given increase in that risk (Ehrenberg and Smith 1982, 217). Still other studies, however, support compensating differentials by pointing to specific offsetting aspects of jobs, for example, greater absenteeism allowed (Allen 1981) or more generous pension provisions (Schiller and Weiss 1981), that compensate for lower wages. All in all, one can only be struck by the inability of careful economic research to establish clearly and unmistakably the case for equalizing differentials.

This research, taken as a whole, indicates that equilibrating processes are decidedly more complex than ordinarily presumed. Yet can such a strongly commonsense notion as equalizing differentials not be reflected in powerful forces operative in labor markets? Rather than refutation, these anomalies suggest the need for refinement and exploration in greater detail. Although labor markets do not operate in simple and uncluttered ways that speedily lead to equilibrium outcomes, a richer specification of relevant job and worker characteristics, and of their interaction, does suggest that observed outcomes, when interpreted within that richer framework, do indeed reveal distinct equilibrating themes. Two broad and seemingly contradictory conclusions will eventually emerge: (1) on the one hand, equilibrating processes will, in general, be incomplete; for several reasons the presumption that observable states will be very close to equilibrium outcomes is untenable in the circumstances of a richer and more relevant labor market framework; and (2) nevertheless, on the other hand, this more complete description does show that equilibrating tendencies are operative in areas and ways that are frequently not taken into account. In short, complexity broadens our understanding of the equilibrating process, but undermines our belief in equilibrium outcomes.

As its very name implies, compensating differential theory implicitly assumes that the relevant job characteristics will be relatively few and sharply defined and that workers will be a fairly homogeneous group. Further, jobs and workers are also presumed not to change very much, and, hence, the analysis can be focused on money wage movements as the equilibrating mechanism. But these presumptions can be misleading for two reasons. First, worker heterogeneity and job multidimensionality—significant (but frequently overlooked) variations in job and worker characteristics—are so extensive in both scope and frequency of change that simplicity and invariance assumptions will be highly inappropriate. Moreover, such variation will, in fact, be an integral part of the adjustment process; there is really no reason to single out money wages as the only, or invariably the most ubiquitous and frequent, equilibrating mechanism. Second, firms, in defining jobs, and workers are constantly reacting to and in conflict with, rather than being independent of, each other; such interactions are also an important element in equilibrating adjustments. Worker heterogeneity and job multidimensionality, and their mutual interaction in a conflictual context, are thus all likely to leave a definite imprint on what happens in labor markets. Inadequate analysis of their full impact is likely to be the basis for the observed inconclusive results; they deserve more complete investigation.

Worker Heterogeneity
Several factors are relevant with regard to worker heterogeneity. First, differential talent, capabilities, and tastes may both be often overlooked and matter very much. Brown's suggestion that differentially advantaged workers will "buy" better job quality will be part of any answer; strong bargaining positions, based on differential capabilities, will find expression in improvements in job quality. If a marvelous chef can't stand the heat, then rather than getting out of the kitchen, air conditioning can be insisted upon as a condition of continued employment. Brown's research may indicate that, in many workplaces, indigenous possibilities for improving work conditions, as a response to strong pressures from a highly valued work force, are likely to be very great, and thereby may explain the positive association between high wages and desirable job quality. As mentioned earlier, this result does not undermine the compensating differential hypothesis, since the relevant comparison wage would be even higher if such workplace amenities were absent. It should, however, increase awareness of those worker attributes that can stimulate, as a maximizing response, great ingenuity in redesigning jobs. Using summary and broad aggregate measures of worker characteristics (educational achievement, general work experience, skill indices, etc.) across job classifications to explain wage differentials may tell only part of the story. They need to be supplemented by more carefully and specifically delineating the potential for varying job duties and conditions in response to less obvious forms of worker differentiation.

We are all familiar with extreme cases of heterogeneity whereby star performers—athletes, entertainers, outstanding executives, legendary academicians—are afforded, as a matter of course, highly individualized and preferential treatment and working conditions. Similarly, less dramatic kinds of worker heterogeneity in more ordinary kinds of work situations will also induce concomitant, if less grand, variations in job quality. The fabulous chef's air conditioning may be, switching metaphors, just the tip of the iceberg. The pervasiveness of worker heterogeneity and its impact on job quality should not be overlooked just because such heterogeneity arises from more subtle worker attributes and workplace distinctions such as tenure, motivational intensity, specific experience, personal characteristics, or very specific and idiosyncratic local plant customs. For instance, in concordance with worker status differences, ostensibly similar jobs can vary greatly: in inclement weather, less senior carpenters do outside framing, and senior ones ply their trade inside; senior airline pilots fly by day, juniors pilot the red-eye. Even workers' job security may be differentiated because their seniority is departmentally based rather than plant based, or because some are protected from being bumped from their jobs when employment must be reduced, or in countless other ways that depend upon local circumstance and custom.[5]

More generally, workplaces are often characterized by considerable variability, from task to task and job to job, in the desirability and attractiveness of ostensibly similar job classifications. Differences in worker attributes can then serve as functional allocators in the apportionment of these differentiated jobs. It is a commonplace of occupational sociology to note that, in group or team work contexts, new workers undergo mild forms of hazing by being assigned the less desirable tasks and temporarily handicapped and more elderly workers will not be assigned the physically most demanding tasks. Somehow, too, experienced and valuable workers can always seem to carve out, often on the basis of seemingly unimportant and obscure differential attributes, special and favorable arrangements for themselves. The creation and apportionment of these kinds of gradations within a nominally uniform workplace, and the existence of such pleasanter niches and shelters, will thus reflect difficult-to-detect worker heterogeneity. Furthermore, such heterogeneity should not be viewed as just another example of omitted variables in a regression equation explaining wage differentials. That would not capture the much more complicated and interactive process in which workers are constantly striving to better their local work arrangements, and firms must respond by judging whether such job quality changes are desirable or harmful and whether they should be accepted, modified, or resisted. Even the careful measuring of differences in worker characteristics and working conditions may, unless forewarned, miss these sometimes subtle and elusive distinctions.

Second, although differential worker characteristics may not be transparent to outsiders, worker heterogeneity implies substantial benefits to insiders, firm and worker alike, from a greater emphasis on more thorough selection and screening processes. Despite the fact that only experience on the job can reveal the full range of possibilities for this mutual adjustment process between multifaceted worker attributes and variations in job quality, the parties' awareness of their more highly differentiated circumstances will inevitably influence prior matching procedures. Indeed, recent controversy over the propriety of genetic screening for susceptibility to chemicals and toxins in the workplace illustrates, in particular cases, how far such trends can go. Firms have powerful incentives to cull worker distributions for desired characteris-

---

5. As the examples indicate, and as common sense and casual observation suggest, whatever other differentiating characteristics might influence worker assignments and job quality, seniority is usually closely tied to gradations in job attributes.

tics.[6] By choosing workers favorably predisposed toward seemingly adverse job conditions, firms can offer a lower wage, thus again generating a positive, rather than an inverse, relationship between wages and generally perceived job quality. Equally significant, workers likewise have, other things being equal, an incentive to choose especially suitable jobs and workplaces. Self-selection, based on self-recognized heterogeneity, is always at work in the labor market. Accordingly, our observations are inevitably censored because firms and workers make prior choices rather than being randomly mated. From both sides, then, selection bias will be a more powerful force affecting labor market outcomes than is commonly supposed. Observed compensatory differentials are generated by a structured, rather than random, selection process.[7] Nevertheless, because matching procedures will inevitably be imperfect and restricted (and are also at least partially influenced by presumptions similar to those causing differential worker characteristics to be overlooked by outsiders) this structured selection process still leaves considerable room for improving job-worker matches.

Worker heterogeneity thus has very important labor market consequences, but its basis in human variability and its matter-of-course treatment in de facto work arrangements are both often insufficiently recognized.[8] Difficult-to-detect variations in worker characteristics, numerous oppor-

---

6. My favorite and long-standing example of imaginative matching is Charles Fourier's idea for his utopian phalansteries to reserve all the dirtiest jobs for children since they love to play in the dirt anyway; I doubt whether modern child-rearing authorities would endorse his proposal. Also in this connection, the "greenfield syndrome," whereby firms deliberately choose nonurban locations and less sophisticated workers as screens for desirable workforce quality, should be noted. In particular, the Japanese automobile transplants in this country, both for their locations and extensive psychological testing and evaluation, are a good example of the influence of strong prior preferences in selecting a desired workforce. Finally, since every job applicant is, for many firms, a medical insurance applicant too, screening for high-risk health factors becomes an important consideration, especially in connection with controversies over the risks associated with AIDS.

7. See Willis (1986, 535): ". . . the basic behavioral hypothesis of economics is the hypothesis that economic agents select the most preferred alternatives from their opportunity set. If the full opportunity set cannot be observed and opportunities vary across agents, then the act of optimal choice implies that market data are systematically censored and there is no guarantee that estimates based on interpersonal differences in earnings and schooling will accurately estimate the opportunity set of any individual in the population."

8. Some recent examples where differences arising from heterogeneity were found include the following: Levy (1988) found that income losses in recent periods were disproportionately suffered by less-educated males; Kletzer (1989) similarly showed that, among workers displaced as a result of the 1981–82 recession, blue collar workers had a much worse time finding reemployment; and Noyelle (1987) argues professionalization and paraprofessionalization are reshaping labor markets by conferring greater independence and bargaining power upon such groups. Similarly, a lively controversy over purported bias in the regression estimates of the relationship between wages and tenure directly involves selectivity factors relating to both worker heterogeneity and worker-job match quality (see Hutchens 1989, 59–61).

tunities for reshaping work arrangements, and the normal exercise of foresight by firms and workers condition labor market outcomes. Greater awareness of their impact can account for otherwise inexplicable job circumstances, and greater recognition of their importance can lead to a better understanding of job quality adjustments. Such adjustments could be highly beneficial, and result in lesser compensating differentials than would be the case for a homogeneous work force. Although an ounce of prevention, in the sense of adapting jobs to worker heterogeneity, might be worth pounds of compensating differential cures, insufficient appreciation of the full range of worker heterogeneity makes doubtful whether such potential gains have been fully exploited. Greater awareness of and sensitivity to worker heterogeneity could lead to both better matching on the job and greater variation in working conditions to fit the reality of substantial differences among workers.

Job Multidimensionality

Job multidimensionality—almost limitless potential variations in work arrangements—similarly confounds any simple application of the theory of compensating differentials. To begin with, the theory itself does not usually embrace the notion of changing job characteristics. Indeed, by making wage adjustments the universal offset of first, and usually only, resort for whatever ails the job, it implicitly assumes almost fixed and immovable job attributes. Yet job characteristics could, in principle, be readily adjusted to obviate the need for either greater selectivity in choosing workers or offsetting wage changes. In practice, however, although variations in job content, as the chef's air conditioning example illustrates, certainly do occur, their scope and completeness are likely to be limited. For reasons that I will outline, firms have been slow to undertake job quality adjustments and need more convincing of their benefits to overcome this reluctance and inertia. Moreover, accommodating workforce aspirations and skills through job change is easier said than done. Economists have generally shown little interest in the specific details of job restructuring, taking for granted its smooth and effortless accomplishment. In contrast, concern with the nature of job redesign has been a major preoccupation of managerial theorists and consultants. Several considerations are relevant in explaining why changes in work conditions have lagged.

First and closely related to the presumption of worker homogeneity, firms also generally assume that whatever new work arrangements are induced by economic and technological change, an assured supply of workers will be available and, consequently, no special adjustments concerning those arrangements are necessary. Who needs a tailor to alter garments that fit anyone and everyone? Workers, firms believe, accommodate themselves with relative ease to whatever the job requires because either existing workers are completely malleable or suitable workers are abundantly available. (Perhaps recent explicit concern about the quality of primary and secondary education and the increasing attention by business leaders to the social and economic implications of such failings might indicate a weakening of confidence concerning the adequacy of the labor supply.)

Further, there is little need to be concerned about the nature of work arrangements, since the technological imperative seems to demand that people must adapt to what technology provides rather than the other way round. Its reductio ad absurdum is when, as Lisl Klein (1976, 16) has so pithily stated, "an engineering designer is likely to feel most pleased that he has found a design solution when he has designed a human operator out of the system altogether, frequently in situations in which the answer is not the most economical one or the one which makes the system work best." The preponderant basis for most job design is to fit the person to the job. First define the job, then search for the appropriate workers to fill the slots thus created. As Michael Piore (1980, 23) has suggested, "labor is treated as a residual variable in planning and engineering. These processes in modern industrial society are essentially sequential (rather than simultaneous or iterative). One aspect of a plan or engineering design is completed before an attempt is made to resolve the next. The labor component is generally the last factor which is taken into account, virtually forcing the labor force to adjust to other aspects of the economic system rather than the other way round." The tragedy is that technology could really be, much more generally and extensively, a liberating force adapting, within the usual economic constraints, the workplace to more adequately fulfill human aspirations. Technology could do much more to make jobs more worthwhile. Instead, all too frequently, technological change has a life of its own, and workers must do all the adjusting.

Furthermore, a problem of interpreting the completeness and adequacy of specific job quality changes arises from the ease with which cosmetic alteration can be undertaken. Although in principle firms are free to adjust all the multidimensional elements of a job, they may emphasize peripheral and easily managed items. Adjustments that may appear substantial to outsiders can be of little intrinsic significance or importance, especially when personnel and public relations departments can always provide pretty packaging. Indeed, as Strauss (1976, 669) has emphasized:

American companies are suckers for gimmicks. Managers are too anxious to find short-cut solutions to complicated problems, particularly in the area of human relations. "The search for quick solutions, particularly to people problems, is a way of life in most organizations and is fueled by managers' need to demonstrate accomplishments rapidly in order to move on and up.". . . Companies try one attractive package after another, just as long as each promises a painless solution to their problems. Human relations, suggestions systems, the open door policy, brainstorming, zero defect programs—all have had their day. Each is tried in turn and then allowed to lapse gradually into oblivion.

Since those words were written, similar notions have come, and, for some, gone too: job rotation, job enrichment, autonomous work teams, quality of worklife programs, employee involvement, and quality circles.

Most significantly, even if firms were of a mind to undertake job redesign more straightforwardly and positively by addressing the underlying anomalies and disparities in job-worker matches, the potential for danger to existing authority positions would be constraining. Because of inherent workplace conflict, if job redesign were to devolve participation to lower levels and confer real control over decision making, it would be highly suspect in establishment eyes. Inevitably, firms considering changing job quality would keep one eye firmly fixed on the strategic bargaining implications of such moves. Changing job characteristics in ways that would lead workers to challenge the legitimacy of the status quo, however desirable and appropriate in enhancing productivity, may be unattractive to those most readily placed to initiate such changes.[9] In sum, for all of these different reasons, adjustments in various job quality dimensions cannot be assumed to occur automatically in just the right way, at just the right frequency, and to just the right extent. The practical limits to changing work arrangements, within the current institutional context, are distinctly narrower than what their theoretical counterparts presuppose.

Job and Worker Diversity: Discussion
Not only do these more subtle and (sometimes) observationally elusive worker and job heterogeneity considerations themselves tend to complicate, and perhaps thereby weaken, the case for equilibrium outcomes, but their ramifications also have this effect. In particular, (1) the sources and nature of worker and job diversity, (2) the tension between such diversity and the desirability of work standardization, and, most important, (3) the interaction

---

9. In Mitchell and Zaidi 1990a, some industrial relations economists (Flanagan, Jacoby, Ulman) make the general point that efficient outcomes generated solely by irresistible market pressures are not a foregone conclusion. Compare Flanagan (1990, 304):

> Many of the practices conjectured to account for higher productivity in union establishments could be implemented unilaterally by nonunion managers without incurring an offsetting union wage effect, but in general such changes are not undertaken. Here the difficulty appears to be a principal-agent problem. Some of the practices that raise productivity in union settings may place constraints on the prerogatives and discretion that managers value in a nonunion setting. Managers may oppose such practices in order to protect their power and discretion. This is done at the sacrifice of profit, and it is not clear whether the market disciplines this deviation from value maximization.

Or Jacoby (1990, 326): "This pattern [of adopting internal labor markets] suggests that external pressure was critical in the shift to more structured employment practices, whose putative efficiency incentives many managers remained skeptical of." Finally, Ulman (1990) stresses the importance of "concerted behavior" by workers, rather than any immaculate efficiency drives or market automaticity, in accounting for observed labor market outcomes. As I will discuss later, the arguments that the market perforce generates optimal outcomes and that those failing to make such changes will be speedily and automatically displaced by others as market forces make themselves felt need to be severely qualified.

between, and process aspects of, changes in job quality and worker capabilities and attitudes, are all important for evaluating tendencies toward equalizing differentials.

First, the sources of worker and job diversity have received insufficient consideration. For workers, too little is known about what produces differences in attitudes and molds preferences about jobs: How innate and deeply held, how malleable and resilient, are such preferences and attitudes? How strongly do workers push for jobs fulfilling their aspirations? How willing are they to settle for how much less? How narrow or wide do they view, and in fact are, their choices? What kind of expectational mechanisms generate preferences, how do they incorporate experience, and how are they influenced by what kind of social institutions and personality structures? Similar interrogatories can be directed toward the sources of job diversity: How technologically driven are job characteristics? What impact do organizational considerations have? How responsive are firms to pressures for changing work arrangements, and from where do such pressures mostly emanate? How free do firms feel to experiment with new forms of work organization? How much consideration is given to the way different job characteristics will affect workers? Who adjusts to whom and in what ways?

Previous discussion has, either implicitly or explicitly, responded to some of these questions; nevertheless, their iteration suggests that rather than accepting worker and job diversity as a datum needing no further explanation, their sources and nature must be more fully comprehended to interpret labor market outcomes. For instance, the questions concerning the sources of worker diversity are likely to generate a wide variety of responses; it would be extremely strange if all workers spoke as one voice on such issues. Yet traditional economic analysis tends to accept preference states, for all workers, as fixed and exogeneous, as unmoved movers influencing outcomes but themselves untouched in the process. Given such unshakable preferences, decision options narrow. Questions, like those above—implying that preferences are not cast in iron, that workers will probe and explore, and responding to their experiences, make extensive midcourse adjustments within a rich choice milieu, and that, in general, attitudes are very much shaped by the actual process of choosing itself—are avoided, if not anathematized. Under traditional presumptions, there is little reason to be concerned with attitude-formation mechanisms and what forces operate to influence them.

Alternatively, if preferences are viewed as more tentative and malleable, then ultimate outcomes become very much path-dependent as interactions between choice and consequence refashion worker objectives. The issues raised by our substantive queries now become very pertinent because how workers choose and what results emerge will depend upon how those questions are to be answered. Some may deride this latter interpretation as leaving the solid bedrock of fixed and exogenous preferences for the shifting sands of momentary desires. Yet if, in fact, such processes more aptly describe behavior patterns, as I believe is the case, then they cannot be ignored. Furthermore, as a practical matter, the level of worker diversity can be greatly affected by pervasive and far-reaching sociocultural trends. For example, in recent years diversity seems to be greatly increasing as a result of increasing labor force participation rates of women, the growing importance of minorities, increasing legal and illegal immigration, more widely ranging educational attainments, and a generally richer and more differentiated cultural environment. One need only reflect upon how far we have already traveled in transforming jobs to acknowledge and respond to this increasing variety in the work force to appreciate the significance of such trends.

Similarly for the questions relating to job diversity; here too it would be extremely unlikely that firms would answer such questions with lockstep uniformity. Circumstances will be determinative, and firms will find different answers best suited to their particular conditions. Moreover, since jobs are designed and not a haphazard arrangement of tasks, they should be viewed as offering an enlarged menu of possibilities. They are not, as discussed previously, inexorably fixed by overriding technological givens. More to the point, even though the full capabilities of technological change to create more desirable work arrangements have hardly been engaged, many countries are initiating promising and encouraging developments along such lines. Because job design offers, in principle, wide latitude for differences in approach and inevitably strikes a balance among numerous conflicting objectives, it must itself be searchingly reviewed as a normal part of the matching process. To turn a blind eye toward such experimentation and ferment concerning work organization is to miss the forces that are shaping its future. Diversity in jobs and workers and its influence on compensating differentials are thus prime candidates for further explanation, and should not be taken as unalterable facts of life. For both firms and workers, observed diversity reflects a continuing process of interaction between desired and actual outcomes that is constantly reshaping, and being reshaped by, ideas about the likelihood and desirability of achieving particular job-centered objectives. The constantly changing extent and character of such diversity will be both cause and result of corresponding movements in labor market outcomes.

With regard to the second issue, too little attention has been paid to alternative ways of resolving the clash between worker diversity and the requirements of workplace uniformity and standardization. Compromises certainly have to be made, because the workplace cannot be individually tailored to exactly fit each worker's requirements. Economists, though, seem to have excessive faith that the relevant trade-offs between cost savings from uniformity and gains forgone from less precise fits will, as an ineluctable consequence of maximizing behavior, naturally occur. In contrast, many others, especially managerial theorists, see work organization as still dominated by a Taylorian "scientific management" bias toward excessive uniformity and systematization, when such procedures are becoming increasingly unjustified and inappropriate. Routinization has become a casualty of both the increased abilities of a more skilled work force and the more rapid pace of economic and technological change. Firms must build into their work arrangements a greater reliance on decentralized decision making in order to respond more quickly and flexibly in a world of greater surprise and change. The rising cost of trying to hammer increasingly irregular objects into uniformly circular holes will eventually be realized by firms. The opportunities presented by greater work force diversity and technological capabilities for taking advantage of more flexible forms of work organization should be exploited rather than ignored.[10] Whatever happened to comparative advantage, anyway?

Furthermore, to the extent that work arrangements are a public good, the standards will be set by the marginal worker. Accordingly, any change in work arrangements, unlike those taking the form of a wage increase, will produce both positive and negative job quality "rents" for the intramarginal workers, since worker heterogeneity implies that not all workers will universally benefit from such a change. For instance, suppose that, in a period of labor shortage, less experienced and qualified workers are hired instead of undertaking a more costly search and, as a correlative adjustment, firms institute increased supervisory and quality control measures. Most intramarginal workers will probably be adversely affected by the more highly supervised and restrictive work environment. The alternative would be to forgo uniform work arrangements and create work situations reflective of the underlying work force diversity. Nonuniform work conditions might have distinct cost advantages compared to either more expensive monitoring or the search costs of attracting better workers through a general wage increase or greater recruiting expenditures.

The third issue stresses that jobs and workers cannot be taken as given; there is constant interaction and change. It is wrong to think of job characteristics as having only positive and negative shadow wage implications, as merely offsetting a low wage or needing to be offset by a high wage. Analogous to efficiency-wage arguments, but perhaps even more so, job quality is

---

10. Dertouzas et al. state:

All the changes in strategy and organization that we have described require departures from conventional job classifications, labor-management relations, career-progression ladders, and policies on employment security, training, and compensation. Best-practice firms have recognized that improvements in quality and flexibility require levels of commitment, responsibility, and knowledge on the part of the work force that cannot be obtained by compulsion or cosmetic improvements in human resource policies. Quality circles do not work unless workers understand the overall production process and unless their wages, job security, or profit-sharing arrangements give them a sense that they have a stake in the firm's future. The most successful firms recognize that quality is the output of an entire production system, and not the result of an organizational gimmick. (Dertouzas et al. 1989, 124).

For a similar view, see Piore 1989.

not solely compensatory; through its impact on worker motivation, it will influence performance on the job itself. Correcting obvious job deficiencies, in other words, will not only lower compensating differentials, but, in more complicated ways, it may enhance worker effort and skill deployment. The compensating differential framework can be faulted precisely because it obscures such kinds of profound interactions between workers and their jobs. The process of changing job conditions as a way of altering worker performance and attitudes can be complicated and purposive maximizing behavior and very much part of the adjustment mechanism.

My previous discussion on changing work arrangements revealed, however, that changes in job conditions are currently and practically constrained by several inhibiting considerations. Can directly changing worker attitudes offer a more promising route? Although economists have tended to stress worker mobility and external labor market pressures as correctives for improving unappealing jobs, as my subsequent discussion of matching will show, employers still devote considerable resources and effort to changing worker attitudes toward existing jobs. Firms believe, perhaps too eagerly, that changing existing workers' perceptions, analogous to screening for innate attributes, is easier and less costly than thoroughgoing work reorganization. My previous citation of gimmicks is clearly a case in point; firms have a strong interest in a happy work force, and the battle for the hearts and minds of workers is continuously being fought. Words are usually cheap, and if they alone could keep workers happy—despite other things about the job—we could expect to be drowned in a flood of oratory.

Changing worker attitudes, furthermore, has a higher purpose than generating a sense of contentment by such stroking; the firm hopes to thereby extract greater effort. The goal of changing attitudes is not simply to get workers to revise their evaluation of reward structures or job duties, but to induce workers to be more effective on the job. Although firms actively pursue such policies, as the numerous and conflicting studies on job satisfaction and job attitudes indicate, their success remains problematic; there is no magic way to guarantee that workers will favorably revise their perceptions of job characteristics, and thus their effort supply, in response to such motivational programs. Effort variability is especially significant where workers are locked into long-term employment relationships and have accordingly built up considerable firm-specific human capital; here, highly valuable effort, leveraged by the workers' human capital, is at stake. Moreover, effort variability implies that the equilibrating process is not a once-and-for-all adjustment at a margin, but rather a search for ongoing sources of productivity growth within the individual worker and workplace.[11] Changes in worker attitudes are not, in short, simply an end in themselves, but are part of an interactive process looking toward dynamic improvement over time; they have an immense po-

---

11. See chap. 4.

tential to yield great benefits, but specific and concrete changes in work arrangements, rather than motivational shortcuts or exhortational appeal, will be the route to their achievement.[12]

A final consideration, bearing on the equilibrating process and adumbrated in previous discussion, is the importance of bargaining—both tacit and institutionalized—in the workplace. Especially because of effort variability, it is apparent that deals have to be struck between workers and the firm, even on an individual basis. When collective organization is involved, then, as I will more fully discuss subsequently, the opportunities for overcoming the inherent public goods character of the workplace to achieve improved working conditions will be greater. Individuals, in other words, always implicitly bargain through the threat of exit or reduced effort, but collectivities expand the ability to use voice, and amplify its power, as an effective bargaining tool. For both reasons, continuous bargaining is likely to be an integral part of any efficient outcome.

Job quality will, in sum, be shaped by continuous implicit or explicit bargaining by a heterogeneous work force, in a conflictual context, over workplace conditions, which themselves are too subtle and numerous to be captured by the usual measures of job characteristics. Analysis of working conditions should be focused on the nature of this interactive, ongoing process, in which jobs and workers are subject to diverse and unequal pressures to change, rather than presupposing conditions that either must be offset by wage adjustments or are themselves easily adjusted by changing a few simple, nonwage elements. There is no warrant to believe that working conditions are infinitely pliable, workers completely malleable, and bargaining arrangements perfectly tailored to the parties' needs such that jobs and workers are thereby exactly adjusted, inclusive of compensating differentials, to each other. Nor can the impact of opposing interests of, and inherent conflict between, employer and worker be overlooked. Rather, if anything, the subtleties and complexities of many job quality facets and worker characteristics on the one hand, and the rigidities and imperfections in the adjustment process on the other, would seem to ensure hedonic disequilibrium.

At the same time, even though equilibrating tendencies do not fully equalize, in a multidimensional sense, the attractiveness of jobs, this richer account of a more complicated labor market framework—specifically embracing job and worker heterogeneity, firm and worker activism—does clarify and extend our understanding of the equilibrating process itself. It heightens our awareness of the multiple channels through which equilibrating adjustments operate. Paradoxically, although recognizing greater complexity seriously undermines the compensating differential story as an equilibrium description of a functioning reality, such recognition does provide a foundation for better matches by forcing consideration of the relevant array of pertinent

---

12. See chap. 8.

job and worker attributes, and range of firm and worker behaviors. Although previous inattention permitted a simpler worldview, the payoff to a fuller appreciation of the internal changes required for this more complicated matching process is likely to be large.[13]

Equal Pay for Equal Workers in Equal Jobs

If wages are so greatly influenced by so many diverse considerations, and compensating differentials so difficult to discover and interpret, it then naturally follows that violations of the "equal pay for equal workers" condition across various organizational and jurisdictional boundaries are to be expected.[14] Who, given those conditions on wages and job quality, could extract any reliable measure (across workers) of what the wage represents or the specific state of job quality? It would take an act of faith that somehow market forces are so powerful and compelling, and human responses so quickly attuned to minute variations, to believe that, even at the margin, the requisite adjustments are faithfully being executed. If the factors accounting for the complexity of wages and the richness of circumstantial variation of jobs were deliberately omitted or exceedingly simplified, then that would probably leave out (at the very beginning) what will prove essential to any explanation of observables. Once more complicated views on wages and jobs are accepted, what previously seemed a simple and irrefutable truth—that like workers are equally compensated—now becomes much less tenable. Thus it is not surprising that the general drift of recent empirical work—after Herculean efforts to control for job and worker characteristics that might systematically cause persistent interindustry wage differentials, and equally heroic theoretical ingenuity to somehow account for them in ways consistent with textbook models of competitive labor markets—has come to the realistic, if unjoyous, conclusion that "perhaps no single theory can provide a complete explanation of inter-industry wage differences because different theories are of greatest importance in different sectors of the labor market" (Gibbons and Katz 1989, 27). Or more simply, as Lang, Leonard, and Lilien (1987, 9) put it, ". . .significant differences in earnings exist between individuals who appear identical to economists."

This position of wage nonuniformity across similarly qualified workers is especially buttressed in the many cases where firms actively use pay policy to further internally set goals and in response to highly idiosyncratic arrange-

13. For a comparable and supporting argument reviewing the more complex processes generating labor market outcomes, see Edwards 1990. His major thesis is very close to my position: the upsurge of interest in how labor markets actually function is a welcome and overdue development, but oversimplifying and trying to fit the new material into traditional ways of thinking produces a distorted picture of "how the labor contract really works."

14. See Krueger and Summers 1988, 260; Gibbons and Katz 1989, 2; Helwege, 1989, 1.

ments inside the firm. Where firms pursue sophisticated strategies for eliciting high-level worker performance and workers can vary their effort and have considerable firm-specific human capital, tacit bargaining over all work aspects is continuous. In such cases the market is only a distant and sometime arbiter rather than a compelling omnipresence. Indeed, the very idea of firm-specific human capital, especially when combined with all the factors that influence effort variability, makes equal-pay comparisons of workers across firms exceedingly problematic. More pointedly, gender and race discrimination could not persist for so many years if the equal-pay condition were so prevailing. Likewise, efficiency wage notions and search theories could not gain such ready acceptance if, respectively, equally qualified workers could not generate diverse productivity outcomes and distributional variation were not so obvious. What seems surprising is that the shoe has not been on the other foot: in the light of all these considerations, should not the presumption be that fairly broad wage distributions across uniformly qualified workers are the norm, rather than exceptions?[15]

Matchups

The anomalies associated with the operation of the external labor market itself—nonclearing, job-worker mismatch, unequal exchange conditions— offer an equally challenging set of circumstances to traditional labor market analysis. And here, too, anomalies can be better understood by considering not only the external labor market but also by more completely describing what is happening inside the firm, as will be undertaken in chapter 4. After all, it should not be strange that markets and firms have to fit together, since they interact and form a mutually dependent system; both external and internal labor market developments drive the new approaches to the theory of the firm.

---

15. Recent studies of wage distributions (Burtless 1990; *New York Times,* 14 August 1990, sec. D; Davis and Haltiwanger 1991) also show that wage spreads across groups of workers having broadly similar characteristics have distinctly widened in recent years, thus enhancing the importance of this issue. Further, as the quotation in note 4 indicates, the point is that a firm's wage distribution will reflect its own internal maximizing logic, based on its own situation, and other firms will not be identically positioned. More sharply, is there a fundamental methodological error at issue here because the notion of wage equality arising from the competitive paradigm compels economists to search (in vain?) for presumptively equilibrating factors? Thus, it will always be possible and tempting to argue that, no matter how vigorous and extensive previous inquiries have been, some yet currently unknown and hence unspecified factor is causally responsible for the wage nonuniformity. The arguments that (*a*) ultimately the answer will be found and (*b*) after diligent search, it has not yet turned up, are never really joined. An elaboration of this point, and the more general contingency argument that organizational design must conform to the specific characteristics defining a firm's jobs, workers, and operational milieu, are discussed in subsequent sections of this chapter.

Nonclearing Labor Markets

Turning to nonclearing labor markets first, it might be thought that the phenomenon of tremendously large ratios of applicants to openings, which is repeated again and again whenever and wherever desirable jobs are to be found, might lead to some doubts about the validity of market-clearing presumptions. Similarly, persistent searching for workers and more or less permanent openings for undesirable jobs suggest the same conclusion. It should especially be noted that such circumstances are not due to, respectively, temporarily loose and tight labor markets but happen under quite normal conditions. As a recent multicountry survey on labor market segmentation summarizes, "'Good jobs' are relatively scarce. There is generally an oversupply of labour for most of the other positions in the economy" (Rosenberg 1989, 385). Further, the ease with which labor upgrading takes place, certainly during cyclical expansions and even at low unemployment rates, might indicate the importance of job rationing. Or more simply, the commonsense appreciation that any worker would always jump at the chance to take a better job, and leave an inferior one, without much subsequent perceptible performance deterioration should make one suspicious about accepting market clearing as a de facto condition. And finally, if the wage multifunctionality argument is accepted, then clearly its corollary must be the recognition that the complexity of factors behind wage change limits its capabilities for unambiguously directing labor flows so that markets will always clear.

The argument for nonclearing is further strengthened by looking more closely at the firm's strategy options. As indicated previously, pay policy is part and parcel of the firm's attempts to extract high-level performance from workers. In this pursuit, firms will pay higher wages and offer implicit long-term employment and working condition commitments for several obvious reasons: to encourage greater effort, loyalty, and cooperation; to create a large queue of potential employables and, hence, greater choice and selectivity in obtaining their work force; and to minimize turnover and its associated costs. Not all firms will pursue such an efficiency wage strategy, since reckoning costs and benefits will vary depending upon a firm's specific environment. In any case, all firms will be cautious about how extensively they make such commitments; they could become expensive in an uncertain world, and they can diminish the firm's authority position. Some firms may even practice a core-periphery strategy that simultaneously provides very desirable jobs for a specific core of workers and much less desirable ones for others. This diversity, within and across firms, in the underlying nature of jobs creates the conditions for queues and long tenure for some jobs and constant recruitment and great turnover for others. Once the complexity and multidimensionality associated with wage determination, job quality, and worker heterogeneity is accepted, then the nonauction and nonclearing nature of labor markets becomes obvious. Again, what is surprising is that this powerful conclusion is so strongly resisted. At the same time, acceptance opens a window on the richness and variety of adjustment variables operating in labor markets. In this sense, complexity and nonclearing are two sides of the same coin.

Job-Worker Mismatch

The notion of job-worker mismatch logically follows from the presence of nonclearing markets. If an all-encompassing, hedonic wage equality was the presumed result of an equilibrating process that focuses on changes in money wages and job conditions, then initially matching jobs and workers is its natural complement. It embraces exactly the same range of considerations, but stresses their impact on sorting activities prior to employment. Wages, jobs, workers: what adjusts to what? In the equalizing differential case, pecuniary rewards are supposed to adjust in response to relatively fixed worker characteristics and nonpecuniary job conditions. In the sorting case, wages are assumed to be fixed and jobs to be relatively invariant in their nonpecuniary structural characteristics; workers move between jobs and firms search over workers, each looking for the most appropriate match. In the traditional interpretation, the matching process was dominated by homogeneous workers with fixed preferences sorting themselves among jobs with fixed characteristics to find a once-and-for-all most desirable match. Changing wage differentials are the most important adjustment variable, providing searchers with a guiding light, and responding to excess supply and demand in particular labor markets to ensure that all markets clear. In more refined versions, the search process also took into account that workers might not be homogeneous and, hence, matching the right worker with the right job plays a more significant role. Once the right match was set, with no further supply or demand pressures for wage change, the system would presumably maintain itself forever.

This idealized and simplistic model of matching has been greatly expanded, although still maintaining its equilibrium presumption, by more thoroughgoing treatment of the participants' maximizing behavior. Job-search theory, based on maximizing expected lifetime income, has been developed to provide a richer account of worker choice; likewise, firms' personnel policies, based on a more comprehensive view of the human resource contribution to maximizing the firm's value, have become integrated into the theory of the firm. Two aspects have usually remained the same: whether workers search for jobs or jobs for workers, the presumption of invariant job characteristics is maintained; once a correct match is made, that is the end of the process and no further developments are considered. On both grounds, as we shall see, the analysis can be improved. But first it will prove useful to explore the expanded matching models.

In an imperfect world where knowledge is costly and the future always uncertain, it obviously pays a worker to invest time and effort to find a more suitable job by job shopping to sample and experience various opportunities to find the right one, or by using the search period as a screening or signaling mechanism to indicate to prospectively desired employers your suitable qualification. Likewise, searching can generate information to find out more about your own capabilities and preferences to facilitate the self-selection process. In all cases, the worker takes the initiative in developing his or her capabilities and bringing them to the attention of job providers, always balancing the costs of doing so against the prospective gains from the improved job fit thereby attained. Jobs do not change, wage adjustments are downplayed, and once a match is made, no subsequent changes in either jobs or workers are presumed to take place.

Looked at from the firm's point of view, the matching process is a matter of choosing the appropriate personnel policies. Okun's (1981) distinction between career and casual labor markets will be useful at this point. For the former, firms set their recruitment activities and wage schedules at levels sufficient to generate a pool of qualified applicants from which they will choose those deemed most suitable. This approach ensures a more-or-less permanent queue, that is, a fringe of unsatisfied job demanders of the desired quality level that can be drawn from in the normal course of personnel replacement and expansion.[16] The quality level is set on the basis of prospective long-term employment arrangements, during which qualified employees would move up the internal job ladder of the firm. Thus, the selection process implies a considerable long-term commitment to those chosen, and the quid pro quo expected by the firm is loyalty and responsive effort supply by such employees. For long-term employment arrangements, current wages are less important, since the bargain is implicitly struck on the basis of expected lifetime income.[17]

For more casual labor markets, arrangements are far less elaborate and current wages and circumstances are much more relevant. But here, too, similar to the queue maintained for career labor market jobs, a significant pool of labor can be drawn upon to meet modest ebbs and flows in market demand, mostly through wage and minor working condition changes influencing participation rates of those more casually attached to the labor market. In sum, for both search theories and personnel policies, even though the matching process is more complicated and the behavior of the parties more purposive, explicit and extensive job restructuring receives little attention as an adjustment variable, and dynamic job and worker changes that can affect the quality of the match over time are rarely considered.

What happens when these latter two considerations are directly taken into account? Conceptually, as noted in the discussion of equalizing differ-

---

16. See Barron, Bishop, and Dunkleberg 1985. In their sample, there was an 83 percent acceptance rate of initial job offers by workers.

17. According to Hall, "wages are installment payments on long-term financial obligations" (1980, 113).

entials, a theory embracing changing jobs and workers has much to commend it. Indeed, once both job and worker changes are considered, the sorting problem becomes conceptually exactly analogous to the equalizing differentials issue, especially since the fit must be maintained over time. For one example, the very notion of firm-specific human capital implies expanding worker capabilities over time, and it would be inconsistent for such potential gain not to be exploited by both parties. For another, experimentation, as mentioned previously, by firms in the area of job redesign as well as continuing technological change itself should alert us to the potential importance of changing the nature of work. Thus, from both sides, continuous pressures for change will be present, and the relevant questions are—as they were before— what kind of change, who adapts to what, and what major influences drive these changes?

One set of issues turns on the relative flexibility of jobs and workers. As previous remarks have shown, economists have been unwarrantedly prone to assume that job characteristics are relatively fixed and, thus, variations in worker preferences and capabilities, either through switching workers or altering existing work force attributes, were thought to be the major adjustment factors in matching workers and jobs. Human flexibility is indeed important, but to focus on it exclusively overlooks the ubiquity of changes in work organization. Other, more fundamental, questions about the matching process arise over how the form and nature of job quality change are affected by the interests of the contending parties. Once it is acknowledged that matching reflects changing job quality as well as workers moving between jobs, and that a good match must itself evolve as both job requirements and worker capabilities vary over time, then matching through work reorganization is subject to the same forces and pressures as were operative in, and is analytically equivalent to, the equalizing differential case.

And just as equalizing differentials in work conditions were only imperfectly realized, so too perfect sorting seems inconceivable—for similar reasons: too little reliance on job quality change, too much faith in worker mobility and malleability. As Scitovsky (1980, 4) has succinctly suggested, with respect to recent U.S. experience, "the upgrading of the labor force ran ahead of the upgrading of jobs"; one-tailed mismatches—overqualified workers and inadequate jobs—were all too prevalent.[18] In brief, the most important reason for such systematic mismatching and deficiencies in job quality is, as suggested earlier, that firms tend to avoid job changes that might erode their control over workers. Yet attaining a good match, and maintaining it over time, may be critical because effort variability and firm-specific human capital are instrumental in determining productivity performance; sustaining a more suitable fit will make workers willing participants rather than merely passive timeservers. Job matching, viewed over time, implies that adjusting

18. See Rozen 1982.

the job quality dimension is indispensable for maintaining a high level of productivity growth.

Further, one very important and powerful implication of mismatches must be stressed: they are overwhelmingly one- rather than two-tailed because firms stand to lose much more by employing workers in jobs beyond their capacities than by not utilizing work force capabilities to the fullest. In linked productive activity, because of substantial interdependence among workers and subprocesses, inadequate job performance would have devastating repercussions because its effects could not be narrowly contained. Indeed, firms operate on what might be called the "Convoy Principle," whereby work rhythms and job standards are frequently set at levels to accommodate virtually all workers. Such arrangements ensure that the work tempo will necessarily be lower than the average capabilities of the group and, as will be argued below, much lower than if work rhythms were more thoroughly considered.[19]

Similarly, previously discussed patterns of excess demand for desirable jobs and excess supply of other jobs are a strong indication that many workers are more qualified for, and aspire to, better jobs than are available for them. Differential rates of turnover, quits, vacancies, job continuity, and the like across the job distribution would not occur if mismatches were not one-tailed; no regular patterns would be observed, queues would not exist, and upgrading would be very difficult. Flows into and out of jobs would exhibit more random behavior; vacancies, turnover, and quits would be as likely for one job as another. There would be only appropriate and inappropriate matches between jobs and workers, with no bias one way or the other, and, furthermore, their incidence pattern would have to be equally probable across all jobs. That observed labor market behavior and flows tend to show these systematic differences over the job distribution strongly indicates the importance of one-tailed mismatches.[20] Large numbers of qualified workers could be, but are not, working in jobs that fully tap their productive potential and are consonant with realistic job expectations and career goals. Improvements in the matching process promise a very high payoff. Economists should properly be very

---

19. To anticipate the obvious objection, I will subsequently more fully discuss why rational economic agents would not quickly move to a superior position. Let me simply say here that, in addition to the authority-maintenance issue, other distributional, cautionary, and inertial considerations also stand in the way.

20. Compare the following:

Krueger and Summers . . . discuss the evidence that there are queues for jobs in industries in which wages are high. If workers in high-wage industries were earning rents, we would expect them to have low quit rates and that there would be queues for high-wage jobs. On the other hand, if high-wage industries merely hired better workers or paid high wages because of undesirable working conditions, there would be no reason to expect lower quit rates in these industries. They report that this expectation is confirmed, suggesting that workers in high-wage industries earn rents and that therefore there are queues for jobs in these industries. Lang, Leonard, and Lilien (1987, 13).

skeptical concerning such free lunch arguments, but the economics of organizational choice nevertheless suggest the possibility that internal rearrangements within the firm can produce great gains at very little cost.

Certainly some economists would argue that not utilizing workers to the fullest extent of their capabilities is inconsistent with maximizing behavior, since both workers and their firms could gain from doing so. Laggard firms, in this view, would soon perish as their more enterprising competitors take advantage of these mismatch lapses. Others will disagree, and maintain that such mismatches may be consistent with maximizing behavior. First, such overqualification can be viewed as an insurance premium against future production uncertainties, functioning as a potential bank of talent to be hoarded and drawn upon if needed. Second, firms might, for the convoy principle reasons discussed previously, find it too costly to make the requisite organizational changes that better matching implies. Finally, one of the virtues of being able to select from a queue of applicants is that firms are able to control for the degree of overqualification and, on the grounds of retention/turnover costs if no other, they will impose an upper bound. All of these arguments can provide a transaction cost rationale for retaining overqualified workers, and thus the firm's actions can be interpreted as consistent with maximizing behavior.

The more profound issue, however, is whether this latter position is more like ex-post rationalization than ex-ante theorizing. As Mitchell and Zaidi (1990b, 163) have noted, "There is indeed a timeless quality to the theoretical studies; a tendency to assume that what exists is optimal at the moment it is observed; and a tendency to assume unique solutions to problems which potentially may have multiple outcomes." As I have suggested previously, institutional blockage—arising largely from the unwillingness of management to jeopardize its dominant position and the ability to make that stick—rather than optimal behavior may be the more salient consideration, and hence may keep the free lunch option open.

Nor should it be thought that matching is a once-and-for-all process. The quality of the match evolves over time as both jobs and workers naturally and inevitably change in the crucible of experience. Apart from consideration of the creation of firm-specific human capital and the tournament implications of promotion and hierarchy, not much attention has been paid to what happens after the match. Yet that may be a critical factor. For one thing, both jobs and workers are responsive to the influence of broad social trends on work organization: the changing legal framework regarding conditions of work, the role of gender and race in defining job opportunity sets, and the pervasive influence of advancing technology on job design and skill requirements, to mention a few. The world of work can never be hermetically sealed and self-contained; it is part of a larger social system and it will influence, and be influenced by, that system.

For another, subtle changes also occur as people and jobs adapt to each other. Like a new pair of shoes, jobs become remolded and reshaped as workers exercise their individuality, within the broad discretionary limits surrounding most jobs, and align the job more to their liking. Likewise, firms are ever alive to possibilities for cost savings and innovative change, and will find it in their interest, consistent with their other goals, to promote the growth of their work force's capabilities. Thus, jobs and workers undergo more-or-less continuous change, and concern for maintaining the goodness of fit between job and worker must accordingly not be too far behind.

The care and attention lavished on the matching process, despite its one-tailed outcomes, is both a testimonial to its importance and an indirect confirmation of the irrelevance of viewing labor markets as auctions. If workers were perfectly homogeneous, or their variation inconsequential, it would be illogical to go to great lengths to arrange good fits and to worry about maintaining them over time. Nor would we ever observe the phenomenon of immensely large numbers of job applicants for desirable job vacancies. Those long lines of qualified people or flood of applications whenever good job openings are publicly advertised convey significant information about the matching process. They are a very crude index of its continuing disabilities.

A recent article (Akerlof, Rose, and Yellen 1988) joins together these nonclearing and mismatch arguments and, in the context of a job-rationing model along implicit contract lines, strongly supports the positions I have taken and provides a convenient point of departure for some extensions. Akerlof, Rose, and Yellen argue that "models with job rationing exhibit a significant market failure: a characteristic of equilibrium models with rigid wages is that some individuals covet jobs held by others who are no better qualified. When wages are sticky, people cannot obtain jobs they desire by offering to work for lower pay. As a result, the autonomous departure of an individual from a job creates a sequence of opportunities that we call a vacancy chain. The vacancy chain concept provides the key to understanding why quits are procyclic" (1988, 496).

In their model markets do not clear, and workers are stuck in jobs they dislike and unable to bid on jobs in other firms, because those firms will not accept lower wage offers from outsiders. That would be too disruptive, lowering the morale and productivity of their existing workers. Many workers are thus "unhappy campers," biding their time until something better comes along.[21] As a famous New York city clothier pithily expressed his sales pitch,

---

21. For the sake of completeness, risk aversion is also relevant, since even a less than satisfying existing job in hand has some advantages over a probably more desirable, but still only prospectively attainable, new job. Note that the "unhappy camper" image starkly brings out the difference between equilibrium and disequilibrium approaches. Equilibrium theorists (see Carmichael 1989) accept the idea that unemployed workers will always better themselves by taking a job that pays more than their reservation wage, but do not usually consider the possibility of unhappy jobholders waiting to move to a better job. Yet the same logic applies when a worker moves from unemployment to a job as when from one job to another. Empirically, job-to-job

"choose, don't settle"; such workers are settling rather than choosing. In an economic upswing, jobs more to their liking open up, better matches ensue, and psychic pain is lessened. Akerlof, Rose, and Yellen stress the psychic gains to workers from better matches: "At low unemployment rates, high turnover enables workers unhappy with the nonpecuniary aspects of their jobs to trade places more easily, resulting in higher average job satisfaction, even if quitters do not, on average, experience wage gains" (1988, 498). Important as such psychic gains may be, their argument can also be given a work organization "spin" to generate output expansion, and thereby a rich vein of implications can be mined.[22]

After all, if workers are unhappy in their jobs, why cannot the jobs themselves be changed rather than using mobility as the only avenue? And if jobs are changed, can that not have extremely beneficial productivity and output consequences? Arguments stressing those possibilities can be strengthened by taking the importance of rhythm, pace, and tempo into account in explaining economic activity. This approach can be justified by a distinction emerging in the theoretical literature between "thick" and "thin" (or high and low) equilibrium situations, whereby differentially ranked multiple equilibria are likely possibilities under realistic specifications of alternative prevailing states of nature (see Hall 1988, 587-91). The basic idea is that economic behavior is situationally sensitive, and hence variation in circumstantial specification, that is, work organization, can generate differential outcomes; for instance, inherent in the idea of efficiency wages is the possibility of both a high wage–high productivity and a low wage–low productivity equilibrium. Efficiency wage concepts can establish close linkages between performance and reward, between effort and compensation.[23] Accordingly, multiple equilibria would be possible since all economic agents can freely choose which particular pairs are best for them. High wage–high productivity firms would coexist in equilibrium with low wage–low productivity firms, as pay and effort are easily adjusted to one another. All the various labor markets would be cleared as both wages and effort in each adjust in line with participants' choices.

It is thus sensible to accept as a general proposition that human activity does not proceed on a steady and even course at all times. Partly, this reflects the inherent variation in the level of performance across the menu of our assigned activities—a marathon is not run like a hundred-yard dash. Perfor-

changes occur more frequently than moving from a job to unemployment or out of the labor force (see Akerlof, Rose, and Yellen, 1988, 526–530.)

22. It should be noted that Akerlof, Rose, and Yellen explicitly assume that all matches are equally good in other than the psychic dimensions and, hence, consciously choose not to explore the possibilities for output change. (See 1988, 521–22.)

23. Sometimes efficiency wages are viewed as a variant of rent seeking because they are higher than alternative opportunities. This idea should be rejected if such higher wages flow from superior performance and not from merely differential positional advantage.

mance intensity is highly situation dependent. Partly, it is the product of externalities arising from group and team activity. Apart from the natural complementarities determining effort interdependence within group activity, pace is also infectious, as each team member responds to what other team members are doing. By being able to assign activities and influence their average level (think of a coxswain stepping up the stroke pace in crew racing) through adjusting job quality, differential outcomes are indicated. Outcome variability occurs as the result of whatever job quality changes drive these patterns of assigned high or low team activity.

Although in this case outcome variability and equilibrium go hand-in-hand, a disequilibrium variant, based on the distinction between choosing and settling, is a natural modification and has broader implications. There is a world of difference, as Akerlof, Rose, and Yellen suggest, between a whole-hearted and enthusiastic acceptance of a job and a resentful and grudging for-the-moment accession until something better comes along, between choosing and settling. If efficiency wages are now interpreted as a shorthand expression for more complicated forms of work organization designed to extract the best possible performance from workers and not as simply balancing a wage-effort alignment, then reaching equilibrium becomes a much more difficult and chancier matter. Now all the conditions determining high-level worker perfor-mance, and not just the wage, are relevant, and they are unlikely, across all firms and within any one firm, to all be fulfilled to exactly the same extent. Workers then confront a restricted, less-than-desired set of options. They will thus have to accept various combinations of settling and choosing, and their productive performance will be correspondingly affected. Their "efficiency terms of employment" will not match their aspirations, and their performance on the job will not reach its productive potential.

Outcome variation can then reflect not only multiple equilibria due to simple efficiency wage factors but, more controversially, the disequilibrium states arising from the extent to which existing work arrangements do not fully tap worker potential. The presence of such disequilibria implies a greatly enlarged role for job quality changes. Now output itself will be affected by the specific details of work organization, and, unlike the cyclical upgrading model, the disequilibrium variant cannot be easily dismissed as merely a transition arising from a less-than-full employment state because it persists even at full employment. And since at issue are not psychic gains for workers, but output gains all can share and be made better off thereby, it deepens the mystery of why such relatively free lunches are turned down.

Two further implications deserve consideration. First, a testable applica-tion of this line of thought is found in the asymmetrical reaction of good and bad jobs to a tightening labor market as high employment levels are reached. Good jobs, by being able to draw from the pool of qualified applicants, are far less pressured to make further improvements than bad jobs, which become increasingly harder to staff. Hence, the latter will be changed prior to the former, and the wage and working conditions gaps between good jobs and bad jobs narrows in a cyclical expansion. That, in turn, eventually puts pressure on the good job sector to reestablish customary differentials. Work reorganization is thus generalized and proceeds more quickly in such circumstances.

Second, there are profound public policy implications. Certainly a thick equilibrium connection between work organization and worker productivity is preferred. As just discussed, a high-employment economy tends to raise job quality, and that alone would justify its more vigorous pursuit. If in addition, however, firms drag their feet in reorganizing work, then additional public measures to overcome that resistance are called for. Potential gains from work reorganization raise the stakes and justify third-party intervention to overcome the inhibitions that prevent the economy moving from a thin to a thick equilibrium.[24] Innovative institutional change may be a pretty close substitute for a free lunch.

"Choose, don't settle" is, therefore, not an idle semantic distinction, but rather expresses a very important operational difference between relatively free and open and greatly constrained choice. Of course, some might argue that wider choice is never a free good, and the fact that tighter choice constraints will narrow options is simply expressing the underlying realities of harsh and difficult conditions. But that argument misses the point that, in a great many instances, work reorganization that permits choosing rather than settling is a very live, and not particularly resource-costly, option. In any case, surely the issue is the factual one of relevant circumstances and not a linguistic dispute about the meaning of free and open versus constrained choice.

Certainly the implied free-lunch—great gains from seemingly trivial or difficult-to-ascertain changes in work arrangements—makes economists very reluctant to accept such outcome variability. After all, if maximization is presumed, then once equilibrium is reached and given stable and settled conditions, the possibility of further gains is unthinkable because that would be inconsistent with the initial presumption. In equilibrium, all potential gains must have been realized. The usual counterargument would be that some significant structural element that explains the variability has been overlooked, and hence the sin of misspecification has been committed.

This issue is aptly illustrated in an exchange between Schmidt and

---

24. See Hall 1988:

Although the traditional view has been that workers gain and employers suffer when unemployment falls, this view should not be taken for granted. Employers are not deserting the drum-tight labor markets of the Northeast, even though unemployment is now close to zero. In a true thick market . . . there is a net benefit in a thick market to those on both sides. . . . An interesting question raised by the Akerlof-Rose-Yellen paper is whether a tight, low-unemployment labor market is truly a thick market in the same way. And if a particular labor market, such as the Northeast, is truly a thick market, can the national economy achieve the benefits of a thick market by expanding the overall economy with monetary and fiscal policy? (589–90)

Greene (1986), in connection with the former's review article on the econometric estimation of frontier production functions, which are attempts to define an efficiency locus for maximal possible outputs. Greene argues:

> It is worth remembering that this entire literature stands in opposition to the assumptions of classical microeconomics. We should keep in mind the difference between what we *estimate* and what we are *estimating*. Before we attach great significance to the difference between least squares estimates of the "average technology" and maximum likelihood estimates of the "best practice (i. e., frontier) technology," we should step back and ask whether the underlying theory doesn't tell us that this difference is just a red herring, a mere statistical artifact. (1986, 337)

Schmidt replies:

> One issue raised in my paper. . .is the extent to which efficiency measurement is a reasonable objective. . . .Greene is quite right when he says that "the existence of inefficiency flies in the face of the classical microeconomics," and I believe this explains the lack of enthusiasm for the efficiency measurement exercise on the part of most economists. (By way of contrast, there is no such lack of enthusiasm on the part of management scientists.) Given a strong enough faith in optimizing behavior, measured inefficiency *must* represent the effects of unmeasured inputs, unrecognized constraints faced by the firm, and so forth. . . .As an economist, I have sympathy for these arguments. On the other hand, people who truly do not believe in inefficiency must live in a different world than I do, because I see it as a pervasive fact of life. People make mistakes, and people manage firms. Their mistakes have consequences, and these may be measurable. (1986, 353–54)

Stretching notions of inefficiency to include not only those arising from human error, but also those caused by correctible organizational considerations defining the firm's range of available choices would seem a logical and reasonable extension. I have called the contrary position of those who a priori exclude any possibility of inefficiency the economistic fallacy, or economisticism. (For elaboration, see n. 3, chap. 2.)

But like the philosophical arguments over free will versus determinism, resolution of this thorny issue is impossible since the parties are arguing from different epistemological bases. Thus, the arguments that, on the one hand, if I knew more, all would be explicable, and, on the other hand, since I already know a lot, the variability I observe does not seem explicable, are never really joined. Each is right within its own sphere. Similarly, the belief that some omitted variable or other misspecification will account for what is presumed to be a free lunch, and the argument that difficult-to-explain gains persist despite exhaustive, but necessarily incomplete, efforts to determine their sources are likewise in mutually exclusive spheres. Nevertheless, the prominence of shifts in pace and tempo and in organizational arrangements in accounting for observed outcome variation is manifest, even though our knowledge of explanatory mechanisms is imperfect and crude. If one feels more comfortable referring to such variation as stochastic uncertainty or the result of innovational change, well and good—as long as labeling is not confused with explaining.

Unequal Exchange Relationships

Most labor market analysis proceeds on the assumption that the exchange of work for pay is a simple quid pro quo and takes place on a completely individualized and voluntary basis among relatively equal economic agents. All are free to choose; what each party offers and demands is patently clear; compliance and enforcement flow smoothly; all presumably have numerous alternatives; no one has a gun at anybody else's head. Even introducing trade unions ordinarily changes relatively little in most formal analyses. But this view of labor markets is being seriously challenged. For one thing, in line with the long-term nature and underlying complexity of the employment relationship, relational contracting becomes the concomitant of associational continuity between worker and firm. Where, as discussed previously, productivity must be elicited rather than commanded, the parties are locked in a more complicated strategic embrace that calls for great subtlety and sophistication in negotiating contested and difficult terrain. The quids and the quos are anything but patently apparent; compliance is not automatically forthcoming, and enforcement may not be simply a matter of command. Under such conditions, exchange will be neither easy nor simple.

For another, as is likely in a great many cases, where substantial disparities in the parties' relative strength exist and where, especially, an individual worker's alternatives may be extremely exiguous, the notion of voluntary exchange among equals must give way to contested exchange among unequals. At a minimum, this ensures that the struggle over shares will make its presence felt in all dealings between the parties, and more likely it will raise great doubts in the minds of the weaker party, usually the worker, concerning the legitimacy of such arrangements. Fair swaps among equals allow all parties to share the inherent gains from exchange; unequal exchange ensures a process of struggle and conflict, the ramifications of which penetrate to every aspect of the parties' dealings.[25] Such conditions are not likely to lead to productivity heaven.

---

25. In particular, in the great majority of cases, the one-sided dominance of employers is the source of such disparity. Assuming free and voluntary exchange among relative equals finesses all discussion of relative economic power. Yet from the anticonspiracy statutes, solicitous

How much, if at all, do trade unions change the picture? As adumbrated in the discussion of equalizing differentials, traditionalists would argue that, if trade unions are able to command a wage premium, then in an equilibrium solution it would follow that other conditions on the job must be worse in some ways, since trade unions do not generally restrict entry. But several arguments, in line with the general tenor of this chapter, have recently challenged this accepted view. First, to the extent that linkages exist between working conditions and performance on the job, any worsening would be cutting off one's nose to spite one's face. As we appreciate the enormous influence on productivity of workers having a greater say and sense of participation and of team effort, the notion of working conditions as a pure reward (or penalty) with no integral connection to production processes becomes more and more tenuous. No hard and fast line can be drawn between on-the-job conditions as motivaters that positively influence workers' efforts and as unavoidable circumstances that are offset by a higher pecuniary reward if unpleasant, or themselves compensate for a lower pecuniary reward if pleasant.

Second, as mentioned previously, many aspects of the workplace are covered by the public goods argument. Workplace conditions and job quality are likely to be common over broad groups of workers; all who work are affected (negatively and positively) by the physical conditions prevailing, the style of supervision, the rules of the shop, etc. Any individual who views such job conditions as undesirable can either try to change them (voice) or leave (exit). Individual action, in this context, poses the classic free-rider problem: since benefits accrue to all, each individual has an incentive to let others do it and not take action herself or himself. The result is that, as long as only individual action is considered, work conditions can be affected only after prolonged exit indicates a serious problem. No individual has a sufficient incentive to take actions that will largely benefit others. Collective action adds a new dimension to voice, and a channel for overcoming the free-rider constraint. Thus, job quality will improve to the extent that collective organization is an effective mechanism for eliciting, articulating, and achieving workers' true desires.

---

injunctive relief, and yellow-dog contracts of the past to the more sophisticated legal and public relations strategies of the present, it is fair to say that the circumstances defining the labor contract are usually tilted in the employer's favor. If that were not the case, labor history and the legislative and legal struggles of workers would be far different than what we observe. Economists seem to have a blind eye for such power disparities: "Neoclassical economic theory has a strong presumption against any beneficial consequences of inalienable worker rights" (Kruse 1990). Perhaps this stems from an Olympian view whereby such untidy and stubborn considerations are thought to be merely transient and temporary, not mattering in the long run. Hence, like Solow's "fleas on the thick hide of an ox" to be brushed away with a quick swish of the tail, they can be safely disregarded. For a very good summary of employee rights and their economic justification, see Kruse 1990.

Third, as noted previously, the implicit presumption of bargaining equality between the individual worker and firms is frequently not true in practice. Collective organization can redistribute benefits, along bilateral monopoly lines, in situations where bargaining disparities previously held down the share of workers. Perhaps more important and certainly more surprising, the redress of obvious inequity in bargaining conditions may lead to a joint gain. The parties can now address each other more constructively as equals, thereby making possible changes and bargains that the previously dominant party would not have been willing to consider (because they threatened that dominance) and that the previously subordinate party could not bring about (because it lacked sufficient strength). It would not be the first instance of firms opposing that which they subsequently found to be in their longer-run interest.

Finally, consistent with the previous discussion of heterogeneity, some economists have emphasized worker quality as an adjustment variable because firms would respond to a wage premium by being more selective in their hiring policies. Thus, work force quality would be raised to match the higher wage paid, and, presumably. the resulting higher productivity would provide the incremental output gains to make this a stable equilibrium solution. In this case, there would be no necessity to downgrade working conditions. Taken together, these arguments seem sufficiently strong to overturn the orthodox presumption that trade union wage premiums should result in compensatory downgrading of job quality. More important, they explicitly raise questions concerning the parties' relative strength within a conflictual context and, thus, force consideration of a wider range of labor market behaviors with a potentially far-reaching impact on outcomes. Excluding such considerations imposes severe and unnecessary handicaps on labor market analysis.

Concluding Remarks

As my discussion has shown, labor market equilibrating processes are more complex and possess more potential dimensions of adjustment than commonly believed. Wage adjustments are far from being completely dominant; changes in job attributes are an important and overlooked adjustment mechanism and can have profound productivity consequences. Anomalies abound: wages and productivity are not tightly bound together in any kind of one-to-one relationship; equalizing wage differentials to offset variations in working conditions cannot be assumed with certainty as an easily reached equilibrium position; broadly similar workers will not receive equal wages; labor markets often will not clear; jobs and workers will not always be correctly matched, or stay that way over time even if they once were—indeed workers are likely to be frequently overqualified for their jobs; and collective organization can expand job restructuring options. New approaches can thus lead to a richer and fuller understanding of, and explanation for, what happens in labor markets. In particular, the view of the workplace as contested terrain plays a very important role in accounting for these unconventional departures from traditional appraisals.

Similarly, some of the issues raised, especially those emphasizing interaction effects between jobs and workers, have extremely important policy implications. If motivation, effort, and performance are affected by job design and variable working conditions, then it is not permissible to view labor market adjustment processes as simply and solely a matter of adjusting pecuniary rewards to clear markets in the context of unchanging worker preferences and capabilities and invariant job quality. Instead, job restructuring will be an important adjustment variable as both a natural, but perhaps tardy, de facto consequence of equilibrating tendencies and, in the context of one-tailed mismatches, a potentially significant policy option.

The microtheoretic implications of this more complex picture of jobs and workers also need to be spelled out. Not unexpectedly, once the simplicities of a flat, one-dimensional view of jobs and workers are jettisoned, it soon becomes apparent that job design matters very much, its consequences reach into areas ordinarily left unexplored, and adjustments in jobs are essential elements of the equilibrating process in labor markets. Similarly, worker heterogeneity plays a much greater role in the labor market as both a datum for job selection and turnover and an important component of the adjustment process. Together, the expanded options generated by multidimensional jobs and heterogeneous workers imply reduced significance for wage adjustments as the possibilities for job and worker change take on enhanced importance; the limits on what wage change can, or even must, accomplish are narrowed.

Multidimensional jobs and heterogeneous workers certainly make the interpretation of wage-productivity relationships, equalizing differentials, and the dynamics of wage patterns more diffuse and complicated. Worker diversity robs them of their conceptual simplicity, and job multidimensionality robs them of their easy and accurate discernment. These underlying attributes of jobs and workers also complicate, by greatly enlarging the possible number of combinations and making their identification more difficult, the process of labor market clearing and job-worker matching. And collective organization might possibly improve the parties' joint position, rather than simply imply a search for narrow advantage in a zero-sum process.

Recognizing greater diversity in the nature of jobs and workers changes many things. Maximization now embraces many more dimensions, and that enlarges the space, and hence payoff, for search and adjustment. The adjustment process is spotlighted because matching jobs and workers is a much more complicated fit. The full range of working conditions must be considered; no longer can it be assumed that wages, as the only adjustment variable, will neatly compensate for whatever failings might exist elsewhere and are an unerringly accurate proxy for worker productivity.

As chapter 4 will show, the impact of working conditions on effort supply can no longer be ignored, especially where firm-specific human capital is involved. In other words, the necessity for explicitly changing job quality is a vastly more important labor market concern. But how job quality is to be changed is much less clear-cut. The different dimensions of job quality affecting on-the-job performance; the limits, both technical and those arising from the institutional circumstances of conflict, on job quality change; the full extent and pervasiveness of one-tailed mismatches; the scope for departing from traditional roles and relationships; and the tension between worker diversity and pressures for on-the-job standardization—all need much further examination before definite answers can be expected. It is thus no great surprise to learn that work reorganization must proceed gingerly and experimentally in response to this limited state of our knowledge.

Two broad propositions can be put forth. One is that the complexity of the employment relationship has many ramifications in many different areas of labor market activity and work organization. It is unwise to take jobs and workers for granted in a simple and idealized version of their status and relationship; leaving out essential aspects of how work organization changes and labor market adjustment processes interact is not likely to give us a true or useful picture of what actually happens. Whatever complexity and difficulty are thereby introduced are likely to be worth it, as they mirror and enhance our understanding of the actual processes themselves. The other is to recognize that beyond complexity lies conflict. As argued earlier, as long as the workplace is largely bitterly contested terrain, then the consequences for that struggle of any action by the parties can never be ignored. Although this may limit some actions, especially those where the fact of firm dominance must be squarely faced, a more conscious awareness of conflict might, paradoxically, make possible its more expeditious resolution.

Finally, by far the most important conclusion to be drawn from this chapter's discussion is that supreme confidence cannot be placed in the ability of the external labor market to achieve the standard equilibrium and implied optimal welfare outcomes concerning wage determination and its smooth matching of jobs and workers. Contrariwise, many factors conspire to generate results that depart greatly from those positions. These factors comprise an imposing list: (1) the great complexities associated with worker heterogeneity and the many dimensions of job quality; (2) the active intermediary role for firms and the greater range of discretion for workers, which both come into play to fill in those penumbral voids where the market cannot quite reach; (3) the transcendant authority and legitimacy issues raised once conflictual exchange among unequal agents is accepted; (4) the heightened importance of high-level performance by workers for achieving potential productivity gains and the many and various barriers standing in its way; and (5) the free lunch implications that flow from one-tailed mismatch and the economics of organizational choice. They all support a Nordhausian view of labor markets where adjustment lags, and the interaction and interdependence of these many complicated factors indicate that how work is organized will matter greatly. In chapter 4, the spotlight shifts to consideration of the internal labor market and further clarification and resolution of many of these issues.

Internal Labor Market Complexities: Effort, Know-how, Honesty, and Job Design

New thinking about developments occurring within internal labor markets has also produced a rich crop of anomalies and complexities that have likewise spurred theoretical innovation. Remarkably, before this theoretical resurgence, the nature of job-worker relationships within the firm and the extent and significance of possible variability in worker performance were long considered, especially by economic theorists, as relatively inconsequential items. Workers, it was thought, would always have few opportunities not to put forth a standard quantum of effort, deploy their firm-specific skill, knowledge, and experience commensurate with the remuneration thereof, and be other than honest, cooperative, and forthcoming in complying with transactional arrangements defining the labor contract. In part these attitudes reflected the judgment that any such variability would yield fairly small deviations of no great matter. They lacked salience. After all, workers are not paid to like what they do, nor to do what they think they do best, nor even to do their utmost; rather, they are paid simply to do what the firm requires on the job, certainly no less and, given coordinated activity, arguably no more.

In part these attitudes reflected the judgment that any deviations were bound to be transient because they were incompatible with optimizing behavior by economic agents. In their own interest, firms would be forced to eliminate errors by overseeing workers, letting incompetents and malcontents go and reshuffling others, revising jobs, adjusting wages, and generally aligning work duties with worker capabilities and aspirations. Likewise, workers would gain by correctly matching themselves to the proper jobs. With each of the parties relatively free to better itself, observed slippages—departures from presumptively ideal outcomes—could only be momentary and evanescent events, destined to be overborne by the powerful equilibrating force of self-interest. The labor contract and adjustments in the terms of exchange were at one with all other economic transactions.

Recently, there has been increasing concern over whether such complacency about the employment relationship is justifiable, and questions of work organization and the labor contract are receiving fresh attention. Notions of transiency and lack of saliency are both being reconsidered. The simple injunction of ensuring that workers do what the firm requires is, under modern production conditions, a more formidable undertaking in both of its parts. What is required of workers is not always completely specifiable; monitoring individual worker performance, in group activity, is never simple and can be quite costly. Instead, worker performance depends more upon ability deployment and effort intensity than upon simply carrying out assigned tasks, and questions of motivation and tapping potential productivity through appropriate incentives become vital and can greatly affect outcomes. Moreover, it cannot be assumed that workers will always fully utilize their firm-specific human capital and that transaction costs associated with fulfilling labor contracts will be inconsequential. Nor, as I suggested in chapter 3, can it be safely assumed that external labor market pressures ensure desired performance.

Many economists are now rising to the challenge of recasting the theory of the firm, especially larger firms, to more adequately reflect these aspects of the employment relationship. They have inevitably focused on the complexities of the labor contract, and have uniformly rejected the view of it as a simple, unequivocal, unidimensional wage payment, easily adjusted to compensate for all other job facets, in return for a standard quantum of homogeneous effort. Rather, efficient worker performance must be induced through adjusting all the circumstances that determine willing participation, instead of being taken for granted as a normal quid pro quo for an offered wage. Effort, skill development and utilization, and honest, forthcoming, and cooperative behavior will be strongly influenced by the internal organization of the firm and the underlying quality of jobs. Although new approaches to the employment relationship may vary considerably in other respects, as subsequent discussion of the specific and closely interrelated issues of effort variability, firm-specific human capital, transaction costs, and organizational rent will reveal, they all agree on the importance and relevance of organizational arrangements in determining workplace outcomes. The first section of this chapter will focus on effort variability; the second will address the issues raised by the growth of firm-specific human capital and notions of organizational rent; and the third will cover transaction costs. Some concluding observations will be offered in the final section.

Effort Variability

Given the strategic role allotted to effort supply, analyzing its determinants becomes an obvious and natural point of departure; whatever the differences among the various approaches, the supply of effort is not usually taken for granted as an invariant and easily controlled activity. (A discussion of effort supply leveraged by firm-specific human capital will be deferred to the next section.) More specifically, in these new approaches to the employment relationship, some or all of the following conditions obtain: effort is variable; workers define jobs; tasks are not rote; information about job duties and worker performance is incomplete; uncertainty, transaction costs, and attitudes toward risk may be important factors in shaping work arrangements; enforcement is difficult and costly; and compliance is not automatic. In such circumstances, the nature of the work contract and modes of work organization must allow for much greater scope and flexibility in job specification and for much more interaction between workers and their jobs.[1]

Approaches most closely related to traditional theories have stressed enforcement mechanisms. For instance, Alchian and Demsetz (1972) and Stiglitz (1975) have emphasized the innate rationality, in group work activity, of individual workers withholding their effort or shirking, because each thereby appropriates an entire leisure gain but forgoes only a pro rata share of the consequent income loss. Thus, workers have a rational incentive to "turn off." Alchian and Demsetz accordingly conclude that the efficient detecting of shirking is essential for the firm's success; it can be achieved only by allowing the shirker detectors, the firm's owners or their agents, the incentive of sole claim to the residual left after meeting all contractual obligations. These conditions, for them, are satisfied by the classical capitalist firm.

Stiglitz similarly argues for the necessity of supervision and hierarchical organization, but with a different emphasis. Nonshirking workers themselves want shirking detected to avoid the loss thereby otherwise imposed upon them. They also support hierarchy because it economizes on the otherwise prohibitive costs of acquiring and utilizing information if it were not thus concentrated within a relatively small group. Lazear (1981) has argued that, in order to avert withholding of effort supply by workers, an upward sloping lifetime wage schedule is required. A deferred wage payment schedule, contingent on workers maintaining specified levels of performance as determined by the firm, is the proper incentive to encourage high levels of effort supply. Since workers would be dismissed for shirking, deferring rewards results in heavy penalties, and workers will thus be deterred.[2]

More recently, Carmichael (1989) has extended this approach by suggesting that, in principle, no wage premium would be required to deter shirking. Firms, themselves presumptively deterred from cheating by reputational considerations, would pay a worker her or his opportunity wage at all times and, contingent on the worker never shirking throughout her or his tenure, pay a bonus at the end of the worker's last period. At the same, time workers

---

1. For a more detailed and complete exposition of many of the approaches that will be discussed here, see Rozen 1983, chap. 2.

2. Mention should be made of other ingenious mechanisms designed to deter shirking that have been offered in the literature: posting forfeitable performance bonds, imposing nonrefundable employment fees, establishing schedules of sanctions and financial penalties, and front-loaded pay premiums combined with automatic dismissal. All such devices impose a substantial cost on workers detected shirking, either as a direct financial charge or an indirect loss by having to move into inferior employment. They all, however, raise moral hazard issues on the employer side or pose considerable problems of implementation. See Shapiro and Stiglitz 1984; Yellen 1984.

would compete for such jobs, since the bonus gives them an edge over alternatives, by paying an entrance fee. This competition would force up the entry fee until the net returns to workers, inclusive of both end-period bonus and entry fee, would exactly equal their alternative wage offers. The result would be self-enforcing agreements with no shirking and also no premium; the lifetime wage schedule would be completely flat, but would include an entry fee and end-period bonus. It should be noted that, throughout this one-firm work career, neither habitual behavior nor trust and loyalty would affect the worker's shirking propensities.

In contrast to these approaches, which have focused on workers' more negative proclivities (i.e., preventing them from "turning off"), other economists have been more interested in exploring what "turns on" workers. Leibenstein (1966, 1976, 1987), in introducing the concept of X-efficiency, argues that, because effort variability is of such overwhelming importance, motivating workers to perform more effectively is what distinguishes the successful firm. The chief function of management is, therefore, to define jobs in ways that will coax more and better effort from workers. Management must constantly strive to adjust the various elements of work organization so that workers will be consistently motivated to do their utmost. Such views are also commonplace among both managerial theorists and practicing managers.

Some economists have formalized conditions of work most likely to generate consistently high levels of effort intensity by reference to the concept of either a wage norm (Annable 1984) or job norm (Rozen 1983). Such norms embody more or less shared expectations concerning what is fair and equitable treatment, and usually imply various sorts of premiums with regard to wages and conditions of work, respectively. The desired levels of effort will be supplied if the resulting criterion of "a fair day's wage for fair day's work" or a "good job" is met. More neutrally, this process can be viewed as setting an efficiency wage whereby effort levels are conditioned on wage premiums. As should be evident, the operational utility of the norm concept relies heavily on a relatively stable and shared expectation set prevailing for an extended period and thereby making sense as a common reference point. It is greatly influenced by customary and traditional considerations and tends to stickiness. It cannot withstand, however, very sharp and sudden changes in the underlying economic environment (see Flanagan 1984). Recall that Nordhaus (1984, 420) captured its essence (under normal economic conditions) very well: ". . . if the speed of adjustment in auction markets is the speed of light, then that of contractual labor markets is 55 miles an hour." Wage stickiness and wage norms have, in particular, important macroeconomic consequences (Perry 1980 and 1983).

Some approaches have stressed the inherent bargaining tension, arising from workers' ability to control their own effort levels, in the workplace. Whether workers will do their utmost depends upon what kind of bargain can be struck. For instance, Williamson, Wachter, and Harris (1975) have emphasized the idea of job idiosyncracy, the notion that each job is the exclusive, up to a point, domain of its practitioner. The firm cannot, therefore, order workers to undertake specific tasks, but must instead induce them to provide what they alone control. Thus, obligational markets are created that involve more complex interactions than command-and-obey, and firms and workers are locked into a long-term, give-and-take relationship. The essence of that relationship is to establish an atmosphere of trust and codes of conduct ensuring that mutual long-run benefit will not be sacrificed by either party for a short-run advantage. Similarly, Aoki (1980) stresses that associational continuity builds up organizational rent over time in the sense that the "unique and lasting interaction of the organizational resources" produces economic gains beyond what is "possible through mere casual combination of marketed factors of production." Organizational rent is generated because workers embody firm-specific human capital, in the form of specialized skills, knowledge, and experience, as a result of their quasi-permanent association with the firm. Accordingly, as will be more fully explored in the next section, a bargaining process over the amount and disposition of organizational rent will determine not simply pure effort supply, but also how intensively workers will jointly utilize their firm-specific human capital.

Efficient, or simple implicit, labor contract theory (Hall 1980) also focuses on long-term employment arrangements that are determined, as again Nordhaus has suggested, on the basis of the economic climate rather than the particular economic weather of the moment. These contracts reflect a bargaining process supported by a mutuality of interest derived from institutionalized comparative advantage. Firms, because of various structural features relating to their superior ability to bear risk, engage in financial intermediation, achieve transaction cost economies, and forecast economic trends, can provide some combination of insurance, in the form of employment continuity, and income smoothing, in the form of stable growth in money wages largely unaffected by sharp profit variations, in exchange for the traditional managerial prerogative of control over the workers' effort. The exact terms of such bargains can either be explicitly bilaterally negotiated or take the form of more implicit understandings to which both parties are committed.

Finally, the workplace public goods argument (Freeman and Medoff 1979; Duncan and Stafford 1980) is very relevant in connection with optimal effort supply. As I argued in chapter 3, workplace conditions and job quality are likely to be common over broad groups of workers and, thus, pose a classic free-rider problem. Each individual has an incentive to let others try to change workplace conditions and not take action himself or herself. The result is that, as long as only individual action is considered, work conditions can be affected only after prolonged exit indicates a serious problem. Collective action, however, offers a channel for overcoming this free-rider constraint. Collective bargaining can provide an effective mechanism for eliciting and articulating worker views and aspirations and for internalizing workplace

externalities. The parties can, accordingly, achieve a more comprehensive and superior agreement that, in turn, will positively affect worker performance.

All four bargaining approaches supply the theoretical economic glue that binds the parties to the employment relationship together for extended periods of time. The essence of maintaining that relationship is to ensure that, in the bargaining process, the opportunities for mutual, long-run benefit will not be sacrificed by either party for short-run advantage. The source of the economic glue—job idiosyncracy, organizational rent, institutionalized comparative advantage, or workplace externalities—can assume considerable operational significance in defining the modalities of bargaining and levels of effort intensity. Some kinds of economic glue will bind the parties more strongly and surely than others, and some will be to the advantage of one party over the other. For instance, it is one thing to argue, as in the institutionalized comparative advantage case, that the nature of the employment relationship simply expresses a natural division of responsibility and position, arising directly from innate structural features and leading to a straightforward quid pro quo arrangement; it is quite something else, as in the organizational rent case, to stress constant and inherent conflict as each tries to gain a decisive advantage. Accordingly, some approaches suggest that bargaining can take place within fairly circumscribed limits that leave few opportunities for radical shifts in position, whereas others indicate a much more open-ended context and potential variability of outcome. Thus, a connection exists between the breadth and nature of bargaining and the particular approach chosen; organizational rent implies the least restricted bargaining option, institutionalized comparative advantage the most cut and dried, and bargaining associated with job idiosyncracy and collective voice would probably lie between these extremes. Possibilities for varying effort levels should be similarly ordered.

The labor-managed, or cooperative, firm, in which labor hires capital, is another approach (Vanek 1970; Jones and Svejnar 1982; Pryor 1983) that directly raises issues of effort supply. This approach argues that increasing the level and intensity of participation will lead to greater effort because of greater worker control over job conditions. Only by having a direct say about one's job, because workers are now also the managers, can work be shaped in accordance with the wishes of those involved in it. Similarly, the neo-Marxist critique of contemporary work organization (Marglin 1974; Edwards 1979; Gordon, Edwards, and Reich 1982; Bowles 1985) also stresses control over job conditions. The workplace is contested terrain; employers seek to control the job in order to prevent worker solidarity and unity. Work organization is not designed for efficiency alone, but rather more importantly as an instrument for maintaining the employer's dominance. Where there is a conflict between introducing a more efficient production technique and a consequent potential loss of control, firms are likely to suppress those modes of work organization and job quality changes which may threaten their control over the work process. Thus, even if potentially favorable effort consequences are likely, desirable improvements in job quality, such as enlarging the responsibility and participation of workers, will not be pursued because they may alter existing authority relationships.

Finally, Akerlof (1982) views the labor contract as a "partial gift exchange": the firm does nice things for workers, such as paying wage premiums, and the workers respond in kind by stepping up their effort. Subsequently (Akerlof 1984), he suggests several rationalizing paradigms that provide theoretical support, as maximizing economic behavior, for such compensation plans and their indicated consequences. In summary, in each of these various approaches, a particular view of the employment relationship is central to its analytical framework. The effort bargain—what a worker will do in exchange for what considerations—is not a simple well-behaved relationship that can be neatly expressed as a supply curve of effort related to a uniquely defined real wage; the labor market is not an auction where continuous bidding and recontracting takes place. Rather, as these approaches suggest, influencing what happens on the job is of tremendous importance in determining effort supply and worker performance, and work conditions reflect varied and complex pressures.[3] Some approaches emphasize the significance, in defining jobs, of managerial performance and ingenuity in either monitoring or motivating workers; others emphasize the necessity for continuous bargaining to induce workers to do their utmost; and some lay stress on the role of collective action by workers. Although an exceedingly wide spectrum of views, all agree that attention must be paid to the effect of on-the-job conditions, whose specification is at the core of each approach, upon worker effort-supply (chapter 5 will discuss these issues further).

Firm-Specific Human Capital and Organizational Rent

Issues concerning firm-specific human capital and organizational rent are closely related to effort supply, because variability in the extent to which firm-

---

3. Some skeptics may argue that concern over effort intensity is much ado about nothing unless reliable measures of its quantitative significance are produced. Weitzman and Kruse's survey (1990) of numerous studies on the relationship between productivity and variables that might be proxies for effort is suggestive and supportive in this regard, but more conclusive evidence is needed. If effort levels were an insignificant matter, one would be hard put to explain both the extensive interfirm variation in observed behavioral variables (e.g., productivity, morale, turnover, absenteeism, grievances) that must be closely linked to effort, and heightened managerial interest in monitoring technology and worker-control techniques. Further, the discussion of the importance of rhythm, pace, and tempo in chap. 3 is very relevant for underlining the significance of group and team activity in determining effort intensity. Finally, it should be noted that, in analyzing effort intensity, much depends upon a prior view of whether effort is predominantly elicited on the basis of shared commitments (i.e., flows relatively freely as a consequence of identification with and loyalty to the firm), or extracted by virtue of a relationship of authority and dominance (i.e., grudgingly provided under threat of effective sanctions for nonperformance.) For the last issue, see Walton and McKersie 1989; Bowles and Gintis 1990.

specific human capital is electively deployed affects subsequent outcomes enormously; such issues have been of central importance in several recent developments of great theoretical and practical interest. The prevalence of long-term employment arrangements and highly sophisticated recruitment and training programs, the pattern of lifetime wage schedules and profit-participation schemes, and the pace and incidence of technological progress and productivity growth have all been tied to the growth of firm-specific human capital, and have sparked a more intensive investigation of its ramifications. Paralleling this appreciation of its significance, however, has been a greater awareness of the increased complexity and interpretive challenges that firm-specific human capital and organizational rent introduce into the analysis of labor market issues. How firm-specific human capital is financed, its rewards shared, and the behavioral options opened up thereby must be more searchingly reviewed. The set of conditions linked to firm-specific human capital—that production is a joint and coordinated activity, that, by definition, firm-specific human capital cannot be quickly reproduced and is embodied in the existing work force, that it can be financed in a variety of ways, and that its translation into tangible and concrete productive activity, and therefore on-the-job performance, can be influenced by both workers and the firm—creates a rich mixture of possible outcomes associated with its development. Determining what lies behind worker deployment of firm-specific human capital and how organizational rent is divided is a natural extension of the question of the pure effort bargain itself.

Three seemingly distinct, but actually closely related, issues arise in connection with firm-specific human capital: (1) optimal separation—either party may terminate the employment relationship in ways that make the other party, and society, worse off; (2) optimal performance—labor contracts are necessarily incomplete; accordingly, to directly improve its own position and/or as a bargaining tactic, either party may change on-the-job behavior or arrangements—the worker through shirking or the firm through degrading working conditions or falsely evaluating worker performance—to the detriment of the other; and (3) optimal sharing—as Aoki has stressed, the parties are inevitably locked together in a continuous struggle over dividing the organizational rent, the synergistic-experiential surplus that exceeds what a similar collection of just-hired factors could produce. It will prove useful to discuss these issues sequentially, because that order mirrors the logical evolution of the problems raised by firm-specific capital; discussion of optimal separation will directly lead to behavioral issues, including effort supply and promise keeping, in a nonseparation context, whose resolution, in turn, will depend upon how organizational rent is shared.

Optimal Separation

In a firm-specific human capital context, this issue arises because each party is vulnerable, to the extent of its financing, to the other party terminating the relationship for its own reasons (Mortenson 1978; Hashimoto and Yu 1980; Hashimoto 1981). Suppose, in the postinvestment period, that either workers received a higher wage offer from elsewhere even though their firm-specific capital would not be utilized or the firm's actual sales would fall below anticipated levels. In the former case, if the firm financed the buildup of firm-specific human capital and therefore received the entire incremental return from it, the worker would receive only the basic opportunity wage and could blithely leave for any job offer that paid more than that; the firm's investment would be lost and society's total output would fall. In the latter case, if the worker financed the buildup and that was fully reflected in the wage the firm must pay, then the firm would dismiss some workers anytime sales fell short of projected levels; those workers would lose their entire investment and, even if reemployed elsewhere, total output would fall because they would not be utilizing their firm-specific human capital. Whenever either of the parties pursues its own interest, under the stipulated circumstances, without taking into account the impact on the other, the possibility arises that one or both of the parties will suffer a loss, as will society in general, as total output falls.

In order to prevent such an outcome, various contractual possibilities have been suggested. The simplest would be some joint financing arrangement, since that would narrow the range of outcomes that would trigger nonoptimal separations. To the extent workers shared in financing, and were accordingly compensated, they would unjustifiably leave only if the external wage offer exceeded this larger magnitude; to the extent firms shared, they would not unjustifiably dismiss workers as long as quasi-rents were positive, thus enabling some portion of their investment costs to be recovered. A more sophisticated variant would be to set the financing to guard against the most likely deviation. If the worker were more likely to quit, then putting the burden of financing on him or her would ensure his or her departure only if productivity elsewhere, and thus (assuming, as in chap. 3, a very rough rather than precise linkage) the offered wage, were larger; and likewise, if the firm is more likely to dismiss because of a sales shortfall, then ensuring that it financed the investment would entail that only in the socially desirable case that postinvestment sales fell below what was previously produced would the firm dismiss the worker. In both cases, the socially correct decision to continue production as long as quasi-rents were positive would be made. Similarly, forms of near indenture, such as exclusive service contracts, could prevent unjustified quits by workers and tenure provisions could prevent unjustified dismissals by firms. Unhappily however, indenture-like provisions would also prevent the worker from quitting, as would tenure the firm from dismissing, when those actions would be socially desirable. Finally long-term contracts, with periodic renegotiation, could also reduce undesirable separations by permitting revisions to accommodate unforeseen change.

All of these contractual arrangements could only limit, but not completely eliminate, the possibility of private, and social, loss from one party exclusively pursuing its own interest. Some have argued that indemnification mechanisms—employment bond forfeitures, severance clauses, payback arrangements—would ensure socially correct choices and not impose unwarranted losses on the other party. If either party had to indemnify the other for its share of investment costs, then any better wage offer or sales shortfall would have to be sufficiently large to make the separation socially correct. If, however, either party could, with relative impunity, evade adhering to contractual terms, then in practice indemnification could be avoided. And indeed, as my previous discussion of effort supply indicated, such an option exists for workers; they can shirk in utilizing their firm-specific human capital to encourage their dismissal, rather than quit and have to pay the indemnity. Nor are firms without similar countermeasures; they can, despite contractual obligations, do many things to worsen working conditions or reduce remuneration, putting pressure on workers to quit and thereby avoiding indemnification. Perversely, indemnification would provide incentives to take socially counterproductive action to avoid paying the indemnity. In sum, as long as either party can, relatively free from retribution, take on-the-job actions harmful to the other party, then indemnification, and any other contractual agreement depending upon positive compliance, will be impotent. As Parsons has stated this idea, "Both parties can alter other, less observable aspects of contract performance to induce the other to break the match. A firm can make a worker's life quite intolerable by varying the nonpecuniary returns of the job. The worker on the other hand can induce the firm to break the match by an appropriate display of sloth or ineptitude" (1986, 825). Human ingenuity ex post will dominate seemingly iron-clad ex ante agreements.

Optimal Performance

The ability of the parties to control, each in a different way, on-the-job activities directly raises the issue of optimal performance. In effect, firm-specific human capital "leverages" effort supply by greatly augmenting the on-the-job areas within which effort intensity plays a critical role. After all, if the parties have the option of worsening each other's position through on-the-job adjustments that cannot be effectively deterred, then such capabilities can be deployed at all times, not simply in connection with indemnity avoidance or achieving a desired separation. Not only can such tactics be employed in pursuit of other goals, but, in and of themselves, they promise some advantage to their initiators. Shirking and withholding effort does provide workers some (temporary?) leisure utility, and allowing job conditions to worsen, or subtly and unilaterally worsening compensation terms, can bring the firm (temporary?) direct financial relief. Because neither party can effectively deter such determined action by the other, contractual arrangements will be of little help. If the optimal separation problem arises because one party ignores the other's investment in firm-specific human capital, optimal behavior must deal with the possibility of either party "squeezing" the other precisely because that investment creates an incentive for quasi–rent seeking.

If the worker knows, in the firm-financed case, that the firm will continue to produce as long as a positive quasi-rent is earned and he or she is relatively free to adjust the provision of his or her firm-financed, firm-specific human capital with little fear of reprisal, then a little bit of shirking might not only be welcome on its own, but it could also induce the firm to be more sharing. Similarly, in the worker-financed case, if the firm knows that the worker will stay as long as he or she earns more than elsewhere and it is relatively free to adjust working conditions without greatly affecting output and worker performance, then the firm might discover previously undiscernible workplace economies and exotic forms of de facto downward wage flexibility. But such processes cannot go very far before exploding; "squeezing" should induce highly destabilizing reactions. Each party will want to be the first off the mark to gain the direct advantages and make the bargaining point, and retaliation by the other in kind is likely to be very swift.

The limits to this process in the form of output being drastically affected by such negative behavior may be soon reached, but much damage will have already been done. In the short run, also, countermeasures in the form of harassment of presumed shirkers by the firm, and effort withdrawal turning into outright sabotage by workers—what Veblen called the "conscientious withdrawal of efficiency"—will embitter the employment relationship. Over the longer haul, workers would shun firms whose reputation for squeezing would spread, and firms would redesign work arrangements to reduce their vulnerability to effort withdrawal by workers. In sum, there is a great potential for very destructive and destabilizing relationships to develop, and both parties will have to weigh very carefully the dangers of starting down this road. In any case, society has an overwhelming interest in persuading the parties to resist the temptations for squeezing afforded by the growth of firm-specific human capital. What is required, then, is a mechanism that makes cooperative behavior more attractive. To respond to that issue, first consider the sources of their power to make on-the-job adjustments.

To begin with, inherent in the notion of firm-specific human capital itself is the inability to look to external markets for quick correction; the worker cannot get the same kind of job, and the firm cannot get an identical replacement. Indeed, being stuck with each other generates those tempting quasi-rents. Thus, the external market establishes very wide limits on what the parties can do. Although the question of who then has the stronger position to vary on-the-job performance or conditions clearly depends upon particular circumstances, nevertheless some general considerations imply a rebuttable presumption of firm advantage. First, to the extent that teamwork and interdependence on the job imply large linkage effects, triggering heavy losses from minor malfeasance, then any malingering on the job is likely to be fairly disruptive. The loss to the firm is likely to exceed whatever gain accrues to the worker. Knowing that, however, firms accordingly have very strong prior incentives to arrange production activity so that small disruptions would not have large consequences. Second, alternatives matter very much. Highly firm-specific workers do not have much bargaining power, and firms would much rather be faced with individual defections, which can more easily be absorbed, than a collective challenge that would pose far greater problems. But when push comes to shove, and even though collective action can be a meliorative factor, the contest is ultimately between a lonely and isolated individual and a large, impersonal organization, and thereby is tilted, for the usual reasons relating power to size, in the latter's favor.

Third, the qualitative characteristics of opportunities for exercising on-the-job adjustments are clearly relevant. The easier it is for workers to adjust levels of effort and performance and the harder it is for firms to detect such deviations, the stronger will be the workers' position. The same argument holds if firms can degrade working conditions in ways that workers can neither follow nor do very much about. But even more important in this connection is the generally acknowledged job-design prerogative of firms. That is a powerful lever, since on-the-job activities can be shaped with prevision to narrow the workers', and enlarge the firm's, flexibility in these respects. There is thus a strong component of endogeneity in job design for precisely these reasons; firms in general have considerable freedom to design the workplace the way they want it to be, and over the longer haul that is, for them, a more subtle and useful instrument than using their power to make adjustments in ongoing jobs. Finally, broader considerations must be mentioned. The parties' ability to achieve their objectives depends not only on what is happening on the job, but in an important way on the more indirect pressures emanating from the legal-institutional environment within which these struggles take place. The firm's greater influence in shaping that environment in its favor confers a tremendous advantage.

Whoever has the advantage in using on-the-job adjustments, some have viewed this issue more as a question of morality than as a matter-of-fact, everyday struggle. If only contracts could be more readily enforced, or the offending parties could be more summarily and certainly punished for their breaches, then this disturbing and unpretty picture of widespread deceit, misrepresentation, and dishonesty would have little force. But as job design endogeneity indicates, if struggle is the motive force that dominates the relationship, then judgments on tactics cannot be derived from homilies on morality, but must be evaluated in the light of the actual process being described. In that context, as my subsequent discussion of optimal sharing and transaction costs will show, quite a lot, if not all, of what the parties do will seem justifiable— certainly to themselves. Consideration of optimal performance, then, suggests that behavior and motivation depend upon the underlying character of the employment relationship: its perceived fairness, equity, and legitimacy. What each contributes and how the relationship reflects changing contributions over time will enter into the parties' evaluation of its legitimacy, and thus determine the spirit in which they maintain their understandings. Or to put it more simply, performance will depend upon how organizational rent is shared.

Optimal Sharing and Organizational Rent

Focusing on behavior, and what motivates the parties, leads straight to the organizational rent issue: what determines how the parties share the joint gain arising from associational continuity and the consequent growth of firm-specific human capital, and how does that sharing affect the parties' on-the-job adjustments? In the end, organizational rent raises fundamental issues of legitimacy and perceived equity; in a context of inherent distributional conflict and dynamic change, the parties must wrestle over who contributes what to, and thereby receives what from, their joint gain. And especially where efficient production processes are characterized by local initiatives and greatly devolved responsibilities, and rely heavily on coordination, teamwork, and information sharing by workers for their success, the parties will be in a bargaining situation with inherently wide limits. For one thing, one cannot stress an enhanced role for workers in generating organizational rent and, at the same time, narrowly restrict their bargaining strength and aspirations. Why should workers, if they contribute so much, be satisfied getting relatively little? For another, how organizational rent is shared clearly depends upon specific technological and organizational attributes, for example, the extent and distribution of firm-specific human capital among workers and the importance of cooperation and teamwork, and the parties cannot help but seek to influence the development of such attributes in their favor. If bargaining strength is sensitive to variations in technological-organizational features, how can the parties remain indifferent?

More specifically, I will argue the following five points: (*a*) a major source of, and accordingly claim upon, organizational rent is the workers' ability to vary their work effort; such variability both underlines the overriding importance of incentives and can be instrumental in strengthening the workers' bargaining position; (*b*) asymmetry in worker and shareholder interest in the growth in the firm's value is unnecessary and arbitrary and arises from the common condition that no equity interest in such gains is ordinarily available to workers; in fact, devising property rights mechanisms for equity sharing can be an integral and essential part of bargaining; (*c*) bargaining is consequently likely to range more widely, involving the pattern of technological-organizational change, growth policy, and equity sharing, rather than being confined, say, to dividing a residual that is net of growth-inducing expenditure; (*d*) absent specific countermeasures, the bargaining strength of workers would become greater over time; and (*e*) largely as a result of all the foregoing considerations, the strategic nature of the consequential bargaining game will be uppermost in the parties' minds. In essence, once the workers' role in organizational rent generation is conceded, issues not normally and traditionally considered in the theory of the firm become central.

Variable Effort

As indicated previously, a view of workers as automatons carrying out easily specifiable and predetermined activities with minimal costs of monitoring and supervision does not accurately describe contemporary work. Especially where workers build up considerable firm-specific human capital over time, such capital can be either more or less intensively utilized and cooperatively employed; its services do not flow uniformly and automatically. Workers do not necessarily, in other words, utilize their skills, energies, and experience completely and fully at all times; instead, they will be responsive to the pattern of incentives, and organizational rent depends in a very fundamental sense on the extent of workers' willingness to use their firm-specific human capital and cooperate as a team. Whatever, under such circumstances, proper incentives might be—an area of much disagreement—the fact that workers can substantially define the character, pace, and intensity of their efforts strengthens their hand in any bargaining situation. Likewise, it expands worker options and introduces much greater subtlety into the bargaining process, since workers are not forced into the either/or position of completely providing or withholding their services. The devastating consequences of work-to-rule job actions are a case in point. Management must either find ways of eroding this kind of control over effort or accommodate to the bargaining posture thereby implied. Thus, one of the corollaries of accepting the importance of firm-specific human capital is that motivating high-level performance by workers will dominate enforcing contractual obligations as the chief managerial responsibility. After all, if contractual obligations could be easily and costlessly enforced, organizational rent would not arise in the first place. The rule of the workshop would be "tell 'em what to do and see that they do it"; there would be little basis for attributing outcomes to actions dependent upon worker initiative and human capital.

An important and often unrecognized consideration with regard to work rhythms and pacing is greatly significant in this context: namely (and as previously mentioned), the externalities associated with the infectious nature of work routines. The group nature and inherent interdependence of work arrangements forge strong links within the workplace. Any one worker's pace will be affected by the pace set by all other workers, and thus organizational arrangements that encourage high-level and cooperative effort by many in the work force will lead to pressure on laggards to keep the pace. By the same token, if organizational pressures are in the other direction, it becomes that much more difficult to overcome the consequent inertia. These considerations of pacing and work tempo and of coordination, information sharing, and cooperative teamwork imply, accordingly, an enlarged multiplier effect on effort levels from success or failure in setting dominant work rhythms.[4]

---

4. A very important issue of time duration arises in connection with pacing and intensity. Although considerable elevation in work intensity for relatively short time periods can usually be

Asymmetry in Worker and Shareholder Interest

In the usual model of the firm, workers live by the wage alone. They do not directly share in the firm's growing (or declining) value; such growth (or loss) accrues entirely to shareholders. The bargaining focus, as a result, is determined by this particular institutional specification. But on grounds of both productivity contribution and risk assumption, workers have a legitimate claim on, and stake in, the growth in the firm's value. Because their human capital is firm-specific and its intensity of use is conditional upon proper incentives, an equity share may be a motivational necessity. Outcomes will vary depending upon workers' substantive contribution, and the supply price for all-out effort may include a share of incremental gains in the firm's value. Likewise, workers' incomes are also at risk; they have a considerable interest in the firm's fortunes, since that influences the return to their firm-specific capital. If the firm fails, that input becomes worthless; if organizational rent diminishes, its return is lowered. Except for risk diversification, there is no reason against, and strong argument for, enabling workers to become shareholders on the basis of their functional role in providing firm-specific human capital.

Indeed, in order to ensure the optimal contribution from workers with firm-specific capital, precisely because of its deployment variability, some mechanism for fixing the present value of all the future consequences of their current actions must be put in place. Otherwise, workers would have a systematic incentive to adjust their provision of firm-specific human capital in ways that accelerate revenues and defer costs. Ceteris paribus, for instance, a research worker would use his or her knowledge to deliberately choose a currently cheap, but costly-to-replace, piece of equipment over something that

---

accommodated without very adverse consequences, sustaining fast-paced and high-intensity activity indefinitely is an entirely different matter. If firms view, especially if replacement or alternative arrangements were not too difficult, workers as being highly expendable, and therefore require them to perform at a sustained, excessively rapid and intense pace over long periods, then, as a consequence, those workers' subsequent capabilities and future work careers could be severely impaired. The history of labor relations reveals that where firms do not have to bear these real costs of decisions about pace, and in the many cases where workers are weakly positioned to resist such demands, the overall intensity of work activity can be excessive. If that were not the case, much labor legislation would be redundant; simply recall the struggle for the eight-hour day. Nor should such possibilities be casually dismissed on the economistic assumption that either the right compensating differential will always be forthcoming or individuals always operate with perfect foresight concerning the future. Like athletes who play "hurt" or ingest dangerous substances to perform better, workers too can be subject to various pressures to take actions not in their long-term interest. Indeed, precisely such pace and monitoring issues are at the heart of the "management by stress" controversy swirling around the work practices of the Japanese automobile manufacturers in this country. More generally and in brief, there is likely to be an "optimal tautness" target for work pace (and monitoring too): not too slow (or sufficiently absent) to permit great slack, and not too fast (or suffocating and heavy-handed) to be harmful and unsustainable for workers and induce counterproductive reactions. Under conditions of employer dominance, that target is likely to be missed.

would initially cost more but be cheaper over the longer haul; the gains would accrue to that worker now, and the higher future costs would presumably be borne by those who come after. If the worker chose the equipment that would yield a higher present value, he or she would bear the larger current costs and others would benefit from the prospectively greater future returns. The socially desirable time rate of discount would be exceeded because, in the circumstances, the relevant future consequences would not enter into the calculations of the providers of firm-specific human capital.

In principle, remedies for this deficiency could take the form of workers being allocated participation shares, ab initio and subsequently, in relation to both their risk-bearing and productivity contribution. After all, there is a complete analogy between such "sweat equity" and, say, founders' shares for a firm's original promoters, or stock option plans for its current executives. Workers would then have incentives to properly take into account the future consequences of their current action, since they would be reflected in the value of their shareholdings. Although the small size of any individual worker's share will obviously attenuate the relationship between action and consequence, nevertheless the collective interest of all workers will, through horizontal monitoring, generate considerable counterpressures.[5]

What Is Bargainable?

Both the importance of effort variability and teamwork in augmenting the significance of firm-specific human capital and the correspondingly greater legitimacy for the workers' claim for an equity share in the firm's appreciation greatly expand the scope of bargaining. Immediately, dividing the growth in the value of the firm between worker and shareholder becomes a major bargaining item. More important, the details of technological and organizational structure also become bargainable, since such arrangements can be instrumental in determining the strength of the parties' bargaining position. For instance, the amount and kind of firm-specific capital embodied in workers and the extent to which work organization conduces toward cohesiveness and unity among workers can both be very influential. To the extent that technology can be directed toward minimizing firm-specific human capital (say, by substituting capital for skilled labor) and organizational structure can be adapted to stratify and artificially divide workers (say, by manipulating job design), the position of shareholders will be strengthened.

In other words, many kinds of actions, some perhaps seemingly oriented toward wholly other objectives or even largely unrelated, may, in fact, have great consequences for the parties' relative position. Potentially, every action, even symbolic ones, can have an impact on their relative strengths. Hence, bargaining must embrace a much wider range of considerations than merely

---

5. For a related discussion, see Schlicht and von Weiszacker 1977. Issues concerning worker shares are discussed more fully in chap. 7 .

being confined to profit sharing. This consideration enormously increases the importance, and complicates the interpretation, of the parties' strategic behavior.[6] Those who view, in this context, all worker-management interaction as explicit or tacit bargaining have captured an important insight.

Trends in Bargaining Strength

Closely related to the enlargement of the bargaining agenda is the likelihood that, in the absence of specific countermeasures, the position of workers is likely to become increasingly strong over time. This development reflects changes over time in risk and capital-supply positions. With respect to risk, three points are relevant. First, as both their equity share and amount of firm-specific capital grow over time, workers, in fact, will be bearing more and more risk. Indeed, precisely because their human capital and equity holdings are both tied to the same enterprise, some have correctly viewed their risk position as too undiversified, and hence excessive.[7] Second, the overall degree of risk associated with the firm declines, at least up to a point, over time; the early period of any enterprise is always the chanciest. Third, as workers become wealthier over time, as a function of the firm's success, their willingness to bear risk becomes commensurately greater. For all of these reasons, workers will be in an increasingly stronger position to assume more of the risks of enterprise, and, in any case, they will have greater risk thrust upon them in the normal course of the firm's development. Both considerations reduce the importance of the shareholder's risk-taking function.

Likewise with respect to capital supply. First, arguably because knowledge, experience, and skill are both rapidly acquired and augmented rather than depleted by their use, firm-specific human capital is likely to grow more quickly and uniformly over time (and also depreciate more slowly) than physical capital; its relative importance to the firm will increase. Second, the firm's growth usually generates its own internal sources of accumulation, thereby lessening dependence upon external sources. Third, external debt capital (and equity for that matter) becomes, in fact, more available over time partly because survival attests to the firm's inherent worth and partly because the workers' ownership stake attests to their commitment to and concern for the enterprise.

---

6. Kochan, McKersie, and Cappelli (1984) make a similar point, from an industrial relations theory standpoint, by emphasizing the increasing importance and impact of strategic choice at higher levels that determine bargaining agendas and outcomes at lower levels. "Strategic decisions are those that alter the party's role or its relationship with other actors in the industrial relations system . . ." (22), and ". . . we believe that it is largely management strategic decisions that have initiated the process of fundamental change in the IR system" (23). In their view, industrial relations systems are being reshaped by more or less unilateral management decisions relating to such things as investment location, union recognition policies, new technology, degree of vertical integration, and work arrangement. Decisions in those areas subsequently condition what happens at the level of specific bargaining.

7. See Meade 1972.

As a limiting case, it is possible to argue, à la Keynes, for the euthanasia of the pure (i.e., nonworker) shareholder. If his or her major function is to supply capital and bear risk, then, as workers take on more and more risk, and are able to supply more and more capital, the functional role of the pure shareholder becomes progressively attenuated. Ultimately, the workers could threaten to leave en masse, rent similar equipment, and start anew unless the shareholders supply capital at its rental value as a pure debt obligation. This would be the true polar opposite of the case where pure shareholders completely control a firm because its easily replaceable workers possess no firm-specific human capital. As long as workers operated en bloc and physical capital is reproducible, the same counterthreat by pure shareholders would be nugatory. (See chap. 7, however, for a discussion of the functional utility of nonworker shareholders.)

Strategic Behavior and the Bargaining Process

The prospect of being progressively displaced in influence and importance over time cannot, ordinarily, be appealing to pure shareholders; naturally, strategic behavior to avert that outcome would become a very important part of the bargaining process. Self-preservation implies the need for counter-measures. As suggested previously, both technological and organizational strategies can be followed. Organizationally, strategies of cooptation and stratification become techniques for siphoning away the natural leadership of the work force and opening up routes for some workers to achieve personal goals through individual, rather than collective, action. Any organizational measures that make worker solidarity and unity more difficult will inhibit conscious collective action. Technologically, firms have an incentive to minimize the amount of firm-specific human capital embodied in the work force. In practice, this would imply designing the great majority of jobs to be performed with little skill or training, to contribute little to the career development of workers, and for which replacements could be easily secured. Correspondingly, more desirable jobs, and a chance to move up the organizational ladder, would be reserved for a small minority of privileged workers.

Workers, too, would engage in strategic behavior, seeking to build up class consciousness and solidarity. Their strategic interest in organizational and technological structure, and in job design, flow directly from the importance of these elements in determining their bargaining strength. Workers can also challenge actions by firms in these areas as being inconsistent with truly maximizing the value of the firm in the socially relevant sense. Policies that deliberately distort organizational and technological structure to maintain control cannot be in the best overall interests of the firm or society.[8] It may be in the pure shareholder's interest to robotize jobs and minimize firm-specific human capital, but the consequences for both the quality of worklife and

---

8. Compare the contrary position of Williamson (1979, 255–56).

allocative efficiency would be strongly adverse. If the answer to Marglin's question of "What Do Bosses Do?" is that they perpetuate their ownership position no matter what, then society can legitimately ask whether the resulting arrangements and outcomes justify that particular regime of property rights. Such shareholder strategies would most likely lead not to their euthanasia, but to their social expropriation. In sum, an approach that focuses bargaining solely on residual sharing fails to recognize that all factors bearing upon the relative strength of the parties become, of necessity, grist for the mill of strategic decision making; bargaining truly becomes almost coextensive with all interactions between the parties.

Once the idea of organizational rent is accepted, it follows that workers as a group have an exceedingly strong claim on both a share in all gains accruing to the firm and a right to participate in firm decision making. Such a view is consonant with, broadly interpreted, some emergent developments in labor-management relations and bargaining trends, and is a more relevant framework for explaining multidimensional bargaining strategies in complex choice situations than an approach that confines the bargaining process to dividing a diminished residual. It is likewise inconsistent to stress the importance of firm-specific human capital and not have the parties try to influence its form and extent in their favor. At the limit, enlarging the bargaining process makes the disposition of organizational rent seem less like a ritualized contest and more like a war in which the parties seek to eliminate, in a functional sense, each other.

Less melodramatically, optimal sharing implies that workers can claim a "piece of the action" and a greater say in what goes on in the firm. If their contribution is so instrumental to the generation of organizational rent, then these stipulations do not seem excessive. In any case, if long-run equilibrium mandates a rough equality between contribution and reward, then pressures for institutional arrangements for achieving those outcomes will be strong. And if the description of generating organizational rent accurately mirrors the underlying production process, then a greater degree of residual sharing, an equity stake, and worker participation in decision making will become increasingly important for firms. This conclusion certainly seems strengthened, despite some recent contrary trends, by even the most cursory examination of the evolution of employment relationships over the broad sweep of modern economic history of industrialized countries. All this still leaves a tremendous bargaining range, within which the qualitative and quantitative details of settlement will be negotiated by the parties.

Firm-Specific Capital and Organizational Rent: Summary

The issues raised by the existence of firm-specific human capital reveal a clear progression: from (*a*) concern that the parties, by not taking each other's interest into account, would non-optimally dissolve their relationship, to (*b*) preserving motivational intensity and integrity on the job in the face of incentives to shirk or worsen pay and working conditions, to (*c*) ultimately realizing that such questions can be discussed only within an organizational rent framework. Additionally, there is no magic formula, no contractual mechanism, to override the inherent conflict between workers and the firm.[9] Although society would gain if the parties were able to resolve the tensions associated with the provision of firm-specific human capital, there is no assurance that such resolution automatically occurs.

Each party has a distinct measure of control over what happens on the job, and utilization of that capability in furtherance of each one's objective may be incompatible with collaborative efforts to maximize their joint gain. In this process, the parties' positions are not necessarily symmetrical. Firms will be somewhat constrained in degrading working conditions because of possible negative consequences for output itself, but they usually possess powers of control and initiation, whose maintenance will be, in the firm's view, essential. Toward that end, the firm has considerable independence in managing the evolution of work organization and the related extent and character of firm-specific human capital to buttress its long-run position. Workers, contrariwise, can only exercise their more limited powers of not working to their full capabilities. It is important, moreover, to note the process aspects of this issue. Each party is aware that any particular decision and state of affairs is but a temporary phenomenon, a stage in an ongoing struggle, and hence must be evaluated with an eye to its future implications. This notion of long-term struggle expands the relevant conflict area to the political arena, and makes the extent and quality of workers' collective organization an important factor in its overall evolution.

Finally, enough has been said already to understand that firm-specific human capital magnifies the critical importance of the determinants of motivation and their relation to organizational design. If either of the parties view their relationship as dominated by struggle and conflict, within a framework of perceived inequity and illegitimacy, then each one's influence over the deployment of firm-specific human capital will be exercised in negative ways; strategy will be formed as part of an ongoing pattern of warfare. If, alternatively, the parties view their relationship as honest and cooperative with joint responsibility, fair sharing, and functionally relevant demarcations, then more forthcoming and trusting behavior will prevail.[10] Where contracts are necessarily incomplete in the sense that transactions cannot be exactly prespecified and monitored with precision, enforcement must take a back seat to motivation.

---

9. See Mitchell 1982, which, in a similar context, suggests gain sharing for attenuating this conflict, thereby achieving greater employment stabilization.

10. History thus leaves its mark on the present. The importance of trust and the way in which the past affects the present cannot be overemphasized in such matters. For a stimulating argument on the pervasive consequences of low trust in modern industrial societies, see Fox 1974.

Nor should it be thought that, as will be discussed more fully in the next section, overcoming deceit, dishonesty, and contract default can be neatly packaged as an inevitable cost of doing business, a transaction cost to be considered with all others in economic calculation. Rather, as my discussion suggests, the nature of the employment relationship will determine how the parties behave. It is one thing to assume an invariant quantum of dishonesty within a workgroup and ask how and at what cost, by varying forms of work organization, it can be offset; it is something else to think that behavior on the job may be shaped by conditions of work itself and the parties' overall relationship, and that honesty, cooperative teamwork, and effort are themselves responsive to those circumstances.

Transaction Costs

Although transaction costs have always been an inescapable feature of economic exchange, only recently has there developed, as Williamson (1979) suggests, "the growing realization that transaction costs are central to the study of economics." Furthermore, "the new institutional economics is preoccupied with the origins, incidence, and ramifications of transaction costs. Indeed, if transaction costs are negligible, the organization of economic activity is irrelevant, since any advantage one mode of organization appears to hold over another will simply be eliminated by costless contracting" (1979, 233). The ubiquity and importance of transaction costs matter very much for the labor market, since the employment relationship, especially where firm-specific human capital is involved, is influenced greatly by them. Significant idiosyncratic and nonstandard aspects of the job itself, dependence upon complicated reward and sanction schemes to affect worker performance, the complexities and uncertainties of the environment within which work takes place—all lead to contracting behavior that cannot easily be standardized and rote replicated. For better or worse, the labor contract is neither self-executing nor costless to arrange; the costs of transacting will play an important role in determining the nature of such contracts.

Specifically, with respect to the employment relationship, the conditions that make agreements costly to arrange and maintain need to be defined more precisely. Three possible sources of difficult and costly contracting can be distinguished. First, contract breach, or opportunism, is an ever-present and, frequently, quite likely possibility; as Williamson states, "opportunism is a central concept in the study of transaction costs . . . [and] is especially important for economic activity that involves transaction-specific investment in human and physical capital" (1979, 234). In other words, innate human propensities to lie and cheat, or "self-interest seeking with guile," in a milieu where such behavior will not ordinarily be easily detected will take the form of worker shirking or withholding effort on the job, or analogous conduct by firms, with disastrous and disruptive consequences for output. Second, the

inherent complexity of the labor process—a result of unpredictable and unforeseen outcomes, the inability to establish precise causal connections and
mechanisms between different kinds of labor input and output, the prevalence
of coordinated team activity, and the difficulty in assessing costs and benefits
and their distribution—ensures that fully responsive and complete contracts
can never be drawn up. Specification and performance evaluation of many job
facets will frequently not be possible; all contingencies cannot be foreseen.
Third, fundamental and basic differences between workers and employers,
and the consequent climate of struggle and conflict, add a further dimension to
the costs of contracting. The workplace is, to a smaller or larger degree, a
combat zone; if the parties' objectives are sharply inconsistent, if each denies
the other's legitimacy (in the sense of accepting its basic position and role), or
if their differences are exceedingly difficult to bridge, then any transaction
will be evaluated not only by its ordinary and immediate consequences, but
also by how it swings the balance of the ongoing conflict. In effect, a conflict
"tax" is imposed on transactions, since each of the parties must always keep in
mind the longer-run consequences for its respective position of any current
action.

The traditional interpretation of and response to these conditions defining
the basis for transaction costs is to emphasize (1) opportunism, mostly by
workers,[11] and (2) complexity as unalterable states of nature, and to ignore or
downplay (3) conflict as either minor and unimportant, or easily offset by
mobility and the existence of alternatives. Given this version of why transaction costs arise, the usual operational response is to adjust and adapt to the
presumptively immovable causal circumstances. This means a firm hand and
eternal vigilance, as well as formal compliance and enforcement mechanisms,
to contain opportunism, and a clearly defined authority position to best both
adjust to hard and unyielding circumstances and override minor conflicts.

An alternative, and to me more cogent, interpretation lays much greater
stress on conflict as a major force in defining the extent of transaction costs
and, in addition, as partially responsible for generating opportunism, which is
consequently viewed as a form of strategic behavior rather than innate moral
deficiency. Adhering to contractual terms cannot be judged in isolation from
consideration of their provenance. The relevance of complexity is not denied,
but the traditional response is arguably motivated more by control maintenance desires and as a strategic move in an ongoing struggle, rather than as a
more neutral adjustment to unalterable conditions; in this alternative view,
there are more effective ways of dealing with the inherent obstacles that a
tough world places in the path of agreement. This alternative position implies
that center stage is occupied by conflict resolution, especially to deal with all
the ramifications of the struggle over shares, and thus society's major policy

---

11. For instance, both Stiglitz (1975) and Williamson (1979) focus on worker transgres-
sions and assume that firms cannot or will not behave likewise.

thrust should be to encourage an atmosphere of trust and cooperation through devolving greater responsibility and creating more participative work arrangements rather than to rely solely on the empowerment of authority.

Oversimplifying by viewing them to be mutually exclusive—when, in fact, they can, up to a point, peacefully coexist—these two approaches can be called contract-enforcement, which seeks to deter contract breach and assert the prerogatives of authority, and motivational, which seeks to create a participative and cooperative work situation. Is work best organized by subjecting workers to the threat of powerful sanctions and to carefully modulated reward structures to ensure that precisely defined tasks are accomplished, or by motivating workers to define and pursue their jobs in ways that call forth their greatest effort? In this context, the importance of variable effort and the utilization of firm-specific human capital can truly be appreciated; the more the worker controls his or her effort supply and utilization of human capital, the more willing participation rather than coerced acquiescence will be required. Yet the traditional approach stresses enforcing compliance as the key consideration, necessitated mostly by innate human duplicity.[12]

Over time, these differences in approach become more and more important, because firms will alter the nature of work organization to fit their conception of the problem. Rather than move in the direction of enlisting the talent and energy of the worker by arrangements stressing trust and cooperation, firms will move the other way—more and more seeking to circumscribe and bind the worker within a rigid framework that more completely controls his or her actions, and where his or her performance will receive minute scrutiny. But, in turn, this is most likely to set a vicious cycle in motion whereby firms, in trying to deter shirking, will create conditions in which doing exactly that will be an irresistible challenge.[13]

Furthermore, the upside-down character of traditional interpretations of transaction costs is revealed by its Panglossian approach to the explanation of

---

12. For a similar dichotomy, see Aoki's comparison of the J-firm (Japanese) and the A- or H-firm (American or hierarchical; 1988b and 1990). Likewise in the very important context of the impact of technological change on work organization, Walton and McKersie (1989) stress the profound implications of an analogous distinction between a mutual compliance/adversarial and a mutual commitment/cooperation scenario.

13. Compare Jacoby (1990, 334): "Even for Williamson, however, trust is an add-on rather than an integral part of the analysis because his operating assumption—like that of most other NEO-ILE theorists—remains that of pervasive opportunism. Yet, as industrial studies have repeatedly shown, the presumption of innate opportunism is fatal to trust. . . . It leads to proliferation of control structures—supervision, rules, and deferred rewards—intended to inhibit opportunism. These create resentment and distrust among employees, who correctly perceive the controls as expressions of their employer's distrust. Expectations fulfill themselves when worker resentment breeds opportunism and the employer is forced to implement additional controls, now with the conviction that his initial beliefs were justified." Walton and McKersie (1984), Dickens, et al.(1989, 341-42), and Edwards (1990) also offer strong support for the position I have stated. For an illustrative example along these lines, see Lupton 1976.

institutional development. In that view, existing labor market arrangements are the response that both parties jointly make to the common external difficulties and objective reality posed by ostensibly neutral transaction costs; present institutional arrangements have best measured up to the challenges of experience—otherwise how could they have survived?[14] The parties have faced a common danger and have adapted optimally in a Darwinian sense. Alternatively, it can be argued that what we observe in the labor market and work organization arises from the efforts of the dominant party, the firm, to maintain its authority and power in the face of persistent struggle and challenge. To the extent that such actions by the firm thereby suppress and dampen the springs of worker motivation and talent growth, the socially optimal outcome moves further and further away. Far from being an optimal response to transaction costs attributable solely to real world complexity and human duplicity, existing labor market arrangements instead condone a counterproductive approach, geared to maintaining existing authority patterns.

The resolution of transaction cost issues is certainly not simple and easy; we live in a tricky and complex world, and contractual agreements cannot be costlessly reached and maintained. No one is arguing for zero transaction costs, nor prescribing transactional arrangements designed for a populace of saints. But if forced to choose between approaches where, in one, the problems are seen to mostly arise from dishonesty and duplicity and the vagaries of nature, from unwise challenges to the boss's authority, and where the paramount emphasis is on the person in charge making the hard calls, telling subordinates what to do, and closely monitoring their activity; and in the other, transaction costs reflect the inevitable conflict arising as each side struggles to achieve the upper hand, and accordingly the major task is to divert that conflict into more productive channels, then the latter seems more persuasive. Transaction costs arise from the fact of conflict at least as much as they do from human failings and unalterable complexity in nature; and moreover, it is insufficiently recognized that transacting difficulties caused by these latter factors are themselves exacerbated by conflict. Offsetting and guarding against presumptive moral deficiencies should concern us, but mitigating and turning to productive account the inevitable struggle and conflict between firms and workers over how work is organized and its fruits distributed should matter more.[15]

Emphasizing deterrence of dishonesty and opportunism focuses on what

---

14. For a recent clear statement of this underlying presumption by a respected practitioner, see Ashenfelter 1982.

15. In the last decade, the literature on agent/principal relationships, shirking, cheating, and moral hazard has grown by leaps and bounds. Its general thrust has been to emphasize the need for elaborate institutional arrangements to guard against immoral and dishonest behavior. A cracker-barrel, and perhaps excessively naive, philosopher might argue, however, that if offsetting mendacity implies going to such great lengths and great cost, perhaps the returns to devising jobs and work arrangements that conduce toward honest and truthful behavior might be very high.

might be symptoms and avoids addressing important sources of such conduct; denying conflict means that its consequences are left unattended. If the struggle for control is overlooked, too little attention is paid to its attrition of productive efficiency; if, from time to time, an armed truce is shattered, the intensified combat stifles what little confidence and trust may have sprouted; conflict itself justifies, and even induces, as a legitimate tactic under the circumstances what would otherwise be judged duplicitous behavior. How much transaction costs are a strategic behavior problem, rather than arising from moral deficiency, is naturally hard to accurately determine, but the more effort variability and firm-specific human capital are neglected, the more these presumptively desirable and potentially output-enhancing aspects of on-the-job performance will be directed toward the power struggle. To not view transaction costs as arising from inherent interest conflict and to ascribe them solely to deficiencies in human character and a tough world, is to build perversity directly into the resultant work arrangements, as firms will then seek to diminish their reliance on individual discretion and effort and on the development of human capital.

The Importance of Internal Organization

What emerges most vividly from each of the areas discussed is the internal organization of the firm as the thread tying seemingly disparate issues together. Effort, skill development and its utilization, and the level of transaction costs are all affected by job design and work organization. Here too, the simplicities of a flat, one-dimensional view of jobs and workers have to be jettisoned. That economists' magical black box, in which homogeneous inputs are magically and easily transformed into standard output, misleads as well as instructs. Ensuring efficient work performance is as difficult and complex as organizational theorists have long contended, as new approaches by economists now recognize. Work organization, including organizational rent sharing, is important in creating the incentives required to generate optimal effort supply, the circumstances in which the potential contribution of firm-specific human capital can be realized, and the climate of trust, honesty, and cooperation that can sharply reduce transaction costs. Each issue makes the same point: work organization matters, its consequences reach into areas heretofore little explored, and adjustments in the nature of jobs are an essential element in both improving firm performance and equilibrating internal and external labor markets through better job-worker matches. The necessity for being explicitly concerned with changes in work organization is a labor market issue of paramount importance. Although I have stressed that the motivational aspects imply a sharper break with traditional approaches, others, as I will discuss in subsequent chapters, argue for greater continuity.

Again, microtheoretic implications flow from this more complex picture of work organization. For one thing, as I argued in chapter 3, because of worker heterogeneity and the multidimensionality of job quality, maximizing behavior is now a much less straightforward and easily modeled process, but the payoff to search and adjustment is potentially greater. Although ensuring that jobs and workers are properly matched must now be viewed as a more continuous and consciously undertaken process, it is likely to be more worthwhile since work reorganization will explicitly scrutinize previously ignored differences. For another, as I have stressed in this chapter, once the implications of work organization are explicitly recognized, the dominant and initiating role of the firm becomes apparent.

The labor contract is not usually drawn between equal partners; in a systematic sense, the firm has numerous advantages. It usually has more resources and options; it initiates most of the action; it has relatively complete freedom with respect to job design, organizational arrangements, and investment policy, and hence can utilize those powerful tools to strengthen its position, and even promote control-maintenance at the expense of economic efficiency; it can intentionally segment and stratify the work force as a technique for weakening group cohesion and making collective action difficult; it can coopt the workers' natural leadership by offering tempting prospects for individual gain at the expense of the larger group; and, finally, the legal and political status quo provide it with many advantages in this unequal contest. In sum, whatever the underlying logic for eliciting superior worker performance by a larger income share and meaningful participation, firms have so far been clever and powerful enough to avoid such drastic change without apparently also having to pay a very high price in the form of a great reduction in worker productivity.

As a result of the firm's dominance, desirable changes in jobs might not be undertaken where that conflicts with the firm's narrow interpretation of its self-interest. As examples, in periods of labor surplus, firms might tend to change workers when jobs need redesigning; when justifiable and challenging worker complaints arise, firms might tend to use job redesign to eliminate the worker rather than the offending cause for concern; and, in general, firms might forgo job changes, especially those devolving greater responsibility to and promoting greater teamwork and cooperation among workers, whenever authority and control are thereby endangered. Most significantly, control over job redesign would restrict the range of potential forms of work organization to those more in consonance with managerial predilection; the usual entry barriers facing de novo firms as well as some ideological ones suggest that alternative organizational forms will be few. If automatic market processes are thought to yield optimal outcomes, these tendencies make their attainment certainly more difficult.

Likewise, views on the nature of the employment relationship need to be substantially revised. Labor contracts embracing the need to cope with variable effort, firm-specific human capital utilization, and minimizing transaction costs are obviously not easy to arrange. Once these conditions are accepted as ruling on the job, then worker discretion and performance variability are central in the determination of efficient labor contracts, and the entire area of incentives and motivation, and their work implications, opens up. As I will discuss more fully in subsequent chapters, these aspects interact with each other in complicated ways. In particular, the possible internal contradiction of accommodative changes between their promise of productivity gain and their potential negative impact on the position of existing authority is an obvious factor inhibiting desirable adjustments.

Finally, the practical implications of focusing on internal labor markets deserve some mention; indeed several considerations impart a special urgency to innovation in work organization. First, disjunctions between traditional work arrangements and the abilities and aspirations of the labor force are growing larger and their consequences more serious as a result of cumulative changes in work force attributes. Second, the need for greater flexibility and adaptability in work organization, in an economy where the growing proliferation and increasing organization of competing interest groups entail more complex, and greater resistance to, adjustment processes, is becoming increasingly apparent. More rapid and dislocating changes in regional production activities within the domestic economy, an increasingly integrated world economy, and the continuing impact of occasional major shocks and swift technological change, combined with the greater recognition of the social waste of relying solely on market forces to bring about the consequently increased scale and tempo of adjustment, make it imperative to devise more creative responses to the ebb and flow of economic fortune. Work reform is a vehicle for responding to such change imperatives by methods that can draw upon the work force's contributory potential.

Finally, work reorganization must be viewed within an even wider context. Work is so central a part of our existence that it cannot fail to affect all else that we do. The externalities that spill over into our lives from jobs that match neither our capabilities nor aspirations exact tremendous social costs. Although the lines of causation may be complex and indirect, work reform should also generate many positive benefits for the general quality of our lives. In these practical ways, greater attention to job quality is likely to have beneficial consequences as we learn more about its implementation and as new and more effective channels for realizing human aspirations are opened.[16]

---

16. See the (visionary?) comments in Dertouzas et al. 1989, 134–35.

CHAPTER 5

Employment Relationships and Organizational Choice

What happens inside the firm? What kind of organizational arrangements best achieve the firm's goals? Where should the firm's domain begin and the market's writ end? Are differences between a firm's internal contractual obligations and its spot market exchanges matters of degree or kind? Are its explicit and formal contracts worlds apart from implicit and relational contracts? Are its long-term economic relationships simply a succession of short-run agreements? More generally, how does the firm's internal organization, when viewed as something more than simply a nexus of spot exchanges, affect its behavior and performance? Such questions concerning the economics of organizational choice extend to many areas—the degree of vertical integration, franchising policies, subcontracting arrangements, sourcing considerations, transfer pricing, divisionalization, make-lease-buy decisions, debt-equity proportions in capital structures, and more—but this book is focused on the employment relationship, or the labor contract, as the fundamental building block of all organizational structure.

My previous discussion of both external labor market anomalies and internal labor market complexities is very relevant for organizational choice. If the external market were totally unremitting and compelling in its disciplining function, then there would be much less leeway for experimentation by and diversity among firms. Similarly, if firms' internal organization were constrained to be as simple and alike as peas in a pod, then labor market anomalies would be far fewer. Indeed, the connections between internal and external labor markets are, in fact, close and organic. Firm-specific human capital and impaired mobility go hand in hand; skill hoarding and one-tailed labor market mismatches are two sides of the same coin. In general, as will be developed in this chapter, organizational choice is very much a response to the perceived salience of the various external and internal labor market characteristics discussed in the two preceding chapters. Views on proper organizational structure are determined by the interpretation of and significance attached to those labor market elements. Much has been written, from diverse points of view, about organizational choice; reviewing and synthesizing these contributions and accommodating their many insights will provide a new and stimulating perspective.

That such attention from economic theorists has been of fairly recent vintage is, as suggested earlier, mildly embarrassing since swapping labor effort for remuneration is so elemental that, in retrospect, not to have explored more deeply the terms and circumstances of that exchange is hard to understand. After all, what could be more fundamental, what quid pro quo could be more basic, than the labor contract, and yet, until quite recently, the simple neoclassical view prevailed that the quid of a precisely specified money wage (adjusted, in principle to be sure, for whatever compensating differentials were required) was swapped for the quo of a well-defined quantum of labor effort. The employment relationship was viewed as straightforward exchange, nothing more and nothing less; even the complicating Pandora's box of compensating differentials went largely unattended.

For the most pressing of both practical and theoretical reasons, such as those discussed in the previous chapters, such innocence has been blessedly overtaken as it became apparent that much more than a simple exchange was going on. And indeed the story is still unfolding, driven by both ongoing real-world events and continuing theoretical inquiry. The former operate in many different ways. The scope and pace of recent acquisitions and mergers, the changing face of industrial relations as the power of labor wanes and that of management becomes stronger, the emergence of the mean-lean firm forever seeking a competitive edge through pressuring its labor force and restructuring its organizational arrangements, the more sporadic outcroppings of the participatory firm trying to intensify worker loyalty and commitment—these trends are apparent to even the most casual observer, and they carry with them far-reaching implications for the continuity and character of the employment relationship. Similarly and closely related, the transformational imperatives arising from an accelerated pace of technological change and a more competitive and tightly integrated world economy, and the inevitable comparisons with the way firms in other countries are organized, also raise questions concerning the best form of the labor contract. And finally, how work is organized cannot be immunized against strong cultural tendencies, generally pushing toward a more educated and engaged work force rather than a detached mass of workers to be commanded and controlled. It is now more or less accepted that organizational arrangements are bound to be, as their operating environment changes, ever-shifting and their worth is constantly being reevaluated; indeed, in the "new institutionalist" view, such movement is the expression of an efficiency principle—a process of dynamic progress where emergent good institutions continually drive out bad old ones.

Likewise on the theoretical front, developments proceed rapidly. It has become increasingly recognized that lines between exchange and contract and between different kinds of contracting, as transactional forms, are blurred and indistinct. In a world of complex and imperfect labor markets and where effort variability, firm-specific human capital, transaction costs, and organizational rent all loom very large, what happens inside the firm offers a disconcertingly large menu of possibilities. As I have indicated, some theorists, designated NC+, have responded to these developments by extending and moderately adapting traditional approaches. In their view, nothing in such increased complexity is cause for sharply breaking away from the main outlines of previous theory. Firms now must simply enforce more difficult and complicated contracts.

Others, designated IC+, go further, arguing that motivating workers can dominate enforcing contracts; trust and cooperation can matter more, supervision and command less. Jobs are not a set routine of simplified and cut-and-dried tasks; workers are not programmable robots and teamwork, cooperation, and information sharing are very important; continuous interaction between jobs and workers within a changing economic environment implies that the matching process and work design require ever-vigilant oversight. The labor contract should not be thought of as simply establishing conditions whereby the parties reach a gains-exhausting terminal point; rather, conflict and bargaining, in the context of continual change, endogenously create new situations, and lock the parties into permanent contestation that takes many forms and whose outcomes cannot be foreseen. These theorists thus suggest that the employment relationship dances differently, so to speak, to the new rhythms of these varied themes.

The agenda for discussion of these issues will be as follows. The next section will classify, within the two broad and encompassing NC+ (contract enforcement) and IC+ (motivational concern) categories previously specified, the alternative forms of the evolving employment relationship. The following section will analyze the determinants of those forms, locating them in the underlying nature of jobs and workers, and the environmental conditions within which the matching process takes place. A final section will compare the two general approaches and also summarize some observations of general import and interest.

Classification Exercises

Stripped to its essentials, the employment relationship reduces to a swap of human effort for, to use the legal term of art, consideration, and it will be most useful to analyze the various forms assumed on both sides of this swap. Surprisingly, a quid pro quo, consideration-for-effort framework can pull together a lot of different threads relating to such swaps and generate, in the process, a detailed classification of a great many alternative forms of the employment relationship. The traditional neoclassical view, as mentioned earlier, posited a simple exchange of a money wage, perforce adjusted for whatever compensating differentials were required by all the circumstances relating to the job, for a presumably standard amount of effort. Thus, assuming the resolution of the compensating differentials problem, no ambiguities were associated with either the quo of what the job required from the worker or the quid of what the worker required for his or her performance. This was a do-what-you're-told, command-and-control framework, with no latitude for deviation in the nature of either tasks or rewards.

Departures from this simple framework can be conveniently grouped into the two previously indicated classifications: those emphasizing individual contract enforcement (now under much more complicated and even ambiguous circumstances), or "neoclassical plus" (NC+) because they are generally consistent with and extensions of traditional theorizing; and those stressing, within a similarly complex environment, whatever kind of employment relationship is necessary for motivating workers as a group to align their interests with the firm's goals, or "implicit contracting plus" (IC+) because they are more willing to explore nontraditional areas.[1] Although specific approaches within these categories overlap and have many common points, fundamental differences in the most important dimensions persist and justify the basic distinction.[2] First those approaches stressing enforcement will be discussed, and then I will discuss the motivational approaches.

---

1. Jacoby makes a similar distinction in Mitchell and Zaidi 1990a, a symposium that is explicitly devoted to assessing the influence of the "New Economics of Personnel" (NEP) on the fields of human resource management and industrial relations. He distinguishes two views (1990, 316–17). One is a "new efficiency-oriented institutional labor economics" (NEO-ILE), analogous to NC+, which "takes efficiency-oriented concepts derived from neoclassical theory—human capital, agency theory, transaction costs—and applies them to the analysis of various real-world institutions, chiefly those that support employment relations in organizations. Yet many of these institutions had been identified and analyzed by an earlier generation of economists whose approach can be called simply "institutional labor economics" (ILE). Thus, the NEO-ILE has a mixed parentage. It has roots in the ILE approach, but it draws more heavily on neoclassical theory and is more rigorously analytical than was the ILE." The other view, similar to my IC+ classification, is more closely related to traditional ILE and includes "economists who work on NEO-ILE issues as well as others whose research is less efficiency-oriented. . . .Members of this group need to be more assertive about what it is that makes their work distinctive and differentiates it from both the neoclassical and the NEO-ILE approaches." Jacoby's summary statement mirrors my own position.

> [M]odern institutional labor economics is complex. It includes those who carry on the ILE tradition and assert the necessity of middle-range theory and eclectic approaches in labor economics, and others who believe that a neoclassical efficiency (rational actor) approach can and should be extended to cover the field. In some respects the tendencies are similar. Both are in contact with and borrow from neoclassical theory, and both operate at a lower level of generality than neoclassicism's hard core. But they diverge on the issue of whether labor economics' distance from the core should be minimized or maintained. This essay has argued that distance as well as contact between the two is inevitable, necessary, and valuable. Although distance creates theoretical tension, it is something that institutional labor economists, whether NEO or not, should acknowledge and maintain, rather than rationalize and minimize. (1990, 336)

2. Some NC+ theorists, especially Carmichael (1989), indeed focus on implicit contracts and argue that such contracts are distinguished by their unenforceability at law; consequently, self-enforcement mechanisms must be created whereby each of the parties, construed as individual entities, never has a superior option and, thus, no incentive to breach. Reputational considerations do this for the firm, and a more complicated combination of entry fees, last-period bonus,

NC+ Approaches

An extremely influential starting point for the contract enforcement view was the introduction, by Alchian and Demsetz (1972), of the idea of rational incentives to shirk, and the consequent necessity for efficient monitoring to deter such shirking. Subsequently, as the discussion of effort variability in chapter 4 indicated, other views also emerged, stressing the importance of individual performance and incentives, and expanding upon techniques for deterring shirking: compensation could be back-loaded (Lazear 1981); the carrot of upward mobility and career progression could be strategically displayed; workers could put up a forfeitable performance bond; a wage premium could be paid or a reserve army of high unemployment could be maintained such that job loss due to shirking would be very costly (Shapiro and Stiglitz 1984; Bowles 1985); most simply, more intensive and sophisticated detection methods could be implemented.[3] Shirking was thus to be controlled through affecting the probability and/or the cost to the worker of its detection. Significantly, it should be added, only workers seemed to shirk, and little attention was paid to the rich variety of possible forms of employer noncompliance and shortchanging.[4]

Other approaches, similar in spirit in focusing on individual contractual compliance but emphasizing circumstantial complexity and, hence, the tremendous range of considerations potentially entering into the labor contract, have extended this line of inquiry. Some theorists have stressed that internal organization is, at base, a principal-agent problem, and organizational forms simply reflect how the strategic environment modifies and shapes the conflicts and tensions inherent in that relationship. Principals can only monitor imperfectly; agents have their own (private and conflicting) interests to pursue. In a setting where various asymmetries in knowledge, risk attitudes, and strategic interest are very important, the principal (employer) must devise least-cost and incentive-compatible surveillance/punishment/reward schemes that en-

---

and flat wage schedule ensures that individual workers keep their end of the bargain. This approach, in my judgment, belongs in the NC+ category because it maintains the traditional ideas of precise calculation and simple maximizing motivation mechanically applied to individuals' standard exchange. Alternatively, IC+ emphasizes trust, motivational complexity, and ongoing bargaining in the more complicated context of relational contracting, associational continuity, and cooperative group endeavor. In other words, it opens the door for a much greater departure from traditional theorizing.

3. I have omitted consideration of piece-rate and commission pay systems as shirking deterrents because the relevant literature is focused on group, rather than individual, activity. In any case, piece-rate systems are of declining importance, and commission arrangements can operate only within very specialized circumstances: ". . . in November 1975, only 1.2% of the nation's workers were paid on a piece-rate basis and only 1.9% on a pure commission basis. . ." (Bishop 1987, S38).

4. For a discussion of "opportunistic" employer incentives and behavior, see Dow 1987; Putterman 1987.

sure the agent (worker) performs exactly as would the principal. But in such complex settings, as might be surmised, incentive-compatibility plans can prove difficult to translate into practical programs.

Simpler implicit, or efficient, contracting notions also fall within the contract enforcement category (including self-enforcement) because, as previously discussed, they were based upon the relatively limited idea that positional differences between firms and workers relating to risk attitudes, knowledge asymmetries, and wealth portfolios, combined with a "missing" insurance market against undue income fluctuations for workers, opened the way for mutually advantageous exchange. The earliest implicit contract ideas could be viewed as comparative advantage swaps that stemmed from these positional differences and were an attempt to account for the stylized facts of relatively rigid money wage rates and the extensive use of lay-offs rather than outright termination. If workers were relatively risk averse and firms risk neutral, then this basic difference, combined with the firm's superior position vis-à-vis risk absorption, information processing and forecasting, and wealth and liquidity portfolios, enabled the firm to offer to smooth workers' income flows through money wage rigidity and long-term employment guarantees.

The firm was positionally well suited to make such an offer at little cost to itself. The corresponding obligation of the worker, however, was not so clearly defined. Presumably, the worker was made sufficiently better off by income smoothing so that, as a kind of compensating differential, the firm's overall wage bill could be lower. Or perhaps more important, the impact on worker morale and loyalty would presumptively yield very beneficial productivity payoffs to the firm that would otherwise not be forthcoming. In this latter instance, the implicit contract would be of the general form of "you treat me right and I will make it worth it for you," as applied to both parties. In either case, the consummation of profitable trades arose largely from the joint influence of the parties' positional differences and the absence of income-insurance markets. The implicit nature of the arrangements stemmed largely from both the workers' putative lower wage bill or greater cooperation and the inability to legally enforce their terms. More sophisticated versions of efficient contracting shift the emphasis from simple, positional differences to the consequences of associational continuity, team activity, and a greatly expanded workers' role, and thus fall within the IC+ category (to be discussed subsequently).

Transaction cost approaches also rely ultimately on contract enforcement, but much more carefully specify the various transactional minefields and obstacle courses the unwary firm must overcome in getting workers to do their jobs. To combat the yawning gaps that could open between what firms want workers to do and what actually gets done, firms must contractually embody institutional safeguards against those dangers, even more than relying on clever surveillance or incentive schemes. For instance, the growth of institutionalized internal labor markets can be viewed as an efficient adaptation to the inevitable condition of job idiosyncrasy, or worker control over tasks. Firms fashion a kind of rough and equitable contractual jurisprudence governing many kinds of difficult workplace "law-and-order" problems, thereby minimizing transaction costs arising from worker foot-dragging and dissatisfaction.

Finally, as adumbrated by the complicated conditions already introduced, some theorists view the firm's internal organization as a strategic gaming problem in contract design; firms must anticipate worker reactions and devise enforceable contractual options to channel them in desired directions. Usually, in this connection, the idea of firm initiation, dominance, unilateral action, and generally manipulative behavior is taken for granted or justified by reference to the importance of reputational considerations for maintaining the firm's integrity. Specifying such strategies, and the underlying environment determining how the parties play their hands, has generated a veritable cottage industry, given the number and complexity of the relevant variables. In this connection, variations on insider/outsider themes are especially interesting, since they directly raise the issue of how closely the market limits the options available to firms.

To summarize: whether stressing the efficient detection of shirking, ensuring agent compliance, institutional defences against excessive transaction costs, or the best strategy for inducing a desired worker response, in all such cases the firm-knows-best presumption prevails, the focus is highly individualized, and the object is to devise contractual arrangements to get a non-complicit and perhaps even fractious workforce to do the firm's bidding. Or, shorter and simpler, rather than accepting the neoclassical position of virtually automatic (or for purists, zero-cost) compliance, NC+ focuses on the firm's search for the best way of enforcing individual contracts.

IC+ Approaches

Alternatively, IC+ approaches stress that motivating workers to high-level performance, rather than contractual enforcement, is most important. IC+, by shifting the emphasis from positional differences to the consequences of associational continuity, opens the door for motivational analysis, because the potential worker contribution is greatly amplified. Some versions stressed the inexorable buildup of firm-specific human capital (Becker 1975; Hall 1980), whose financing and incentives for on-the-job utilization set the stage for having to coax workers to fully deploy their augmented capabilities. Others emphasized the efficiency-wage argument, where workers' effort supply was inherently (quantitatively and qualitatively) variable, and wage premiums (or more sophisticated incentives) were required to elicit higher levels of effort (Yellen 1984).[5] For some transaction cost approaches, the focus of attention

---

5. Carmichael (1990) distinguishes four types of arguments for efficiency wages: sociological/gift giving, selection improving, turnover reducing, and antishirking. The first three are consistent with IC+; the last has been used in an NC+ sense (see Shapiro and Stiglitz 1984) to

became establishing mostly noncontractual institutional arrangements aimed at gaining the workers' full cooperation, rather than setting contractual forms directly minimizing transaction and agency costs. Still others argued that nurturing the shared experience and teamwork that generated organizational rent—the excess output of an ongoing firm over what an exactly alike collection of factors hired de novo could produce—was the critical concern (Aoki 1980).

In all of these instances, the benefits from associational continuity and an augmented workers' contribution become more important, and the process whereby potential productivity gains can be realized becomes the central focus; the possibilities for variable worker performance now drive the system.[6] Workers must be persuaded, by whatever means necessary, to do their best, and bargaining rather than manipulation is inherent in the structure of arrangements. The implicit contract takes on a different coloration; it is less a straightforward individual exchange dominated by positional differences, and more a complicated relational arrangement dominated by a wide-open search for the proper team incentives. Within a bargaining framework where it must persuade workers rather than knowing-best-and-determining-all, the firm must actively tap the workers' full potential by offering sufficient inducements, whose nature and magnitude might abruptly depart from traditional firm practices. Such implicit contracts are still self-enforcing, since each party is free to establish its own level of compliance, but any sustained shortfall is likely to be quickly requited. Both parties are locked into the fundamental swap defining their relationship: "you treat me right and I'll put out."

These versions stressing firm-specific human capital, effort variability, transaction costs, and organizational rent can rightly be called *implicit contracts plus* to draw attention to the vastly enlarged importance of high-level worker performance and team activity and to their more open-ended nature.[7]

---

rationalize wage rigidity and involuntary unemployment equilibrium. A rigidly higher-than-market-clearing efficiency wage must be maintained as an explicit worker-disciplining mechanism to prevent shirking. But efficiency wages can also be interpreted in an IC+ sense of eliciting high performance levels, rather than as simply a premium for minimally preventing shirking, by emphasizing that such desired worker behavior is both more greatly affected by general work conditions and necessarily more important for achieving the firm's goals. For NC+, attaching this much conditionality and importance to workers' efforts matters little; workers do what they are told or they suffer the consequences. For IC+, successful outcomes depend upon creating work conditions that can fully elicit the potentially great contributions of most workers. Accordingly, the text is concerned with efficiency wages in this latter sense, as leading to greater effort and productivity rather than simply preventing shirking.

6. Others have noted a pattern of convergence too. See Putterman 1986b; Green 1988; Yarbrough and Yarbrough 1988; Aoki 1990. For a more restrained and individually focused definition of implicit contracting along NC+ lines, see Mortensen 1986, 914).

7. See the review article by Milgrom and Roberts (1988), and note the following:

[T]he incentive-based transaction costs theory has been made to carry too much of the weight of explanation in the theory of organizations. We expect competing and complementary theories to emerge—theories that are founded on economizing on bounded ration-

Two of their characteristics deserve further comment. First, they are more complicated than a straight transaction based on well-defined positional differences, since they are characterized by continuous interaction in which strategic bargaining to influence the other party's behavior in your favor will always be present. Furthermore, "treating right" and "putting out" are not simple and self-evident concepts, but are bound to be laced with ambiguity and imprecision; accordingly, the parties must exercise constant vigilance, and opportunities for disagreement will be abundant. If the parties wish to preserve their arrangement, they must develop means to limit the damage from real or apparent breaches of their understandings.

Second, conflict in a very fundamental and basic sense will always be present. This will not simply be the ordinary higgling over terms of exchange to get the best possible deal of the moment, the ordinary economics of the little more and little less. Rather, the pervasiveness of strategic behavior charges any action with much greater significance. As I will subsequently discuss, questions of authority and power disposition, of legitimacy, and of basic property rights will inevitably arise as the parties struggle over the fruits of their joint activities. When such issues are joined, stakes become immeasurably higher. Once the idea of inherent variability in workers' contribution is accepted, participatory work arrangements become a logical focus for inquiry.

More generally, as these IC+ approaches become more complex and refined, the parties could be thought of as engaged in ambitious explorations of multidimensional bilateral swapping, with the level and/or quality of effort and the reward for effort jointly synchronized. Rather than coming to any simple quid pro quo agreement, the parties negotiate, implicitly as well as explicitly, an extensive pattern of trade-offs ranging across many aspects of performance and reward and sustained over a long time. Further, the parties must delicately blend together the cooperative and adversarial elements inherent in their relationship. Each party says, "treat me right, and I will do you likewise"; but each party also must be aware that the other party may revert, for one reason or another, to more adversarial behavior. Here too, although perhaps less so, breaching possibilities were looked for more on the workers' side of the bargain than the employer's.

---

ality and that pay more attention to changing technology or to evolutionary considerations. (1988, 450)

Compare also Nalbantian's apprehensions concerning NC+ theorising:

Yet, the analysis presented points out the inherent dangers in simply extrapolating from these models in evaluating real-world compensation systems. The problems posed by the need for incentives in modern organizations are complex and idiosyncratic. Providing incentives usually calls for the application of custom-made incentive plans tailored to the specific circumstances, environment, and objectives of the individual firm. These plans must take into consideration the attributes of employees and employers, the complexity of job function, its vulnerability to external shocks, and the kind of employee behaviors that are most significant for company performance. (1987, 34–35)

Once the IC+ view is adopted, however, both the quids and the quos become more elusive. No longer are jobs able to be precisely defined; workers now have great latitude to vary the level and quality of their performance; and surveillance is likely to be costly and difficult, if not counterproductive. Definitive contracts cannot be written, and workers must be persuaded by more elaborate and sophisticated incentives, not excluding power sharing, to do whatever more inherently complicated undertakings the job requires. To varying extents, IC+ approaches are directly implied when the propositions are accepted that effort is innately variable and incentive dependent, that workers have substantial amounts of firm-specific human capital that, if so motivated, they can deploy more intensively, that transaction costs are heavily influenced by the possibilities for cooperative and forthcoming behavior, and that workers, by virtue of the efficiency gains arising from shared experience and continuous association have, a legitimate claim as a group on the firm's organizational rent. The employment relationship under such circumstances is no longer a matter of simply ensuring, through surveillance-cum-sanctions or sophisticated strategic gaming or complex wage schedules, the fulfillment of specified individual contractual obligation. Monitoring can inhibit obvious shirking, but not compel full-hearted cooperation. Bargaining thus necessarily becomes continuous and complicated as each party tries to move the terms of the swap in its favor by simultaneously seeking to preserve the gains from cooperation while endeavoring to maximize its share thereof. The mix of cooperative and adversarial behavior is very much process dependent.

Beyond the realization that bargaining is part of the the employment relationship, some approaches have also recognized an inherent conflict over authority. Alchian and Woodward (1988) have stressed that control over the firm must reside in the hands of the most firm-specific inputs, since, by definition, they have the most to lose from the firm's dissolution and, hence, the most to gain by its survival as a going concern. Others have pointed out that the more the functional importance of workers' firm-specific contribution is emphasized, and the more it becomes necessary to motivate workers to achieve the full extent of their potential contribution, the greater the pressure for property relationships to be modified to reflect this enhanced responsibility and position. Highly contributory workers, in other words, can claim not only greater financial rewards, but also share, or even become dominant, in authority and decision making.

Thus, Aoki (1988a) envisages a production (rapid technological change) and demand (intensive world competition) context where the imperatives of flexibility and frequent changes in the firm's output mix require, for efficient firm operation, a correspondingly high degree of variability and judgment in worker inputs, whose provision will be forthcoming only if worker authority and pay are sufficiently enlarged.[8] Likewise, Bowles and Gintis (1988 and

---

8. Compare the views of the MIT Commission on Industrial Productivity:

In the longer run, the convergence of market forces, consumer preferences, and technolog-

1990) stand Alchian and Demsetz on their heads, and ask if, indeed, workers so fully control their contribution to the firm's success, and if efforts at monitoring are bound to be so imperfect and costly in real resources, why not turn to intrafirm transfer arrangements? Authority and income would be reapportioned to persuade workers to fully deploy their talents and perform at high levels, thereby avoiding the substantial real resource costs entailed by monitoring. And, of course, labor-managed firm theorists push such ideas to their logical end by making only those who work the firm's owners, hence in full collective control of both share division and strategic decision. Although the literature on the labor-managed firm is both unending and disputatious (Bonin and Putterman 1987), nevertheless such arrangements, as I will discuss in chapter 7, can lead to the desirable and relatively costless combination of "horizontal" monitoring and high effort intensity.[9]

This evolution of views on the employment relationship reveals a pattern of ever-increasing complexity.[10] The quo of required tasks calls for levels of worker performance that are inherently more difficult and complicated to both specify and perform; tasks are harder, more judgmental, and workers have both greater individual and group responsibilities. We have moved from "do what you're told" through "do your job" to "do your best, as only you know how to interpret it." Likewise, the quid of required incentive structure is hardly limited to a money wage, but is extensively multidimensional and needs to be intricately designed to motivate workers in order to tap their acknowledged greater capabilities. As I shall discuss in the following section, the nature of jobs and workers, and the environment in which they are matched, must be more carefully and completely specified before correct forms of work organization can be described.

It might be tempting to draw from this evolutionary process the generalization that we are witnessing a pattern of the fittest surviving, a unidirectional

---

ical opportunities suggests the possibility of "totally flexible" production systems, in which the craft-era tradition of custom-tailoring of products to the needs and tastes of individual customers will be combined with the power, precision, and economy of modern production technology. In such a world the strategic objective will be to deliver high-quality products tailored to each customer at mass-production prices. . . . To achieve this goal, manufacturers will have to move well beyond today's advanced flexible production systems to flexible but fully integrated product development, manufacturing, and marketing systems. (Dertouzas et al. 1989, 131)

9. The issue of the legitimacy of authority is closely tied to concern over who has the ultimate residual claim on whatever surpluses may be generated. The bit of doggerel in the appendix to this chapter lightheartedly probes this question.

10. This pattern of evolution can also be grasped by enumerating six views on the changing image of the worker and nature of the exchange as jointly defining, in roughly increasing order of complexity, the employment relationship: (1) a simple swapper and mechanical exchange; (2) a shirker-cheater and the need for extensive controls and monitoring; (3) a pure instrumentality and reliance on creative incentives; (4) a joint participant and cooperative interaction; (5) an insider and a process of substantive bargaining; and, finally, (6) a challenging proletariat and the presence of contentious class conflict.

movement toward more participative work organization and the extinction of vestigial authoritarian relics. What started out as a simple quid pro quo exchange became a closely monitored transaction, then turns into more complex relational contracting, and seems to end up questioning whether the existing institutional framework is sufficiently flexible to allow for proper motivation. That interpretation, however, would be incomplete. The main message is that work organization will reflect the abundantly diverse circumstances within which it is forged. This is not to say that certain tendencies may not be more prominent and gain in relative importance. Indeed, as suggested above, changes in work and workers (and in the economic environment as well) tend to push in the direction of ever more complex forms of work organization. Yet a cross-section drawn at any moment of time would reveal that, for a host of reasons, all forms are likely to show up in the sample. For example, as mentioned earlier, responses to our recent economic tribulations reveal, on the one hand, extensive employer militancy directed toward a mean-lean position on wages and working conditions, and, on the other hand, considerable interest in more participative and cooperative approaches for enlisting worker support.[11] Although elements of a natural progression are there, situational variety ensures a broad array of different types of work organization. Thus, a fine line has to be walked between being aware of powerful tendencies generally pushing toward more complex forms of relational contracting and being sensitized to particular environmental aspects that thereby define specifically appropriate forms of work organization. A similar caution concerns overemphasizing the distinctiveness and mutual exclusivity of different forms of work organization. Rather, it seems clear that they, perhaps imperceptibly, shade into each other, and that various hybrids will be formed in actual circumstances. Theoretical simplicity and real-world messiness may be an odd couple but, in the nature of things, are a frequently found combination.

Finally, some controversial implications should be pointed out. The role of bargaining and conflict, over both the immediate conditions of work and reward as well as the larger issue of how authority relates to contribution and

---

11. Osterman (1988, vii) makes this point as follows:

Employment security has broad importance beyond the situation of those people directly dislocated, because it is at the heart of another issue facing the labor market: the organization of work within firms. An observer attempting to predict the evolution of employment practices would be struck by two very different tendencies. New technologies and the realities of heightened competition are forcing firms to innovate, but responses differ. Some firms seek to transform their work structures by broadening jobs and gaining a more committed labor force. A key element in this strategy is increased employment security. Other firms attempt to force change in internal practices by aggressive concession bargaining or work force reduction through layoff. In effect, employment practices have reached something of a crossroads since the different models compete. Which pattern will come to dominate and become the new American model is unclear, but in this book a strong case is made that the former is preferable.

Walton and McKersie (1989) make the same point and adopt an identical position.

is shared, is at the center of many disputes over desirable forms of work organization. Tensions over decision-making power are inherent in enlarging the functional role of workers within the framework of traditional ownership-based property relations. Continuous testing of where the boundaries of authority lie rather than once-and-for-all resolution seems the most likely state. A closely related concern arises from the tilt to endogeneity that is the natural corollary of an augmented bargaining process. Outcomes are not determined solely by this or that set of initial specifications, and all the parties will be very much aware of how present actions affect future positions and of the string of implied strategic interactions. The firm's internal organization is thus hammered and shaped through contested exchange, and outcomes are very much process dependent. A final concern of this sort turns on contrasting the relative importance of the group and the individual in explaining internal organization. Does the well-known bias of economists toward methodological individualism founder on, first, the innate heterogeneity of workers' contributory role with regard to effort variability and deployment of firm-specific human capital and, second, the overriding importance of peer and group influence associated with team productive activity and its requirements for coordination, cooperation, and information sharing? The twin assumptions that all workers are alike and groups are irrelevant are not very helpful in explaining how work is actually organized.

This evolution in views of work organization is clear testimony to the influence of real-world changes and the search for theoretical explanation. Beyond that, basic issues of organizational choice are raised. Some view the problem narrowly as arising from run-of-the-mill conflict inspired by positional difference or inherent higgling and requiring this or that modest adjustment in incentives or arrangements. Others consider a wider range of more systemic and fundamental reorganization dealing with issues of coordinated activity, authority, and legitimacy that would radically redefine the firm as traditionally conceived. In either case, more is to be learned by further inquiry into the determinants of such change as they operate on jobs and workers and on the environment conditioning their interactions.

Strategic Factors Defining the Employment Relationship

A natural breakdown for analyzing factors influencing the nature of the employment relationship is a threefold division into jobs, workers, and the associated conditions surrounding their interaction. The causal mechanisms seem perfectly straightforward, and, indeed, my own position regarding the employment relationship has been previously put forward. Nevertheless, a more general discussion concerning how these factors affect employment relationship possibilities will still be helpful. The nature of work tasks themselves and what kind of role they imply for workers will obviously influence the form of the employment relationship. Similarly, the talents and capabilities of workers and the motivational keys unlocking their full deployment will also shape the nature of the labor contract. And finally, the match between job and worker never takes place in a vacuum; inevitably a bargaining process, affected by many specific environmental factors determining the strength of the parties' relative positions, defines many features of the employment relationship. Thus, a rather homespun and simple approach, relying on specifying circumstantial factors, rather than a more abstract, high-theory venture should be instructive.[12]

The nature of the job itself and the implied worker role are of tremendous importance in establishing the outlines of the labor contract. How specifiable are the tasks themselves; how and by whom are they defined; are they rote, simple, and easily monitorable or complex and unmonitorable; are they individually or team assignable; do they fall into a predetermined pattern that must be mechanically and inflexibly performed or do they allow for variation and independent initiatives; are career ladders rigidly constructed and internally filled or more loosely defined and open to outsiders; is compliance enforceable by tight control from above or dependent upon willing and forthcoming workers? These attributes of the job are clearly not to be thought of as either/or categories, but rather as polar opposites with actual conditions capable of being somewhere between the poles. Nor, as will be discussed more fully later, should it be thought that such attributes are inevitably natural endowments, the only way things can necessarily be. Further, changes in job design and human capital development, as well as technology, will be very relevant factors; it has now become commonplace to make occupational outlook projections on the basis of shifting job mixes, and associated worker skill requirements, implied by trends in such factors. This listing suggests, accordingly, that the nature of tasks will be very influential in determining the possibilities of the employment relationship.

Likewise, what workers can do on the job, and what will get them to do all that they can, will greatly affect the employment relationship. How innately capable and talented are they; are they predominantly shirkers or do they conscientiously fulfill obligations; do they seize initiatives and seek responsibility or do they hold back; are they trustworthy and cooperative or hostile and adversarial; how important is team activity, cooperation, coordination, and information sharing; how much firm-specific human capital do workers bring to the job; what is the relative importance for them of pecuniary and nonpecuniary compensation; do they prefer compensation to be fixed or

---

12. For an alternative and broadly similar representation of the bases for work organization differentiation, see the comparison between Fordism (e.g., mass production) and flexible specialization (Toyotaism?) in Phillimore 1989, 81, table 1. For a more formal and analytical discussion that parallels my own in many ways, see Aoki's (1990) comparison of the Japanese firm with a prototypical neoclassical firm. For a critique of my kind of homespun, middle-level sociological approach, see Carmichael 1990.

variable, predefined or contingent on some aspect of their, or the firm's, performance, front or back loaded; and finally, do workers respond rather mechanically to firm initiatives or is the process dominated by strategic inter- actions? Here too, these characteristics have been expressed as polar opposites whereas, in fact, they need not actually be so extreme; they are meant to suggest the range of variation, and not the precise identification of given circumstances. And here too, the implications are very clear for the employ- ment relationship: for example, very different organizational arrangements could prevail in situations where workers are extremely capable and respond mostly to nonpecuniary incentives from those wherein capabilities are limited and concern is only with the money wage.

No less important in determining the nature of the employment relation- ship are all the external circumstances that bear upon jobs and workers. Since this category is unbounded, only some of the more salient aspects will be discussed. First, bargaining processes are very much influenced by whether outcomes reflect voluntary and relatively harmonious, or contested and to some degree compelled, exchange. The latter implies not only the ordinary give-and-take of bargaining, but also one of the parties disputing the legit- imacy of the bargaining framework. They are also influenced by whether the parties are relatively equal or unequal, where unequal means substantive disparities in economic strength, that is, the availability of realistic alterna- tives. Contested and compelled exchange implies the absence of mutual trust and commitment, raises legitimacy issues about perceptions of being unfairly coerced, and gives rise to deep resentments concerning outcomes; unresolved tensions and underlying disagreement will mark the bargaining process. Dis- parities in the parties' relative strength will be associated with imposed solu- tions and also will tend to increase outcome instability as the weaker party strives to redress, and the stronger to maintain, strategic dominance. Or- dinarily, most economists assume the employment relationship is based upon voluntary exchange among equals; its stability is vouched for because, in any given period, the parties seek to do the best they can within an accepted and agreed framework and willingly, even if sometimes grudgingly, abide by whatever outcomes emerge. In situations of contested exchange among un- equals, however, the employment relationship will be less definite and more fluid because there is no joint acceptance of framework and outcomes; a kind of continuing guerrilla warfare goes on.[13] Needless to say, where functional

---

13. It may be useful to remember that classical political economists (Smith, Ricardo, Mill, and Marx) thought very much in terms of underlying social divisions and classes whose interests were naturally conflicting, as compared to the modern idea of vacuous and pale economic agents with little to distinguish one from the other. As Brown and Nolan suggest: "It is stimulating to recall certain features of the classical writers' conception of wages which help counteract the comparatively narrow view offered by orthodox contemporary theory. First, they had a lively sense of the political character of the distribution of wages. Second, they considered market forces in some respects to be subsidiary to this. Third, in their interest in the way work was

importance and the pattern of rewards and authority are ill matched, contested exchange is more likely to be found.

Second, demand and product characteristics must also be factored into the employment relationship. Is demand stable or changing, predictable or irregular; is the product standardized or customized; is the production process mass assembly and routinized or individualized and constantly changing? As should be apparent, the greater the certainty associated with demand and product considerations, the more restricted the role of workers, since routine and continuity permit such delimitation. Third, institutional arrangements defining the legal and social context within which the employment relationship is framed will also determine its form. Broadly speaking, any bias therein toward one party will push outcomes in that party's favor, and spur the other to alter the offending circumstance. Finally and of ever-increasing importance recently, competitive pressure, in both product and corporate-control markets, and technological change will require timely flexibility in firm activities, and hence push for whatever form of work organization conduces toward that end.

It should be obvious that the grand inspiration for choosing the specific determinants of jobs, workers, and associated environmental conditions derives from the view that, fundamentally, the employment relationship is a matching process that harmonizes these elements within a context of mutual adaptation. In other words, once those attributes are exogenously specified, then a particular form of the employment relationship flows most naturally therefrom; but at the same time, particular combinations of attributes will endogenously arise from an interactive process of mutual adaptation. Accordingly, whether attributes are mostly exogenous and given endowments over which neither party has much control, or are largely shaped through conscious and deliberate interaction, is an important issue. The latter option, which certainly applies in many cases, greatly complicates matters. To the degree, however, that directional change in attributes reflects the powerful pull of underlying exogenous forces, then that tilts the employment relationship toward modalities most appropriate and fitting to accommodate them. Any pronounced trend in those underlying determinants of the employment relationship should lead to correlative changes in work organization. Given the previous strictures on interaction, endogenous design and intervention, and the parties' self-interest in retaining advantages, however, nothing will be inevitable or automatic about such changes. And finally, it should be noted that because the parties are not likely to accept the existing arrangements as permanent fixtures, then conflict and bargaining must be viewed in the widest context.[14]

---

organised they implicitly questioned any automatic link between wages and productivity" (1988, 340).

14. There is a tendency among some economists (Alchian and Demsetz 1972; Williamson 1980) to view dominance and survivorship of particular forms of organization as proof positive of

The IC+ View and Its Implications

The IC+ view is a clearly derivative response to the issues raised in the two previous chapters. Jobs comprise more complicated tasks and require definition and cooperation by the workers performing them. Workers bring greater productive capabilities to the job, and more sophisticated incentive structures are needed to elicit their deployment. And the relevant associated economic conditions are changing such that, on balance, high-level and team performance by workers is becoming both more important to the firm's success and more conditional in its provision. These trends are interrelated and support each other, their significance increases with time, and their implications grow more profound. The upshot is that motivational and incentive considerations become objects of much greater concern as trends in work organization swing toward "turning on" workers as a group rather than preventing individual workers from "turning off." The NC+ stress on enforcing individual contracts and control-by-command gives way to IC+ considerations of motivating workers.

But if such functional powers now reside in workers' hands, what are the implications for the underlying theory of the firm and for managerial style and the legitimacy of managerial authority? If form inevitably follows function, then must not new arrangements relating to greater power sharing and reward for workers come into being? And will such radical revisions in property relationships be easily and willingly forthcoming? Or can firms maintain, for the most part, the substance of existing work arrangements as superficial change and rhetorical sleight-of-hand create only the appearance of organizational reform? Whatever the belief in institutional Darwinism, there seems no great movement by those in authority to willingly and voluntarily diminish their powers substantially and no overwhelming rush of genuinely new forms of work organization sweeping over the landscape. Despite that, certainly much lip service and sanitized change offer their homage to ideas of work reform. After all, if the illusion of motion can be created without having to pay its real price, that kind of a bargain is hard to resist. And who knows but that such organizational forms may do perfectly well, as what seems unpromising in theory sometimes works out quite nicely in practice? Whatever the theoretical merit in devolving authority and power in line with functional requirements, their present holders remain, not surprisingly, unpersuaded. A seemingly fundamental contradiction persists.

In this connection, a relevant comparison at the theoretical level can be made between the IC+ views stressing the causality of these underlying interactions among jobs, workers, and the economic environment in shaping

---

Darwinian selection efficiency. For devastating arguments against this kind of ahistoricity and Panglossian thinking that whatever is, must thereby be superior in this only and best of all possible worlds, see Dow 1987; Jacoby and Mitchell 1990.

new forms of work organization, and other mostly NC+ views, like those discussed above, whose organizational features are more traditional and stem from adding to, or refining, neoclassical presumptions. NC+ approaches, by introducing more sophisticated assumptions concerning informational asymmetries, transaction and agency costs, differing risk attitudes, knowledge limitations, and uncertainty into the ordinary analysis of the firm, can be very useful and relevant in explaining previously puzzling work arrangements; no one denies their theoretical contribution in enriching our ability to explain firm behavior.

But such modifications usually do not fundamentally challenge the contractual compliance-via-command framework. Although circumstances are much more complicated, the boss still gives orders and applies various sanctions to ensure compliance, authority is not at issue, and individual workers still must perform circumscribed tasks as defined from above. Hence, these approaches are insufficiently attentive to the possibilities for unleashing the full deployment of worker capabilities and all too frequently simply rationalize and accept existing forms of work organization as already embodying optimal adjustment to the posited circumstantial changes.

Given those more complex assumptions, the NC+ firms evolve more complicated and subtle maximizing command mechanisms for extracting from workers the productivity performance due them. Jobs may indeed be less specifiable, workers more talented and knowing, and the work milieu exceedingly dimension rich, but such considerations only call forth correlatively sophisticated techniques for ensuring that workers fulfill their effort obligations. Some of the agency literature leaves the strong impression that the employment relationship is a high-level, cops-and-robbers game requiring eternal employer vigilance and a hypersophisticated set of incentives and sanctions imposed from above. The focus is thus, in sum, on correcting transactional non-performance; not very much is heard of the potential for an augmented worker contribution and its implications.

Alternatively, by stressing workers' enhanced capabilities, IC+ approaches highlight both the necessity for more tangible incentives to ensure high-level group performance and the workers' central role in determining the firm's success. They also frequently challenge the legitimacy of existing arrangements. Control-maintenance and reward-sharing disputes become crucial and overriding, because once the enlarged contribution of workers is accepted, organizational structure and distributional arrangements cannot remain pristinely inviolate. Thus the traditionally based approaches generally support the organizational status quo as having optimally resolved the effort bargain; the "new IC+ view" implies more far-reaching changes in firm organization are needed to tap the full potential of the workers' contribution. Since consistency requires that organizational arrangements and contributory roles be closely linked, such differences seem quite natural.

Further, the more traditionally minded modifications tend to presumptively posit "stylized facts" as truly reflecting enduring outcomes, universal states of nature, or generic human conditions.[15] Workers naturally shirk for individual gain; transaction costs reflect fundamental human frailty, dishonesty, self-aggrandizement, and perversity; and informational asymmetries and differing attitudes toward uncertainty and risk are predetermined and inescapable endowments. Usually, like the explicit authority structure in the principal-agent models, flaws and inadequacies are ascribed to workers and corrective action is the inexorable duty of employers. Posited worker attributes become more or less fixed obstacles to be overcome or countered by managers suitably redesigning work organization.[16]

But stressing the conflict between the workers' augmented importance and lagging recognition thereof in apportioning rewards and authority can internally generate, rather than having to presumptively posit, many of these stylized facts as the direct consequence of the firm's failure to undertake the required organizational changes. What makes more sense: Workers shirk because they're inherently lazy, or because they're making a point about the disposition of rewards and authority? Transaction costs are invariant because human nature is fixed, or depend upon how willingly workers cooperate? Informational asymmetries just happen, or are deliberately sought because knowledge is power? Attitudes toward risk are genetically imprinted, or reflect variation in relevant environmental circumstance?

In the traditional and NC+ approach, optimal organizational designs are

---

15. Jacoby and Mitchell (1990) argue, from an industrial relations (IR) standpoint and against the "New Economics of Personnel" (NEP), that although in the ongoing tug-of-war between institutionally minded labor economists and their more abstractly inclined NC+ theoretical colleagues, the latter's use of stylized facts belatedly recognizes the importance of actual circumstances, nevertheless at the same time there is a failure to realize the finite temporal span of such stylized facts. By the time theorists incorporate reality within their models, it has changed: ". . . neither institutionalists nor NEP theorists can base their observations on a set of stylized facts, and ignore trends which are changing those facts, without risking obsolescence" (1990, 37). Ulman, also from an IR approach, is even more castigating (1990, 299).

16. Even in a perceptive paper by Kanemoto and MacLeod (1988) that clearly recognizes that all parties can "cheat," the unrestricted right of authority to initially establish the rules of the game is uncontested. But giving any one player the power to set the rules by which all must play would considerably lessen that player's incentives to cheat, since there would be a natural tendency to set rules favorable to oneself. For instance, sometimes top-down piece-rate, payment-by-results, or "scientific" job evaluation schemes are put forward as ostensibly neutral means for ensuring distributional equity; people are presumptively paid according to their precisely measured contribution. But as the high level of controversy over such arrangements suggests, fairness of a payment system cannot be separated from the process and circumstances of who controls its creation and implementation.

More generally, various seemingly neutral motivational and enforcement ideas—the use of tournaments to stimulate effort, peer monitoring to limit shirking, assuming reputational considerations will guarantee firms' agreement keeping—have been suggested with little awareness of the controlling importance of context and origination source for their implementation. Such notions play out very differently according to whether the firm is a "we" or an "us and them" organization.

a consequence of presuming specific, and ostensibly neutral and enduring, job-worker-environmental characteristics; in each case, the ordering sequence can be inverted as those attributes can, themselves, be outcomes rather than causal agents. Focusing on the augmented role of workers and, hence, the importance of motivating them can explain the origins of such presumptions, and thus suggest improved forms of work organization and the employment relationship through their elimination or modification. In other words, the traditional approach relies mainly upon a one-way, direct line of causation from presumptive attribute to observable outcome within an unquestioned command framework. The new view suggests that how work is organized instead reflects interactions among jobs, workers, and their environment within a conflictual framework wherein each party can, to a greater or lesser degree, actively pursue its own goals. Devising optimal monitoring arrangements to contain inevitable and invariant shirking is one thing; if motivation for shirking can be attenuated in the first place, that is surely a superior option.

Perhaps it might also be useful to contrast the NC+ view with an industrial relations approach (IR) that is close to, but whose provenance slightly differs from, the IC+ view. For NC+ theorists, the problem is specifying and enforcing complete and incentive-compatible contracts. For IR theorists, the issue is what practical organizational arrangements can best tap the workers' productivity potential? Although seemingly similar in objectives, in fact they point in completely different directions. Viewed from an IR standpoint, four distinct differences can be distinguished: (1) stylized facts are not bedrock: "Although NEP [i.e., NC+] provides a rationale for various anomalous facts first pointed out by labor economists of the 1940s and 1950s, it appears that this theoretical success has come just at the time when the facts themselves are changing rapidly. Labor markets are moving away from the rigidities captured by those facts" (Jacoby and Mitchell 1990, 35); (2) social norms and customs are useful and relevant theoretical constructs, and should not be lightly dismissed simply because they may not be explicitly derived from or grounded in presumptive maximizing behavior; (3) it is impermissible to neglect contested terrain and conflict of power arguments in the belief that voluntary exchange among equals is the most reasonable assumption; and (4) observed institutional circumstances are not usually superfluous and blindly irrational impedimenta preventing the market from working to perfection, but rather often facilitate achieving greater productivity.

This theoretical dispute turns, in part, on general and long-standing methodological issues concerning the degree of abstraction and the realism of assumptions. The best and shortest answer to such questions is to adopt whatever provides the best explanation, and that, of course, is to say that the arguments will continue. But partly this dispute bears upon more substantive matters: how worker productivity is to be "extracted," and to what extent rigidities and frictions are contributory toward, rather than antithetical to, efficient markets? The traditional view would be that, first, the going wage is all that is needed to ensure the former, and, second, the latter are unmitigated evils that block mobility and smooth transitions between equilibrium states.

Concerning the first issue, industrial relations specialists would argue for

> . . .the importance of the relationship between wages and productivity. Rendered largely unproblematic by the assumptions of modern economic analysis, its complexity is, by contrast, the main focus of concern in industrial relations. . . .what underlines [the study of industrial relations] is a more fundamental concern with the problem of eliciting productivity within that relationship. It is the inherently controversial nature of the employment transaction, including the frequently contested question of what sort of performance is expected for what sort of reward. Whether or not labor is organised, employers use very varied devices in their efforts to raise and sustain the productivity of their employees. Wages feature with greater or lesser significance as one component in these devices. The consequence, we shall argue, is that the relationship between wages and productivity is far from simple (Brown and Nolan 1988, 340).

In brief, as argued throughout this book, the quids and quos of the labor contract need to be more richly specified to resolve productivity questions.

Likewise with regard to the second issue, many such so-called imperfections provide stability and a structural framework for harmonizing expectations, both of which are essential for the effort bargain to be expeditiously struck. Both parties to the employment relationship benefit from their actions being guided by and formed within a shared framework of assumptions; an unbounded spot auction market would prove disastrous in practice. In general, such norms and conventions act as a focusing lens drawing together the always fractious tendencies of individuals engaged in single-minded pursuit of their own divergent and narrow self-interest. Such fixities do not, of course, endure forever and will crumble when they constrain more than facilitate. While they reign, however, they are more functional than obstructive.[17]

There should be, in summary, nothing very startling about these IC+ and IR views; rather, what should be cause for wonderment is the survival and dominance of traditional NC+ views of the employment relationship. The NC+ economist's usual abstraction, though, truly occupies a world all its own. In practice, firms were, and are, very sensitive to the employment relationship's complexities. Not of course as analytical observers, but as

---

17. For excellent statements of the industrial relations approach in general, see Marsden 1986; Brown and Nolan 1988; Turnbull 1988 for the British view; for an American perspective, see Mitchell and Zaidi 1990b; Jacoby 1990; Ulman 1990. Interestingly, although the rationale for norms is similar to that for stylized facts, NC+ generally accepts the latter and rejects the former.

active and self-serving participants, designing and shaping work organization to achieve their private goals. After all, they are greatly interested in getting as much as they can from their workers (while giving as little as possible) and certainly not in relinquishing traditional prerogatives.[18]

What for the firm is the art of managing should be for the economist the issue of setting out organizational relationships that square with the realities of the production process. Adhering to narrow and restrictive views of the employment relationship as solely concerned with contract fulfillment may close one's eyes to more fundamental and underlying issues concerning what is required for high-level worker performance. Specific jobs to be done by easily observed workers, who are most responsive to money-wage variations, and within the context of substantial external continuity and stability yield one kind of an employment relationship. But complex and nonspecifiable work tasks requiring great initiative and experience, team activity, highly motivated workers, and which must be continually refashioned in a constantly changing and dynamic world economy, certainly suggest the need for an altogether different kind of employment relationship. Organizational arrangements appropriate for the former situations will certainly be ill-advised for the latter conditions (conjecturally however, those designed for the latter might conceivably do better for the former).

To grasp the truth of this, observe the sensitivity of intrafirm variations in organizational arrangements across different divisions, activities, and levels of responsibility within almost any large corporation to even *traditional* presumptions concerning corresponding variations in job-worker-environment circumstances.[19] Organizational structure seems to be functionally driven; internal variation in the employment relationship within the firm very closely follows circumstantial attributes. If, however, the workers' role in general is becoming substantially enlarged, then will not what are ordinarily presumed to be the preferred organizational arrangements for a narrow range of jobs have to be similarly extended? How far into the firm they will reach and what the precise modalities of revisions in reward and power-sharing amongst the firm's constituent parts might be, however, are different matters; only the passage of time and circumstantial specificity will provide those answers.

Wherever that process might end, though, the evolution of implicit contracting ideas has transformed the analytical landscape. From a restricted and narrow extension based upon assumed attribute differences between firms and

---

18. For some examples and explanations, see Osterman 1984.

19. For a similar argument by extension, see Weitzman and Kruse 1990, 106–8. Also note the following: "However inadequate the theory, in practice employers (and governments) act as if they are acutely aware of the implications of the open-ended character of the employment relationship. They find it necessary to devote massive and continuing efforts to constructing an institutional context in which employees can be motivated (or, as some would prefer to describe it, controlled) so as to work with the effort, care, compliance, flexibility, or whatever, that enhances their productivity" (Brown and Nolan 1988, 344).

worker, implicit contracting has moved on to embrace all interactions between the parties; it has refocused the theory of the firm on the highly leveraged effort variability of workers and its implications for incentive patterns and organizational structure. Initial concern for explaining wage rigidity has given way to analysis of who should control the firm; identifying precise swaps of specific quid pro quos has been supplanted by exploring the proper ambience and incentives for high-level worker performance; mechanical and robotized views of workers as responding to well-defined commands and rewards have yielded to the recognition of the complexities and conflicts involved in eliciting effort; and the easy invocation of moral hazard to account for self-serving deviant behavior has been replaced by the realization that parties ensnared within a web of strategic dependence and struggle are not likely to reach a common and agreed interpretive framework. IC+ has led us to the fundamental dilemma stated above: once the enlarged role and contribution of the worker in the production process is accepted, then the institutional arrangements defining the firm must be recast to accommodate this functional realignment. What began as an ambitious attempt to explain certain stylized facts within a traditional analytic framework has burst its economistic bounds to enter a more fluid and undefined world. Inescapably, in that new world, will not institutional form eventually follow economic function?

APPENDIX

Who Is the Firm's Residuary Legatee?

Mirror, mirror, on the wall
who can best the residual claim
for contributing most
to the firm's profit and fame?

Me, me, say Knightians believing
that they risk their own
by paying all others
before outcomes are finally known.

Me, me, say Alchian-Demsetzians certain
that they will then better oversee
workers to foil their shirking
should they receive the residual fee.

Me, me, say firm-specific Alchian-Woodwardians
having the most to lose from any breakup
and thus very powerfully motivated
to maintain a going concern's makeup.

Me, me, say Gintis-Bowlesians
whose efforts can not be overseen

else we shall sulk, shirk, and soldier
unless given the most green.

Me, me, cry Aokians who mediate
endless struggle among stakeholder peers
whose bickering and squabbling over shares
requires skillful intervention by overseers.

Me, me, shout latter-day Lockian labor-mixers
believing that only through work's pains
is it possible to savor and contemplate
the just enjoyment of what remains.

Finally, me, me, say those most activated
by visions of surpluses to take,
for without the lure of glittering prizes,
little will exist for others to make.

So what sense to this avid search
for a valued residual claimancy right
when all these seekers have much
logic and justice to support their fight?

Surely the secret must lie
in further inquiry and deeper thought
weaving together these diverse strands
until no further answers are sought.

CHAPTER 6

Further Thoughts on IC+ and NC+

Thus far, I have argued that IC+ is the more responsive approach to the anomalies, complexities, and puzzles actually found in both external and internal labor markets. Not surprisingly, that judgment is vigorously challenged by traditional neoclassical economists as theoretically unsound and empirically inappropriate. Against the assertion that the IC+ view resolves analytical doubts, such as those discussed in previous chapters, concerning the adequacy of completely market-determined explanations, neoclassicists have, as we have seen, incorporated richer and more complex institutional specifications within the more traditional formulation and argued for its greater theoretical coherence and power. Similarly, and perhaps of more immediate interest, if implicit contracting is espoused for its empirical relevance, the emergence of inconsistent and embarrassing countertrends is viewed as cutting the ground from under it; here too, NC+ offers seemingly even more cogent explanations of actual events. This chapter recognizes and evaluates both the theoretical counterarguments and the contrary real-world trends.[1]

Despite these sharp conflicts, the resurgent neoclassical approach and implicit contracting share some common features: they both focus on the market as the analytical core, although one stresses its strengths, and the other

---

1. Compare the similar observations of Mitchell and Zaidi (1990b, 163):

   Yet in certain respects, developments during the eighties have pushed the labor market to behave more as the classical model would suggest. Wages may become more flexible via contingent pay arrangements such as profit sharing. Employer-employee attachments appear to have weakened, as indicated by the growth of a contingent work force (temporaries and similar workers) and a decline in the length of on-the-job tenure. The large bureaucratic firms which may be considered models of implicit contracting have declined in their share of the work force. . . . Such events suggest, ironically, that just when economists began rationalizing the lethargic institutions of the labor market, the lethargy decreased.

   However, the labor market did not become a classical auction market in the eighties, and it will not become one in the nineties. Rather, there has been a move along the spectrum toward more "flexible" labor market arrangements than once prevailed.

In this connection too, NC+ economists often argue that whatever is of value in the nontraditional approaches could easily be, or has usually already been, incorporated in the NC+ analysis. For examples, see Pencavel's review (1987) of Marsden 1986, Kahn's review (1989) of Leibenstein 1987, and more restrainedly, Reder's review (1989) of Kaufman 1988. For an opposite view, see Jacoby 1990; Ulman 1990.

its flaws; they both draw sustenance from real-world trends and events. These differences and similarities set the agenda. Can IC+ withstand substantive and seemingly devastating criticism? Should or can it be modified to encompass NC+ considerations by nesting them within a more comprehensive explanation? What are the possibilities for synthesis or, at least, coexistence? This chapter will first compare these competing and contrasting approaches, then concentrate on their implications for and application to the practical problems of macroeconomic stability and economic transformation, and finally discuss some further aspects of IC+.

The Rise of the Mean-Lean Firm

Any new approach is bound to be minutely and critically contrasted with more familiar and traditional views, and implicit contracting is no exception. NC+ theorists could thus criticize implicit contracting for leaving the underlying employment relationship too vague and unstipulated—too many possibilities and too few restrictions—thereby diminishing its predictive and explanatory capabilities relative to more traditional approaches. It could be further faulted for heretically departing from the framework of strict maximizing behavior and for paying insufficient homage to the role of market forces. In any case, Occam's razor can conveniently excise it, since existing theory already adequately accounts for the relevant happenings. In this view, implicit contracting adds very little and obfuscates more than it clarifies.

Empirically, even its ostensible strength—explaining significant observations that were anomalous within traditional theory, and, yet, arguably not straying too far from the normal confines of maximizing behavior—has been overtaken by events. Real-world developments within the past decade have become increasingly difficult to square with the logic of implicit contracting and certainly contradict its predictions. In this view, a neoclassical mean-lean, and not an implicit contracting, firm occupies center stage. Now as before, authority and command, not cooperation and persuasion, are dominant governance modes; restructuring and change, not continuity, are the order of the day.

In particular, a world of lay-offs, shutdowns, pecuniary concessions, intensified high-tech surveillance, unilateral work rule changes, multitier wage structures and work arrangements, outsourcing, COLA downgrades, plant relocations, decertification pressures, and the assertion and expansion of managerial prerogative in general bears little resemblance to the precepts of internal governance under implicit contracting. Such "mean" behavior is presumptively imperative as the market dictates survival terms; it is not to be understood pejoratively as a firm's character defect. Firms have little choice but to take whatever actions stern and unyielding market forces press upon them. Niceties and perquisites that were perhaps tolerated in palmier days have to give way to new competitive realities. Implicit contracting was a fair-weather theory; when exposed to the rigors of more demanding times, it could not be sustained.[2]

Likewise, although takeovers, mergers, divestment, plant closings, transnational location shifts, hostile leveraged buyouts, recapitalizations, personnel reductions, subcontracting, leasing workers, down-sizing, and other such forms of corporate restructuring seem antithetical to the organizational implications of associational continuity and firm-specific human capital, they too reflect "leanness" in the service of the market's diktat. Here too, the market has its way.

Discontinuity and restructuring, then, merely reflect normal adaptation to the pulls and tugs of market forces, as they themselves are shaped by a ceaselessly and increasingly rapidly changing world economy. It would be anomalous, and even bizarre, if, when all else is in flux, the organization of the firm remains chastely inviolate. The emergence of the mean-lean firm, driven by a demiurgic market, thus challenges implicit contracting's importance and its rationale.

Before examining this critique more specifically and fully, some general comments should be helpful, since controversy over the validity and usefulness of neoclassical theory has a distinguished and long pedigree. Above all, it reflects Solow's natural tension between what perfect markets can theoretically accomplish and the inevitable limitations of real-life markets. Indeed, as Coase long ago pointed out in his classic article (1937), the very existence of the firm is an admission that markets cannot encompass all economic activity, and an ongoing administrative entity can perform a wide and distinct range of economic functions more efficiently than relying solely on a regime of markets. If that were not the case, firms would have disappeared a long time ago. Implicit contracting is, thus, simply a logical extension of Coase's idea, whereby a particular set of conditions relating to the firm's environment and functioning can require associational continuity as an efficiency condition. At the same time, this perspective recognizes that the boundaries between firm and markets are never permanent but continuously shift in response to changing economic conditions. Moreover, for any single firm, choices regarding own/lease, make/buy, and, more generally, the extent and form of the span of control are the stuff of everyday managerial decisions.

---

2. Perhaps nothing is as antithetical to implicit contracting and illustrates this point with such clarity as the increasing frequency with which employers have been responding to strikes by hiring replacement workers, thereby de facto terminating striking employees. This has happened to copper miners, paper mill workers, airline personnel, intercity bus drivers, express delivery people, and others. President Reagan's decision to fire the air controllers pointed the way in this regard. Alternatively, IBM's actions, when it closed a plant in Greencastle, Indiana, in 1987, offer a remarkable contrast. IBM went to great lengths to offer comparable jobs at its other locations to those willing to move, retraining grants to those wishing to stay, and assistance in finding replacement plants and a cash grant to the community in recognition of the dislocating consequences.

Where the writ of the firm ends and that of the market begins can not be determined a priori.

If the placement of the boundaries between the firm and market is shrouded in ambiguity and subject to the vagaries of history's unpredictable evolution, then disputes over the correct organization of the firm should not be surprising. So far as I am aware, no one has suggested that Coase was wrong, that firms should not really exist. At issue is what particular organizational form should firms assume. In that context, implicit contracting is to be judged. Because trust, loyalty, and cooperation cannot be bought and sold on markets as we understand them, associational continuity will be a desideratum where those qualities are essential. The implicit contracting firm comes into being in those circumstances as a consequence of inevitable market deficiency. Where contrary conditions prevail, the firm can operate differently and assume other guises. There is no neoclassical organizational straitjacket into which all firms must be fitted; if being mean and lean pays off in some circumstances, in others it will be inappropriate. NC+ can be nested within IC+, but not the reverse.

Indeed, this endogeneity of organizational design—the process whereby institutional context establishes the presumptively more desirable organizational form—is becoming increasingly recognized, and its manifestations appear in very diverse applications. In a volume on the impact of new technology on work organization (U.S. Department of Labor 1989), two papers present the argument that technological change is greatly reshaping how work should be organized (Osterman 1989; Walton and McKersie 1989). The latter authors suggest that "computer-based work technology has been changing in a way that places a higher premium on an internally motivated and intellectually competent work force. The trend has been away from automation applications that simply substitute capital for labor toward more complex applications that augment the role of labor in the production process or delivery of services" (Walton and McKersie 1989, 37). And Osterman says, "in an environment in which activities are tightly linked and in which the costs of errors are high, it does not pay to risk a labor force which does not understand the system and cannot respond to problems" (1989, 7).

Similarly, Levine and Tyson (1990) propose that to be successful, cooperative forms of work organization require both some very specific internal conditions—gain sharing, long-term employment security, solidaristic wage policies, and fair industrial jurisprudence arrangements—and certain favorable external conditions relating to the economy and public policy. Also with regard to the cooperative firm, MacLeod (1988) establishes formal conditions for the right incentives for effective and low-cost horizontal monitoring to restrain shirking, thereby gaining an advantage over its capitalist twin, which must expend more resources on external supervision.

Others make the same point in an impressively wide array of different circumstances. Ehrenberg (1990) stresses the importance of not viewing pay systems as exogenous parameters in determining productivity performance variations, since pay policies may themselves reflect other more systematic endogenous factors (like superior managers or workers) operating to jointly influence both pay arrangements and performance variation. Hashimoto (1990) tries to link the characteristic features of Japanese work organization to a presumptive lower-cost advantage in investing in the firm-specific human capital that makes such organization possible. Hutchens (1989) explores more limited linkages among the character of work duties, the extent to which they permit shirking, and the nature of required supervisory arrangements. Finally, some economists have sought to connect the general macroeconomic setting to the firm's internal organization. In a British context, Newell and Symons (1989), Layard and Nickell (1989), and Metcalf (1989) have traced a linkage between the generally higher unemployment prevailing in the 1980s and a productivity resurgence along the lines that the fear of job loss is giving firms, at least in the short run, a more tractable work force and a freer hand to reorganize work to raise productivity. Similarly, Mitchell and Zaidi (1990c) survey, in broad detail, how recent macroeconomic conditions in our country have affected, and are likely to further change, the firm's internal organizational arrangements.

What is fascinating about this general agreement that situational contingency defines appropriate work organization is that simultaneously, as our IC+ and NC+ distinction indicates, the specific form that such definition takes can be so widely varied—truly the devil is squarely entrapped in the details. Accordingly, a connection between certain underlying variations in behavioral presumption and consequent organizational form is quite likely to be the answer. Thus, is work to be organized on the basis of: (*a*) hope that workers will do their best or fear that they will do their worst; (*b*) workers being "turned on," cooperative, and energetically industrious or being prevented from "turning off," holding up the firm, and shirking; (*c*) excellent workers being able to do their utmost good or poor workers doing the least damage; (*d*) aiming for the largest gain or avoiding even small losses; and, finally, (*e*) enabling the free exercise of workers' creative potential and variable effort or operating strictly along contractual specification and stipulated performance? Such widely divergent possible positions concerning firms' basic strategic organizational decisions naturally generate controversy over proper organizational form. What divides economists, however, is not whether organizational design must be consistent with underlying behavioral presumption, but what are the right factual premises and on what that judgment depends.

In any case, no matter what one's views on proper organizational arrangements, several additional factors, some currently prominent and others more enduring, have also contributed to the neoclassical resurgence and its challenge to implicit contracting. The conservative drift in the country in recent years provides the appropriate mood music for emphasizing market hegemony and discipline within the firm. Similarly, the generally higher levels of unemployment and more difficult economic conditions prevailing during much of the 1980s offered convenient excuses for unilaterally imposed measures, tougher attitudes, and restructuring initiatives. The natural and almost irrepressible drive for authority-retention by its possessors also finds ample scope for expression in times of greater geographic mobility for firms by reestablishing familiar arrangements at alternative locations. And finally, the comfortable fit of the usual theorizing creates a climate for too easily dismissing unconventional alternatives. In combination, all of these factors greatly buttress maintaining traditional organizational arrangements.

Theoretical Arguments

Turning to more specific theoretico-economic comparisons between implicit contracting and neoclassical approaches, two interrelated aspects are central: how well do markets work, and what role does motivation play? First, with regard to the question of markets, the differences are many and deep. For neoclassicists, the market is swift and inexorable. Firms are left with no choice and little time; they quickly must dance to the market's tune, or face extinction. A single instance of error, inattention, inertia, or other forms of slippage might not bring hair-trigger retribution, but the margin for mistake is very thin. Tough choices are required, failure severely penalized, and market forces omnipresent and omnipotent. The economic environment is neither forgiving nor accommodating; firms are compelled to adjust to its demands as best they can; it is incorrect to believe that cooperation and understanding can always produce happy outcomes. The mean-lean firm is simply the product of market realities.

Implicit contracting sees things quite differently. Market pressures work, in general, more slowly, and firms have more leeway to respond. For better or for worse, firms have some time that can be used constructively or frittered away. Slack can be eliminated, internal reforms activated, and, roused by adversity, the firm's resources can be better mobilized and deployed. As argued previously, associational continuity and firm-specific human capital insulate the firm, to a degree, from close market discipline (in the sense of requiring instantaneous response) and provide the potential space for the firm to creatively react to the challenge of change. For implicit contracting, the market is less a suddenly obliterating and overwhelming force and more a powerful persuader and catalyst for change. More specifically, implicit contracting stresses the possibilities for internal renewal, especially in the workplace where, in a milieu of trust, cooperation, and devolved authority, the latent talents and energies of the entire work force can be focused on the problem at hand. The market does not usually present firms with unexpected and immediate life-or-death situations that require abrupt and destabilizing changes; accordingly, the process aspects ensure a decent interval in which the firm has a chance to draw upon the implicit contract to make itself over.

Motivation is the other key area of difference between the two approaches. For the neoclassicists, the money wage, itself adjusted for whatever compensating differentials are present, does it all; it induces people to always do their best. Whatever slippage exists because of monitoring or compliance shortcomings is likely to be small and inconsequential, and, in any case, market discipline would soon make things right. Implicit contracting is much more concerned with the complexities behind motivation. It has serious doubts about whether decision makers are focused on achieving the best outcomes or, instead, are very jealous and sensitive concerning authority-retention, and about whether their time perspective is excessively oriented toward the short run and the quick fix. It wonders whether top-down managerial styles—tell 'em what to do and see that they do it—can really bring out the full range of worker capabilities, and whether a bias toward methodological individualism overlooks, thereby, the inherent importance of cooperation, mutual assistance, and information sharing in coordinating teamwork and group activity. Above all, as stressed earlier, implicit contracting's central theme is the interaction of effort variability, firm-specific human capital, transaction costs, and organizational rent—all dependent upon worker volition—in determining firm performance. Neoclassicists find the resulting absence of automaticity in outcomes uncongenial and unacceptable.

Furthermore, market failure and motivational variability play upon each other. If the market did, in fact, operate swiftly and perfectly, motivational variability could not persist; the fact that workers can choose performance intensity levels contributes to the inherent variability of market outcomes. For neoclassicists, then, the market works fine, outcomes are mostly predetermined, economic agents can't do anything very much different since presumptively they are already doing the best they can, and bemoaning these results changes nothing and is just so much crying over spilled milk. Certainly it would be nice if, somehow or other, happy outcomes could be achieved through gracious and pleasant means; implicit contracting is irresponsible, however, holding out false hopes based on incorrect theory. Implicit contracting rejects this Pollyannaish interpretation, and insists that it is simply arguing for a more realistic assessment of the market's influence and the firm's options. Of course the market cannot be disregarded, and of course the firm is not free to do anything it wants, but it is foolish to overlook the full range of discretionary choices the market allows and the firm can exercise.

Indeed, at least from an implicit contracting standpoint, the two approaches are not incompatible; NC+ can be nested within IC+. Implicit contracting argues for situational dependence, not for exclusivity. Certain conditions conduce toward it; others do not. Similarly, implicit contracting does not renounce maximizing behavior, but argues that, under very specific conditions, its expression can be realized in that particular organizational form. Nor does implicit contracting suggest that the application of its organizational remedies guarantees a happy outcome, avoiding hard and painful choices. It does envisage a wider range of outcomes when confronting adversity because market leeway and motivational variability expand allocative choice, but that by no means guarantees success. Finally, implicit contracting underlines the importance of job design. Work organization is not predetermined and fixed; jobs can be structured to stress different organizational arrangements. Rather than accepting the Panglossian position that all has worked out for the best, implicit contracting highlights the possibilities for specific improvements in how work is organized.

Empirical Disagreements

But if implicit contracting is thus theoretically respectable, how then are the contrary empirical observations to be explained? Although, as discussed previously, the rise of implicit contract notions flowed directly from the observation of firm structure and behavior, nevertheless the emergence of the mean-lean firm sharpens the issue: of what possible relevance can implicit contracting be if many firms seem to place little value on maintaining organizational continuity? They will, unilaterally and often with little notice, drastically restructure their operations and arrangements and use a suddenly improved bargaining position to press for concessions in working conditions and compensation terms. Don't such actions imply the insignificance of implicit contracting? When hard choices are required, or when opportunities present themselves, traditional managerial prerogatives and techniques are relied upon. So much the worse for implicit contracting; if it can't stand the heat, no wonder that it must leave the kitchen! Being mean and lean is accordingly the right, the normal and natural, condition for the firm.

Nor should such actions be saddled with pejorative connotations. Being mean does not imply repugnant or ethically dubious conduct by the firm. Rather it could signify the absence of vacillation when decisive and quick judgments are required and acting rapidly and surgically, without sentimentality, in doing what has to be done. Likewise, a lean firm could signify the only structural arrangement capable of succeeding when confronted with overwhelming market pressures to get in step with changing conditions; after all, it would be inexcusable for the firm not to change under those circumstances. Put this way, who could object to a firm being lean and mean; has it any choice?

Furthermore, what kind of relationship exists between being mean and being lean? Is being lean as a structural form more forced on the firm as result of market pressures, whereas being mean is more a matter of behavioral choice and style? Proponents of the mean-lean firm would shy away from that distinction since the market, in both cases, determines; attempts to distinguish create the illusion of choice. Lean and mean, however, do usually interact with each other. For instance, down-sizing might occasion wrenching and coldly calculated decisions over who and what goes or stays, and increasing worker responsibilities might eliminate supervisory layers. Distinctions between behavioral and structural will be shaky because structural change will inevitably induce behavioral variations in the firm, and behavioral change will usually set the scene for subsequent restructuring. Mean-lean is thus more than a handy rhyme; it manifests, for its proponents, an organic connection between behavior and structure.

Should the argument for the mean-lean firm then be accepted, on the basis of widespread current observation, as the embodiment of wisdom and virtue? Does it reflect the appreciation of necessity, and the fact that implicit contracting is fatally flawed because its emphasis on associational continuity seems to ill serve the structural adjustments and behavioral modifications required by a rapidly changing economy? For several reasons such a conclusion should be resisted. First, it misjudges implicit contracting's purposes and capabilities. Implicit contracting implies not blind attachment to the status quo; rather it uses continuity as a vehicle for more effective change. An implicit contract does not mean that the firm is frozen into the particular pattern of activity and relations prevailing at some instant of time. Precisely because implicit contracting can build upon the solid pillars of trust and cooperation, it should be able to accomplish resource reallocation tasks more smoothly and with less pain. All parties recognize that change is a constant challenge; where reciprocal obligation and mutual trust lubricate the mechanics of change, greater efficiency and equity will prevail.

An ambience of trust and cooperation also opens up greater possibilities for a longer run perspective and for not, as a first resort, undertaking those adjustments that preserve for some only at the expense of sacrificing others. Sometimes, of course, the trauma of shutdown, selective termination, undesired relocation or reassignment, compensation reduction, more onerous working conditions, and the like cannot be avoided; at least having a voice in determining their implementation and knowing that more desirable options could not be found make them more bearable. Implicit contracting is aware that life offers no guarantee of only happy choices, but that does not thereby entail the acceptance of inferior options if they can be avoided. Although the oft-heard incantation that "we owe it all to our workers" may seem ritualistic and ceremonial, to be trotted out at suitable formal occasions, it nevertheless bespeaks truth. Because implicit contracting can offer, in stipulated circumstances, a more effective way of both responding to the challenge of economic change and moderating its negative consequences, it should not be dismissed as being hopelessly wedded to the past.

Second, neither should it be taken as axiomatic that being mean and lean is the most efficacious response to market pressures. Such actions can be counterproductive for several reasons. They can reflect ingrained and reflexive behavior that often fails to systematically review a more extensive range of options. Moreover, their use as a first resort will inevitably induce a backlash in the form of lower morale and persistent resentment that can hardly fail to have adverse productivity consequences. Furthermore, firms do not usually take into account the sometimes very great social costs of such actions. Communities whose social viability is undermined, terminated workers, especially older ones, whose skills will atrophy and who cannot find comparable employment, and the heavy toll of disruption in personal and family lives must somehow all be reckoned in the balance. Certainly, circumstances may make such tragedies unavoidable, and the only option may be to mitigate their severity. But experience indicates that all too often private calculation of such social costs is given very short shrift.

Additionally and more specifically, being mean and lean can flow from less than worthy motives; the mean-lean firm can do the wrong things for the wrong reasons. The mean-lean firm may, perhaps instinctively, focus excessively on short-run quick fixes; it may simply be interested in retaining authority and command, even at the expense of forgoing efficiency; on the supposition that, in an adversarial context, maintaining precedents and not losing face are presumed to be tactical necessities, its actions may be strategically correct, but functionally wrong; again, largely as an article of faith, the mean-lean firm may unwisely downgrade the prospects of internal renewal; its hierarchical outlook may inhibit it from tapping the energies and talents of its workers; and, more generally, its simplistic mind-set regarding motivation and organization renders it incapable of appreciating the potentially immense contribution of trust and cooperation. Thus, far from being the firm's natural and correct response to evolving market pressures, the mean-lean firm could worsen rather than improve matters.

These contrasting characterizations of the implicit contracting and mean-lean firm suggest no prima facie case, flowing directly from abundant observation, for rejecting implicit contracting. Indeed, a more accurate rendering of the factual situation would conclude that empirical evidence exists for both approaches, and, thus, judgments concerning their respective worth must depend upon further analysis. The choice of the mean-lean approach offers no guarantee of superiority, since it could be based on numerous considerations unrelated, and even antithetical, to efficiency. Alternatively, implicit contracting offers the promise of a better response to market pressures, especially where variability in the performance of the human agent is critical. Those who believe that correct theorizing requires the presumption of market perfection and unidimensional human beings may express surprise at such a conclusion, but the major argument of this book is directed precisely against accepting the universal applicability of such beliefs. Situational contingencies will largely determine which approach is best suited.

Macroeconomic Stability and
Structural Transformation

It thus becomes pertinent to consider these two approaches in the context of the very important issues of macroeconomic stabilization and transformational imperatives. For both issues, my previous discussion of responsiveness to market pressures is very relevant, but the focus here is changed to explicitly consider the macroeconomic consequences of what is happening at the microeconomic level. This perspective offers new dimensions for evaluating efficiency concerns and is also justified by the overriding importance of those issues.

Perhaps most noteworthy is that the neoclassical approach has much less to say about them than does implicit contracting. Neoclassicists believe that such problems have already been addressed by pointing out how effectively the market works. If, for some reason, rigidities and frictions impede the smooth workings of the market, then the proper remedy is to go to the source of such disturbance and allow the market to do its job. That will both stabilize, in classical Say's Law fashion, the overall economy and, at the same time, allow whatever shifts in the pattern of resource use are required to quickly take place. Certainly there may be practical difficulties in unclogging the pricing mechanism, but that is surely a second-order problem that can be resolved without too much strain.

Implicit contracting views these issues very differently. First, with regard to macrostabilization, important linkages are manifest, especially if one accepts the position that inflation is the main challenge and upward labor-cost pressures the major driving force. For one thing, the productivity gains accruing from reliance on the implicit contracting firm offer some welcome supply-side relief. Higher productivity stems partly from being better able to tap workers' creative talents and energies, and partly from the smoother transitions in the pattern of resource use. For another, the generally more desirable working conditions under implicit contracting substitute for higher wages in many ways, and upward wage pressures are moderated. Implicit contracting offers a very close approximation to the economist's unthinkable free lunch in the sense that a cooperative and participative work climate not only is more productive, but at the same time is more finely attuned to what most workers want from their jobs. Hence, the edge is taken off the scramble for higher pay to compensate for all that is wrong with the job.

Finally, it is not too difficult to imagine connections between on-the-job conditions and how workers relate to broader social concerns. Incomes policies, for instance, have not been notably successful, in large part because of the justifiable concern that others would take advantage of one's restraint. But authoritarian workplaces contribute to the prolongation of such self-centered attitudes since their ethos is directly supportive; stressing a narrow version of self-interest does not mesh very well with achieving broader trust and social cooperation. Fundamental changes in workplace regimes, however, can demonstrate the benefits of cooperation and trust by example, and the projection onto the larger society of similar attitudes is not a very large step.

This last point can be extended to include the entire range of social issues where mutual strategic dependency, combined with substantial suspicion and distrust, create vexing and seemingly unresolvable problems. Strategic interaction creates an inevitable tension between parties since each must choose on the basis of supposition about the other's conduct. In a workplace context, this might mean that firms would hedge against allowing too much information and decision-making capability to flow into workers' hands for fear of losing a bargaining edge; workers might deliberately underperform for fear that firms would institute new and more rigorous work standards. They would each be motivated to take functionally unwise actions in an area under their control, certainly to society's, and possibly to their joint, detriment. Where trust rules, such inferior outcomes can be avoided.

All this is not to suggest that implicit contracting is a magic pill that guarantees stability for the economy. Far from it; problems abound. It should be clear that I do not have in mind a cartelized economy in which the gains from cooperation are not passed on. Cooperation in the small should not become a mechanism for extracting rents from the larger society. Vigorous competition among implicit contracting firms should keep any such tendencies in check, but combining competition among and cooperation within firms is admittedly a tough balancing act. Nor am I suggesting that creating and maintaining implicit contracting arrangements is a simple and easy process; I will directly address this issue in the next chapter. Finally, the idea of situational conditionality should never be forgotten; as stressed before, implicit contracting may work better and be useful in some circumstances and not in others. Despite these cautions, the prospect that implicit contracting can assist in the battle against inflation is a strong argument in its favor.

The notion of transformational imperatives was implicit in my previous discussion of adjustment capabilities, but its importance merits greater treatment. Although the realization of change as the economic law of life is not exactly new, recent economic trends have nevertheless heightened our sensitivity to its manifestations. The startling contrasts between the quickly changing economic fortunes of different industries, sectors of the economy, and geographic regions indicate the accelerated pace and broad extent of economic transformation. And the increasing integration of the world economy, spurred by communication and transportation gains, suggests that this process will continue. That transformational imperatives will dominate our economic agenda is beyond doubt. We confront not just the occasional and isolated adjustment to a specific disturbance, but a more or less continuous pattern of systemic shocks reaching far and deep into the structure of our economy—that is why transformational imperatives are a macroeconomic problem.

Again, such a future poses few problems for neoclassical thought since, as always, the market will automatically produce the required resource reallocations. Alternatively, implicit contracting is based, in part, on the recognition that such shifts do not take place so easily, and anything that can facilitate their accomplishment will be a blessing. The argument for implicit contracting, as detailed in previous chapters, is that a firm confronted with the necessity to make such frequent changes will do so more quickly and efficiently in a milieu where trust and cooperation prevail.[3]

Here too, caution is well advised. Change is always difficult; the instinct to protect what one has is strong. No one should have any illusions that implicit contracting somehow produces new and superior kinds of human beings. It can help, but that is all. What seem like firm agreements and mutual understandings can crumble under strain. No internal arrangements can modify the hard and demanding external givens. Implicit contracting does not control what challenges an ever-changing world will pose; it can only respond to them. When all is said and done, a greater possibility for doing the best with what you have is implicit contracting's claim; fulfillment would be a feat, not an inevitable result.

But if there is this good chance that implicit contracting can be helpful in resolving these immensely difficult social issues of macroeconomic stabilization and large-scale economic adjustment, that greatly strengthens its appeal as social policy. Moreover, such accomplishments seem to be a true externality arising from the firm's internal organization. At the same time, the fragility of relationships based upon trust must be remembered. Unfortunately, although trust must be built up over a long time, it can be destroyed in an instant. That is not a reason for rejecting implicit contracts; it does reinforce the need to exercise care and caution.

IC+: Further Implications

As my discussion of various aspects of labor market and on-the-job behavior has illustrated, exploring where implicit contracting leads and what kind of

---

3. In this connection the trends listed in note 2 are very relevant. More and more, it is not disagreements over wages as much as disputes concerning work rules and job duties and the greater freedom generally sought by employers to unilaterally restructure work arrangements that eventuate in strikes and lockouts. But if such disputes lead to new hires replacing existing workers, then, given the union-security and union-busting implications of such trends, that way of trying to reorganize work will be extremely costly and eventually unsuccessful. Current circumstances may very well offer tempting visions of complete freedom in a union-free environment, but a cursory acquaintance with labor history would indicate the illusory nature of such visions, and the heavy social costs from the consequent intensified level of conflict and struggle between labor and capital. Indeed, current work organization rigidities are likely to themselves be the result of reactions to previous attempts at unilateral dictation of work conditions. Implicit contracting can break this vicious cycle.

behavior it covers should be fruitful. The implications are many, and the purpose of this section is to highlight some of these as illustrative of the kinds of changes in thought required. First, those more directly connected with agent behavior will be surveyed, with special attention to theoretical implications, and then some public policy issues will be discussed.

Perhaps the most important insight from implicit contracts is the necessity to deal with the strategic behavior problem as a pervasive consequence of associational continuity. Strategic behavior implies a pattern of continuous interaction within the context of latent or active struggle; the parties deal and/or duel. From the firm's point of view, its problem is to get workers to fully utilize their capabilities without giving up too much of either its income share or decision-making prerogative. For the workers, their problem is to achieve an income share and participative role commensurate with their collective economic contribution, since each is dispensable on an individual basis. The collective proviso is very operationally significant because of all the well-known difficulties of acting in concert. In this contest, the advantages are almost invariably and overwhelmingly the firm's. Although, in the IC+ view, the underlying basis for eliciting superior worker performance is a larger income share and meaningful participation, firms have yet to move very far along those lines.

Nor have workers yet been able to translate their theoretically strong claim into the practical currency of a larger say and share.[4] This partially reflects the traditional difficulties of speaking with a single voice and the blandishments of profitable individual egress; partially, it reflects the lack of intellectual definition of position in a situation where novel action is required—like a sleeping giant, workers are not aware of their potentially enormous powers. Furthermore, the major segments of organized labor have looked to collective bargaining as an instrument for achieving direct and short-run material gains, not as a lever to extract any measure of joint responsibility and participation; moreover, a majority of workers are not even under the collective bargaining umbrella.

Whatever the logic of implicit contracting and the employment relationship may entail for reshaping the disposition of property rights, managerial and shareholder sensitivity concerning power and prerogatives ensures opposition to such implied shifts. After all, at stake is not merely a marginal redivision of income, but the far more sensitive and fundamental issue of who is boss. And that issue must be confronted in situations where, ex hypothesi, no objective market or other standard exists by reference to which the parties can measure their position. Firm-specificity and organizational rent make

---

4. This is true even for a country, like Britain, with a strong socialist tradition. For some British evidence of the extent to which workers have not vigorously pressed for expanded participation, see Edwards and Scullion 1982. It should be added that it is not strange for the spread of unorthodox and unfamiliar ideas to take considerable time.

each firm, with respect to its collection of workers taken as production teams, unique and sui generis. Certainly individual workers may be replaced from time to time without much impairing the firm's performance, but firm-specific talents and skills and the experience of working together as production teams imply the impossibility of completely replacing, within reasonable time frames, groups of workers. Thus the parties must work out their differences without objective market evaluations as precise guidelines.[5] Compared to their alternative opportunities, their present situation generates huge rents, whose appropriation will be a source of constant struggle.

Issues of both power sharing and the absence of market standards are precisely what push the parties to rely very heavily on strategic behavior, but this is in an environment where the firm holds most of the cards, stakes are very high, and rules of engagement very fluid. Any action by either party will be judged not only by what it appears to be on the surface, but also by the sense it makes in a longer run pattern of move and countermove; the game is never over, since each completed round of strategic moves only sets the stage for the continuation of the process. Nor are there any precise limits to contested areas, since each will try to move the conflict to its favored field. Nor does strategic gaming provide a hospitable ambience for compelling moral imperatives, such as honesty and fairness, since the parties are not likely to agree on how such abstract concepts are to be operationalized in a world of ceaseless struggle. As a distinct form of conflict, strategic behavior comes under the rubric of all's fair in love and war.

Strategic gaming is thus pretty much loaded against workers. But if IC+ is correct, the disparity between what should be and what is will ultimately negatively affect productivity as a consequence of inadequate incentives. Although firms will be able to sustain their advantage tactically, the cost in productivity gains forgone will become greater and greater. Workers are unlikely soon to overcome the organizational and inertial barriers to bringing actual motivating conditions into line with the implied theoretical standard, and their disenchantment will make it harder and harder for firms to elicit superior performance. Perhaps public policy intervention can avoid such stalemated and nonoptimal outcomes.

Whatever the future may bring, the value of the implicit contracting approach lies also in the richer and fuller account it provides for otherwise unconnected and truly puzzling phenomena. By strongly asserting the claims

---

5. These observations apply more to labor markets than to product markets, where firms will usually confront other firms. The point being made here is that firms do not have the alternative of replacing their labor force, en masse, without incurring huge efficiency penalties. To some extent, however, the trends mentioned in n. 2 and 3 are exerting a counterforce. Multiplant and multicountry activities, extensive product diversification, and the increased readiness, in various ways, to maintain operational capabilities in the event of a strike have all reduced the dependence of firms on any one group of employees. Having such options strengthens the firm's hand, but the full implications of these trends are not yet apparent.

for situational dependence, it sensitizes us to the circumstances that generate variety in observed outcomes. Economics is done a disservice when essential and important complexity is assumed away in the rush to obtain a spurious generality of result. Wage instrumentality and multidimensionality, worker heterogeneity, local initiative and team activity and their correlative requirements of information sharing, cooperation, and coordinating mechanisms, infinite variety in terms and conditions of employment, sophisticated job-worker matching processes, on-the-job behavior highly dependent upon the pattern and quality of incentives, and the legitimacy of existing structures of property rights—all are proper subjects for more thoroughgoing investigation, once IC+ is accepted. Beyond questions of proper subject matter, it also alerts us to the centrality of conflict in defining how the parties interact; ineluctably, long-standing issues concerning moral hazard and efficient outcomes must then be reinterpreted within that framework.

IC+ notions are helpful in dispelling the confusion created by two blind alleys, relating to moral hazard and efficient outcomes, which theoreticians are prone to enter. For one, moral hazard, in the sense of resort to unprincipled and unethical behavior, can only be interpreted within a well-defined context. Just as a nation does not apply ordinary standards of morality to its own espionage agents and just as one person's freedom fighter is another's terrorist, so in the rough-and-tumble of conflict and struggle between workers and the firm, a higher and universal morality, applicable only to a collection of individuals in basic harmony with each other, cannot be arbitrarily imposed. Formal contractual relations are buttressed by legal compulsions affecting precise undertakings; implicit contracts depend upon mutual forbearance applied to imprecise understandings. A breach of an implicit contract is not so much dastardly and immoral behavior, but rather a sign that forbearance is no longer forthcoming from at least one of the parties.

Interpreting all such breaches as necessarily and prima facie unethical conduct or acts of dishonesty and cheating presumes their precise identification and the prior existence of an agreed moral code against which they can be objectively measured. But in a world of conflict and differences in interpretation, agreement on plain facts and/or unambiguous moral imperatives is unlikely. This is not to say, as those stressing shirking seem to believe, that human beings will lie, cheat, steal, and generally behave dishonorably according to an intricate calculation concerning whether the expected gains from such actions are likely to exceed their expected costs.[6] Rather, it is to suggest

---

6. The notion of shirking as calculated and deliberate individual maximizing behavior within a utility framework is espoused most notably by Alchian and Demsetz (1972). At least three other grounds for shirking can also be proffered. (1) Shirking as innate laziness: human beings are inherently work-avoiders, always preferring leisure to work because of their, respectively, presumptively positive and negative utility. Tendencies toward idleness arise not so much from rational calculation as from the imprinted, innate nature of human beings; hence eternal vigilance against such backsliding is required. (2) Shirking as a competitive gambit: workers

that, in an implicit contract context, trust and mutual forbearance are both precious and fragile and must be patiently and carefully nurtured rather than taken for granted. Conflicting interests create a fine line between legitimate strategic behavior and tactical maneuver, on the one hand, and morally despicable conduct, on the other. Only high trust between the parties ensures that line will not be crossed. Successful implicit contracting thus symbolizes an ongoing cooperative and forthcoming relationship wherein the parties fashion arrangements permitting each to satisfactorily achieve valued objectives, despite a conflictual context capable of otherwise eliciting mutual withdrawal and reflexive hostility.

Similarly, the argument that implicit contracting must necessarily and automatically yield efficient outcomes, in the sense of attaining the best possible results under the stipulated circumstances, is equally misdirected. IC+ offers the possibility, not certainty, of a better outcome. A continuing struggle-for-control and the interaction aspects of implicit contracting presage multiple equilibria and, combined with the impact of associational continuity in insulating the parties from close market discipline, together spell the doom of the Panglossian position. Even some implicit contract theorists, like their NC+ counterparts, have sought to put an irresistible efficiency "spin" on their argument by claiming that observed outcomes do indeed reflect ordinary maximizing behavior under the more richly specified circumstances, hence the parties reach the best attainable results, given those conditions. Such an interpretation, however, fails to recognize the conflict "spin" element in implicit contracting.

Even IC+ cannot rule out the possibility that the parties can be so mistrustful of each other that neither would accept the other's legitimacy and, consequently, strategic jockeying for advantage and for assertion of dominance could take hold. The dominant strategy for both parties will be to protect and advance their own position in the face of worst-case assumptions about the other. Workers could consciously withhold and withdraw their effort if, in their view, incentive patterns were inadequate; likewise, firms could deliberately, to maintain authority and control or to engage in short-run cost shaving, adopt inferior and perverse work arrangements. Implicit contracting can fail; conflicts between the incentives workers require and what firms are prepared to offer can be unresolved, and efficient outcomes will be derailed. The best of all possible worlds is thus not a preordained result; inferior outcomes are all too possible because the parties can move away from constructive agreement, and the market cannot drive them to a unique and best

---

shirk to make a point; shirking is symbolic communication, indicating dissatisfaction and addressing itself to changing specific conditions of work. (3) Shirking as a manifestation of the class struggle: shirking is a collective protest against an unjust and exploitative system, and seeks its overthrow through one of the few avenues open to workers for pursuing industrial guerrilla warfare.

equilibrium.[7] What implicit contracting unerringly teaches us is that, as common sense would suggest, it all depends on the particulars and the setting. Hence, here too, public intervention can steer the parties toward better outcomes.

One factor, though, that can mitigate destructive impulses in the employment relationship is the development of trust between the parties. Enough has been said already to establish the linkage between mutual forbearance and positive interaction, and trust is clearly the lubricant that eases the way for the parties to be honest and forthcoming with each other. Bonds of trust must be forged, however, by specific deeds; the basis for trust lies in whether the actual relationship reinforces the willingness of the parties to afford each other the benefit of doubts, and is clearly very much a two-way street.[8] Thus adversity, if it induces good-faith and cooperative efforts at joint resolution, can strengthen rather than undermine implicit contracting. And trust, of course, builds upon itself; each positive experience lays the groundwork for deepening and extending trust, and with trust augmented, the resolution of difficult and divisive issues then becomes that much easier to accomplish. Perhaps in rare cases, where the implicit swaps are well and simply defined, and their consequences patently apparent and not dependent upon interpreting each other's behavior, trust would not matter. More likely, however, where high trust prevails, the parties can jointly realize the full potential of the inherent gains from associational continuity; absent such trust, inferior outcomes and persistent conflict more logically follow. For achieving joint goals, strangely enough, trust can be an infinitely more compelling force than legal obligation.[9]

---

7. Schultze (1985), quoting Solow, begins his presidential address as follows: ". . . [T]he world may have its reasons for being non-Walrasian," to which it may be added, and non-Panglossian too. This assumes that Walras was not inevitably Panglossian.

8. Substantive parity between the parties, or at least the absence of great disparities, in the relevant dimensions of economic strength is likely to be a prerequisite for trust. Dependency, because it implies one-way flows, corrodes trust. Relevant in this connection is the suggestion by some (e.g., Weitzman and Kruse 1990) that self-interest, in their case via profit sharing, can be marshaled to support mutual trust and empathetic behavior in long-term situations. The underlying position can be modeled as a repeated Prisoner's Dilemma game, in which incentives for self-seeking advantage at the other party's expense can be dominated by the knowledge that resisting such temptations in order to sustain the long-run relationship will confer an even greater gain. Two problems, however, persist. First, and in my view fancifully, a purist would argue that any individual would still have an incentive to cheat, regardless of what has happened before, in that person's terminal period since there would be no further relationship to sustain and, hence, no penalty. Second, and more relevant, the relative parity condition would become even more important for such self-interested behavior since dominance, and therefore the prospect of unilateral and arbitrary action by the more powerful party, would undermine the required sense of mutual confidence. Self-interest and trust can thus support each other, but only under certain conditions.

9. At first glance, mixing conflict and trust may seem incompatible too, but on reflection and where long-term association is the context, mutual dependency creates incentives to establish

The practical importance of trust and cooperation is revealed almost daily as frequent surprises and unforeseeable circumstances in the production process insistently demand instant and on-the-spot resolution, and highly capable and coordinated work teams must respond to such challenges. This valuable reactive facility becomes especially significant when viewed in the light of the impact of pace and tempo on productive efficiency. Consider the following four representative and strategically relevant production process issues: (1) the success of the *kan-ban* (just-in-time) production system that minimizes inventory requirements by very tight production scheduling procedures (Aoki 1988b, 22–25); (2) devolving quality-control responsibilities to production line workers, including the right to stop the line at their discretion; (3) ensuring steady and high levels of effort by recognizing that workers' fears of "working oneself out of a job" can be addressed through guarantees of considerable job security, such as "lifetime" employment contracts at comparable jobs and pay with necessary retraining; (4) achieving extraordinarily high levels of effort intensity by workers in response to periodic, and usually unexpected, demands to accelerate production scheduling in connection with deadlines and emergencies. In each case, worker willingness to take on such very great participatory and initiating responsibilities and refrain from exploiting short run strategic advantage is the critical element in successfully implementing such productivity-enhancing approaches. And in turn, that willingness to respond to pace and tempo demands will depend not so much upon contractually specifying duties, but rather upon drawing from a preexisting reservoir of trust. The returns to trust and cooperation as productive inputs can hardly be exaggerated.[10]

Because mistrust and perverse strategic behavior can both be so socially disintegrative a process and have such socially wasteful outcomes, the public has a large stake in how the employment relationship evolves. As we have seen, the market alone cannot be relied upon to generate socially optimal

---

trust as a way of enabling the parties to accomplish their objectives most expeditiously. Indeed, the presence of trust creates opportunities beyond those prevailing in its absence. In any case, if the parties are stuck with each other, as in a repeated game, they may as well make the best of it, and that is a lot easier done if trust prevails.

10. Two lines of extensive empirical research—(1) regression analysis of the relationship between various productivity and output measures and an augmented menu of regressors that also includes surrogate variables, such as profit-sharing, participation indices, and extent of worker control, for gauging the impact of more cooperative organizational arrangements; and (2) the estimation of frontier production functions that seek to capture maximal possible output, or what happens in best-practice firms, as a current limit on potential productivity gains—should be noted in this context. The latter is less relevant for our purposes; for a recent survey, see Schmidt 1986. For the former, Weitzman and Kruse have done a complete and careful survey of the regression studies, and they conclude: "The general picture . . . is that profit sharing and productivity are positively related. . . It is fair to say that no one study yielded convincing evidence on the relation between profit sharing and productivity. However, the similar conclusions that emerge from all sixteen studies taken together provide fairly strong evidence of a consistent pattern" (1990, 127).

results, and the parties can easily be quite nasty and brutish to each other with consequent dangers for social stability and civility. These unwelcome outcomes suggest a social rationale for establishing a public presence that pushes the parties toward greater trust.

With economic outcomes inherently variable, depending upon the parties' ability to fashion the appropriate internal arrangements, the question of how their choices can be influenced by third-party intervention arises. In this regard, many precedents exist. We have defined a legal structure for labor relations that establishes a support system for encouraging voluntary collective bargaining; we have created mechanisms for mediating and resolving labor disputes; we have established standards and implementation mechanisms for occupational safety and health; we have used the tax code to encourage employee stock ownership plans—in all of these actions, one can discern a broad public purpose to encourage and support particular patterns of behavior based on the belief that society's interests are directly at stake and are thereby better served. Providing incentives for firms and workers to move in more cooperative and participatory channels would be well within these traditional forms of support. Such programs could usefully complement efforts at building up trust and could be instrumental in softening the trauma associated with ongoing economic transformation and institutional evolution.

Indeed, the likelihood of continuing institutional evolution is what should drive public policy and is itself based upon what kinds of firm-worker relationships are ultimately compatible with associational continuity. As I have argued, associational continuity and the strengthened collective position of workers flowing therefrom will be the strongest influence on the future of the firm. The logic of variable effort, firm-specific human capital, transaction costs, and organizational rent imparts a syndicalist push to the firm's evolution. In the face of powerful structural forces and trends that, over the long run, strengthen the workers' position, will not the internal arrangements within the firm have to mirror this increasingly recognized functional reality?

In a fundamental sense, this result can be viewed as the logical and necessary outcome of revisionist theories of the firm based upon implicit contracting and the employment relationship. Expanding the scope and potential variability of the workers' contribution, and making it so sensitively and intimately dependent upon more complicated incentive schemes, must influence both the form and extent of workers' rewards. If effort matters so much, firm-specific human capital is so very much at risk, transaction costs are so important, and organizational rent is so eminently tangible and sharable—if, in a word, the worker has become a virtual principal—then how, and how much, workers are compensated must be confronted.[11] In a nutshell, as a

---

11. Leveraged buyouts, in which operating managerial groups take over firms by borrowing on the basis of their functional responsibility for the firm's performance, have become commonplace in recent years. Extending this principle to embrace larger numbers of employees should not appear strange.

matter of logic, workers have the equivalent of an equity stake by virtue of this interpretation of their contributions.[12] Devising property rights mechanisms, such as those discussed elsewhere in this book, to actualize such claims would seem to be the precondition for efficient resource allocation in both an instantaneous and intertemporal sense.[13] Yet in practice, as I have observed, there is no headlong rush to offer workers the participative responsibilities and augmented income share that would seem to be the natural accompaniments of their heightened productive contribution. Logic and fact seem sharply at odds: theory suggests fundamental alteration in income shares and decision-making authority; practice reveals no such dominant trend.

Issues of authority and power thus become fundamental matters of dispute, once the implications of implicit contracting are followed through; questions of legitimacy flow directly from the theoretical implications of emphasizing the expanded importance of workers. After all, it should not be strange that responsibility, reward, status, and power should all follow function. When so much depends upon properly motivating workers, it would be incongruous to expect that institutional forms and power-sharing arrangements would not be affected by such a drastic shift in relative emphasis. Realigning property rights is, accordingly, the natural outcome of the functional recognition of the collective importance and claims of workers and of their contribution to the firm's fortunes. Theirs is an earned right to a larger income share and to greater participation in firm decision making.[14]

---

12. As equity holders, workers would, of course, be exposed to bearing the firm's losses too. It would therefore be advisable to insulate them, through a reserve fund mechanism, from extreme swings in this regard. Similarly, cumulating equity holdings would mean that both one's human capital and financial assets are narrowly concentrated in a single enterprise. Normal diversification considerations would suggest that workers would want to hold alternative financial assets (see chap. 7 for a discussion of these issues.) For those appreciative of irony, the paradox of implicit contracting as a doctrine stemming from a desire by workers to avoid risk coming full circle to accepting risk as both inevitable and compensable should be noted.

13. Property rights, we should remind ourselves, undergo continuous modification in response to changing legal and political conditions. For instance, collective bargaining has been defined as the progressive erosion of managerial prerogative. Change in the firm's internal governance should be viewed in a similar evolutionary perspective.

14. Such changes represent concrete recognition of what is so often stressed in firms' advertising and public relation efforts: namely, our workers are our most important resource, a company is its people, we owe all our success to our hard-working employees, etc. La Rochefoucauld's maxim seems apposite: "Hypocrisy is the homage that vice pays to virtue."

CHAPTER 7

Is the Labor-Managed Firm an Explicit Version of Implicit Contracting: Or What Lyrics for Voice?

If implicit contracting plus survives the critique from neoclassicism, what about its response to a challenge from the other direction? After all, if worker participation is being stressed, do we not have, ready-made and easily available, the enormous literature on the labor-managed (LM) firm, wherein workers control the firm? Presumably, close, continuing, and trusting cooperation among worker-owners would be the LM firm's automatic accompaniment, and thus it might conceivably be viewed as the ultimate realization of implicit contracting, at least in terms of achieving IC+'s objectives. In this sense, the LM firm could be an explicit rendering of the elements composing the implicit contract, a formal arrangement whereby the structural and motivational features are determined by the workers themselves. Has the empowerment theme arrived at its logical terminus?

As I will make clear in this chapter, the LM firm has not usually been viewed as the fulfillment, or even an extension, of implicit contracting and certainly its origins differ.[1] The LM firm arose partly as an academic interpretation of the evolution of the Yugoslavian form of market socialism (hence its Illyrian designation), and partly from pure intellectual speculation about what happens when traditional arrangements are inverted and labor hires capital.[2] For the most part, this literature has accepted the economist's usual austere assumptions and then explored where the formal logic of maximization leads, especially as compared to the traditional firm, rather than being concerned with more real-life and practical organizational and motivational issues. Moreover, for better or worse, it has usually been tightly bound to the tradition of methodological individualism, despite the intrinsic and functional importance of the collective entity. Nevertheless, as I will show, the IC+ and LM firm do tend to converge toward common ground, since they both ultimately must deal with the internal organizational arrangements conducive to high-level worker performance. At the same time, much of the extensive theoretical controversy generated by the LM firm literature can be largely

---

1. See Ward 1957; Vanek 1970; Meade 1972; Stephen 1984; Aoki 1984; Bonin and Putterman 1987.

2. See Putterman 1984.

relegated to a sideshow, either reflecting some highly inappropriate original specifications or else irrelevant for our purposes. The practical organizational and motivational issues, however, are more persistent and troublesome.

Is the LM Firm a Natural Disaster?

The literature on the LM firm is voluminous, and much of it has stressed that the LM firm inevitably generates perverse and undesired outcomes. As many have demonstrated, however, most of the more sensational results flow from particular assumptions that can, in principle, be easily replaced with more appropriate ones.[3] Three major specification shortcomings are at fault: (1) using average income per worker, or share, rather than aggregate income (or the value of the firm) as the maximand; (2) excluding any kind of tradable ownership claims and an associated capital market, thereby automatically assuming that all capital is debt financed; and, closely related, (3) establishing an arbitrarily truncated time-horizon—a worker's time on the job—as the relevant maximizing period. With regard to the first issue and maintaining the debt-finance assumption, instead of maximizing aggregate income (and the value of the firm) by hiring workers until the marginal product is equated to the competitive wage, the firm maximizes share income in the short run by including additional worker-owners only up to the point where the marginal share equals the average share, with the latter inclusive of an offset adjustment assigning to workers their proportionate part of fixed costs. In essence, the firm balances the impact on share income of the declining marginal contribution of additional workers (reflecting decreasing marginal productivity) against the incremental gain from apportioning given fixed costs over a larger work force. In other words, the firm will produce where the marginal return is equal to the average return, net of one's fixed-cost share, of all workers in the firm rather than to the presumptively lower opportunity cost of labor, that is, the competitive wage.

Consequently, relative to the competitive ideal, firms in the short run will hire too few workers and be too small, and, since share income can differ from firm to firm, workers will not necessarily be allocated to equalize their contribution, at the margin, across firms. Share maximization also leads to other problems for the LM firm. Whenever expansion is desirable, instead of adding new workers and thus reducing the average share (since the marginal gain will necessarily be less than the average share), firms will either increase their subcontracting or expand by substituting capital and/or contract workers for owner-workers. When things go badly (and share income is less than the competitive wage), some workers would rush to be the first to jump ship and

---

3. See Meade 1972; Schlicht and von Weizsacker 1977; Sertel 1982; Stephen 1984; Wolfstetter, Brown, and Meran 1984; Barzelay and Thomas 1986; Bonin and Putterman 1987. For a critique of the LM firm and a statement of its presumptive faults, see Jensen and Meckling 1979.

earn the larger competitive wage elsewhere, leaving those remaining to bear the fixed-debt burden (and any other extant common obligations).

Since hiring only until the marginal return equals the average return limits firm size, relative to the competitive outcome, the equilibrium long-run expansion (contraction) must entail large-scale entry (exit) of many small firms. Such entry (exit) would be induced by the positive (negative) gap between the return to workers in those existing firms and the competitive wage that could be earned elsewhere. Expansion, however, might prove difficult; entering firms could only attract inexperienced workers since, in good times, workers in existing firms are already doing as well as they can and thus would have no incentive to break away and start their own, or join new, firms.

Additionally, as has been fixated upon in the literature that views LM firms as a natural disaster, the response of a share-maximizing LM firm to favorable parametric shifts in demand, uncertainty, productivity, and fixed costs will be perverse. Higher output prices, less uncertainty, productivity increases, or declining fixed costs will all cause the firm to contract, rather than expand, its output; indeed, the logic of income-per-worker maximization implies that fellow workers will be fired under such conditions to increase the returns for those remaining (Vanek has dubbed this a suicidal urge). Conversely, unfavorable movements of those parameters will paradoxically induce output increases and new hires. Although in the long run gaps between share income and the opportunity wage will induce correct output and employment adjustments through the entry and exit of new firms, the bugaboo of negatively sloped short-run supply curves of output has been the symbol of the LM firm's perversity.

Similarly, with regard to the third issue (truncated time horizons), as long as workers derive their income solely and exclusively on the basis of their current work activity, they will have an incentive to defer payments and accelerate revenues. Once they leave the firm, they can have no claim to any income (or, for that matter, any obligation for losses) accruing as a result of actions taken during their period of employment. Arrangements thus blithely disregarding the obviously pertinent consideration that present actions have future consequence are asking for trouble. The present value of those consequences must inescapably enter into any rational decision-making process.

For instance, an investment project will have to pass the very specific test of yielding a competitive return within the average worklife (as a crude approximation) of the existing work force rather than be discounted over its normal lifetime. Indeed, pay-offs from any current expenditure whose fruits will appear largely in the future (e.g., advertising, good will, research and development) accrue only to those contemporaneously working at the time. Because of this focus on extracting current income, all activities would have to be continuously scrutinized against its attempted enhancement through deferring payables, accelerating receivables, and realizing the cash value of assets by either outright sales or inadequate depreciation arrangements. For departing workers, there is no tomorrow; hence, a distributional bacchanalia can be anticipated. Furthermore, investment will be restrained and biased toward quicker yielding projects, as workers will not sow where they cannot fully reap. Such implied work force decisions will hardly promote confidence among suppliers of external finance.

Both of these issues reflect a fundamental error in focusing only on current income sharing, neglecting the future consequences of current activity, and in not separating the return to labor from the return to capital; both can be formally corrected by addressing the second issue and having workers be shareholders and concomitantly creating capital markets. This can be done by the simple expedients of (a) establishing an initial capital subscription, attested to by a tradable, dividend-paying, equity share claim, as an entry condition for original, and, after a probationary period for additional, workers, and (b) revising the income-sharing arrangements to include a return on such equity claims as a residual, after crediting each worker with a notional wage that would ideally approximate the competitive level. In addition, as explained subsequently, allowing nonworkers to hold, with comparable residual claimant status, nonvoting shares would be an essential part of a functioning capital market.

Initially, the original workers would indeed do exactly as before by maximizing share income, which would now consist of the notional wage plus the return on their capital subscription. Once having done this, though, they would immediately see that it would be in their interest to hire, as provisional members for a probationary period without requiring immediate share purchase, additional workers at the notional wage as long as such workers' marginal revenue product is greater than or equal to that wage. In taking this action, aggregate income would rightfully be maximized, the LM firm would mimic the competitive outcome, and only the original workers would receive the additional surplus generated by the newly hired during their probationary period.

The analytical key to understanding why such hiring would be undertaken and what happens subsequently lies in viewing the LM firm as an organizational innovation directly responsible, like any other innovation, for an upward shift in worker productivity. First, those hired would not be ordinary contract labor, since in circumstances where the firm's success is due to the high-level performance associated with an ownership stake and extensive participation, that would be self-defeating. Rather, as an employment condition to preserve the firm's cooperative character and high-level performance, new hires can, after the probationary and familiarization period enables all parties to be more informed, become shareholders. As a form of entry fee and in order to maintain the firm's high productivity status, existing workers must offer the probationary new hires (assuming standard employment eligibility qualifications are met) the chance to become worker-owners by purchasing shares. Contract workers, ex hypothesi, would not be nearly so productive;

indeed, their hiring could start a process leading ultimately to the unraveling of the LM firm itself. But why, it might be asked, would the founding workers do this when they know it means reducing their subsequent share? The answer is that they are compensated for sharing future gains with the new hires out of both (1) the surplus generated by the new hires during the probationary period, and, subsequently, (2) the entry price, or the value of share purchases, the new hires would willingly pay because of the incremental gains over joining a traditional firm at the competitive wage rate.[4]

New hires would be attracted by, hence willing to pay for, this prospect of future higher returns from participating in an inherently more productive organizational form. Both parties would also know that, over the longer run, new entry of like firms would anyhow eliminate scarcity rents—that portion of present above-normal returns stemming from superiority over existing traditional firms—and would take that into account. The new hires know that the notional wage is at least equivalent to what they could earn elsewhere. Furthermore, to encourage the growth of cooperation and trust upon which the firm's success is so much dependent, the entry price for new workers is likely to be somewhat less than the actuarial present value to them of the LM firm's superiority over non-LM firms. Both parties thus stand to gain. The existing workers are currently compensated for accepting a lower future share, and the new hires do better than their alternative options.

This obvious resolution has not usually been suggested because, in part, the LM firm has not ordinarily been viewed as a productivity-raising organizational innovation and, in part, such worker differentiation supposedly undercuts the presumed egalitarian basis of the LM firm.[5] In this interpretation, either there are no potential organizational gains or institutional inconsistency prevents the realization of attainable advantages. The absence of any productivity advantage, which the literature on the LM firm usually accepts, certainly makes a case for the LM firm harder to argue. The primary justification for the LM firm in those circumstances lies in whatever additional personal satisfaction is gained by those working under such conditions, and such gains are most likely to be found in relatively small firms composed of mostly equally talented and skilled people. The absence of productivity advantage

---

4. Two further points should be noted. First, existing workers could be compensated, through either cash bonuses or stock issues, from the surpluses and entry fees of new workers. Second, various deferred payment financing techniques could enable new members to overcome any liquidity problems associated with purchasing shares. For a theoretical discussion of entry fees in an implicit contract context, see Carmichael 1989.

5. Bonin and Putterman (1987, 67) raise an additional issue by stressing the dangers arising from undiversified enterprise-specific risk that is uninsurable because of presumptively unavoidable moral hazard problems. This seems too pessimistic an evaluation. Insurance diversification possibilities are surveyed later in this chapter; moral hazard issues are little different from any principal-agent relation and, given the ethos of labor-management, are likely to be less significant than in systems emphasizing uninhibited individualism.

suggests, however, that either trust, effort, and cooperation do not matter very much, or they are unattainable, as a practical matter, under most observable conditions. I find both of these positions difficult to believe.[6]

With regard to the question of unequal treatment, although all workers will be shareholders, this will be, as Meade has pointed out, an inegalitarian cooperative since shareholdings will not be equal. The equity stake, however, enlarges all workers' sense of commitment and loyalty, and. as I will discuss, continuous share revaluation by the capital market ensures that the future would be properly taken into account. In essence, these arrangements capitalize the founding workers' gain from demonstrating the success of a novel form of enterprise while preserving equal access on terms reflecting current conditions for all newly hired workers. All worker-owners, both original and postprobationary new hires, would subsequently receive higher than normal returns, in proportion to their shareholdings, for as long as inferior organizational forms exist.

Once the LM form becomes universal, returns remain higher than the original situation because of the higher productivity associated with organizational innovation. It does not seem inconsistent with the underlying spirit of a cooperative firm that no member receives any windfall, but always enters on terms equal to prevailing contemporaneous alternative opportunities; situational equity, not pecuniary equality, is the paramount consideration. And inequality itself does not arise from workers receiving different payments for identical work, but rather from various circumstances that lead to differential shareholdings. Furthermore, in order to avoid the extremes of both undue decision-making concentration and merely token shareholding, maximum voting (but not ownership) and minimum shareholding limits for workers would be established.

These arrangements would achieve important objectives and serve several purposes. They advance the interests of the initial group of workers without doing injury to those of the newly hired workers. The augmentation of the former's income through acquisition of the surpluses (above the notional wage) generated by newly hired workers during the probationary period and the revenues from share purchases is simply compensation, partly as a reward for successfully initiating a more effective organizational form and

---

6. It should be noted that this turns the usual argument against the LM firm upside down. For instance, Jensen and Meckling (1979) presume that capital markets and worker shareholding are impossibilities and, hence, allowing workers to control cannot result in the maximization of the value of the firm and will simply mean worker appropriation of what others contribute to the firm. Knowing that, no one would become involved with such a firm, and this tendency for the workers "to eat up the firm's assets" is the reason why the LM firm cannot be efficient. My argument is just the reverse: because the capital market now performs its usual disciplinary function, the higher level of worker efficiency arising from this organizational form can shine through; the LM firm will be a productivity-enhancing innovation and, consequently, outsiders will be attracted.

partly as payment for allowing newly hired workers the chance to share in the firm's future gains from its high-productivity status. In any case, because of free entry, that portion of above-normal returns stemming from its coexistence with inferior organizational arrangements will be sustained only until the latter disappear.

The newly hired workers earn what they currently could elsewhere and would also subsequently, after the probationary period, benefit from being able to participate fully in the gains from a superior organizational form. Two things should be noted: (1) this prospect of potential gain over and above their competitive wage alternative will clearly be worth something to prospective new hires; and (2) the realization of higher productivity performance and increased earnings is inextricably tied to worker shareholding. It seems quite natural to think of the probationary period and share purchases as reasonable payments from new hires to existing workers for the opportunity to realize a preferred position.

Share purchases by new hires are thus not a coercive tie-in, but rather reflect decisions to join a presumed-to-be superior, and thereby prospectively more profitable, form of organization. Those decisions would be wholly voluntary and, indeed, could prove useful in the early stages, when such arrangements are unfamiliar, in selecting workers having a more natural affinity for the LM firm. In sum, both founding workers and new hires are able to improve their well-being on the basis of sharing the gain from expanding the LM firm; the founding workers divide the additional revenues stemming from the new hires, and the new hires stand to gain by being in a higher productivity firm. All workers would earn the competitive wage, and all share transactions would be at what a competitive capital market establishes as their current value. All gains (losses) to worker-owners would accrue in connection with their shareholdings.

Such a scheme accordingly builds upon the distinction between workers' effort contribution and their capital stake. Further, as an additional and helpful refinement that will be discussed more fully, instead of relying solely on external debt finance, equity shares (but without voting rights attached) should also be made available on the open capital market to nonworkers to increase the liquidity of workers' shares and to provide an additional source of funds and an external check on the firm's operation.[7] Within broad limits set by having each worker hold some minimum number of shares as a clear indication of commitment and by also having a maximum limit on voting shares (a voting cap) to avoid undue concentration, workers would be free to split the notional wage as they choose between money and shares. The firm would

---

7. For a similar two-class shareholder scheme, see Barzelay and Thomas 1986. For discussions of various problems relating to buyouts, share issuance and dilution, voting, and incentive structure, see Askildsen, Ireland, and Law 1988; Grout and Jewitt 1988; Bowles and Gintis 1990, 312–13.

maximize the aggregate net of the notional wage bill; part of this surplus would be distributed to all equity holders as dividends and part would be retained by the firm. Initially, worker choices concerning the form of the notional wage merely divides it into a present (the money wage) and future (the equity claim) component; what you do not get as a current money wage, you receive as an equity claim in the form of a specific number of shares whose value just equals what is required to ensure that the total notional wage approximates what could be earned elsewhere.

Subsequently, as differential shareholdings emerge—from varying times of entry and lengths of service, different money wage/equity splits of the notional wage, and capital subscription differences—interest conflicts among workers and between nonvoting shareholders and workers can arise over the size of the return on shareholdings. Workers would now receive their notional wage, consisting of the money wage plus the incremental equity stake and, in addition, a return on their shareholdings. Those with greater shareholdings (and nonvoting shareholders) will want higher returns and a lower notional wage, and those with fewer shareholdings will prefer the opposite. Anchoring the notional wage to the competitive wage, the fact that all nonprobationary workers receive some return on their capital stake, the limited range of differential shareholding among workers, and the discipline of the capital market arising from the need to make shareholding attractive to outside purchasers should all moderate and soften such conflicts. Even the LM firm, however, cannot do away with the inherent tension between the claims of labor and capital.

The tradability and, thus, valuation of equity shares resulting from the functioning capital market will be helpful in dampening conflict by offering an ever-present alternative and an objective indicator of the worth of shares, but it will also be useful to consider other aspects relating to wider shareholding. There are few reasons against, and many arguments for, allowing nonvoting shares to be held by nonworkers. Such shares could be identical in all other respects or could, if desirable or necessary, have special contractual provisions and safeguards as compensation for the absence of voting rights. If a worker sells shares to a nonworker, the voting rights would simply not be attached; if a worker buys shares from a nonworker, they could then be voted (assuming the voting cap on individual shareholdings did not apply).

The most important reasons for allowing such wide share ownership are (a) to overcome the illiquidity limitations and valuation disabilities that would otherwise be present if the share market were thin,[8] and (b) to provide addi-

---

8. Thin share markets could also be mitigated through fair valuation procedures similar to the Internal Revenue Service's valuation of closely held companies for tax purposes. In fact, market-making in and the valuation of shares could be an important function of a central financial institution dedicated to overseeing the labor-managemed sector. Such activities would be a natural extension, for example, of the kind of support provided by the cooperative bank, the Caja Laboral Popular, in the Mondragon system of cooperatives in Spain.

tional and alternative sources of funds and thereby subject the LM firm to the usually salutory impact of external and objective capital market discipline—it is always helpful to see ourselves as others see us. Nonworker trading in shares would be motivated by normal considerations concerning the firm's prospects, and purchases would reflect the belief, inter alia, that such organizational forms result in superior performance. In particular, those outside the firm would be attracted by the productivity implications of the commitment and internal oversight capabilities of worker shareholders. It should be noted that, in the world of corporate finance, different classes of shareholders and restrictions on voting rights are not unknown, and, like any other property right, such differences can be appropriately valued by market trades. Similarly, institutional investors usually base their portfolio decisions on prospective returns rather than any yen for active participation in the firm's operation. Market breadth, low transaction costs, and instantaneous execution enable buy or sell decisions to generally provide adequate investor protection. There are thus both precedents and a continuing rationale for ownership claims not necessarily being tied to participation in the firm's decision making.

Other kinds of conflict can also occur, and later on I will detail further conditions attaching to such shares that can moderate and resolve contentious issues. Despite differential shareholding, unequal voting among workers, and nonworker ownership, arrangements confining total responsibility for decision making to worker-shareholders are well within the spirit of the LM firm. At the same time, properly functioning capital markets will also ensure that both socially correct allocative rules will apply and the time value of returns will be correctly accounted for in the firm's decisions.

Other LM Firm Problems

Beyond the intellectual puzzles arising from spinning out the implications of alternative maximand, financing, and time-horizon assumptions, the LM firm raises other practical and substantive issues.[9] In general, these relate to the broad areas of organizational design, motivation, and incentives. Will workers in the LM firm shirk more? Is there a $1/n$ problem as n, the number of workers, becomes larger, and natural collegial ties therefore are attenuated? What kind of workers will find the LM firm attractive and how will they be selected? Will decision making be incredibly cumbersome? How responsive is the firm to its external environment? Is there excessive risk inherent in workers having both their income flows and their wealth tied to a single activity? Will insider favoritism and oligarchic arrangements pose serious problems? Does the LM firm quickly bump up against severe limitations on feasible size and, hence, on its growth? Is there an endogenous life cycle

---

9. Here, too, there is irony in the fact of the literature's obsession with these relatively minor formal and theoretical issues at the expense of the more important and substantive practical concerns relating to the functioning of the LM firm.

ending in senility and decline, a kind of natural entropy, inevitably pro-
grammed for the LM firm? And finally, how well does the LM firm face
adversity and dissolution pressures?

Two technical arguments lie behind the case for greater shirking in the
LM firm. The first calls upon the income effect on work and leisure. As
income grows in the successful firm as a consequence of greater effort by all
workers (or for any other reason), individual workers will inevitably value
additional income less highly and additional leisure more highly. Hence, after
such greater efforts by all workers (or whatever raises income), each individual worker will have a greater incentive to indulge shirking propensities in
response to the now higher valuation of leisure. The harder one's mates work,
the more incentive for any single worker to shirk. The second is based upon
the presumption that functional hierarchy is entirely incompatible with the
LM firm. Anarchy and chaos must prevail as none take orders from anyone
and all shift responsibility to others; group self-discipline is an impossibility.
Like an army with all generals and no privates, a firm where all workers are
bosses cannot, in the nature of things, function very well; an LM firm is
doomed to the ineptitude and impotence resulting from this absence of order
and discipline.

Both of these criticisms are wide of the mark and neglect a powerful and
overwhelming counterforce. At the relevant range of income levels at issue, it
is hard to take seriously a strongly operational income effect; after all, if that
were really the case, the sustained, secular increases in real wages would have
already yielded a large reduction in effort and mass defection from work that
is nowhere apparent. It is even harder to give any credence to the idea that, as
one's mates work harder, an individual would take that as an opportunity to do
less, or more powerfully, would ever be allowed to get away with such
behavior by fellow workers. In fact, a considerable force in the LM firm
countering any shirking tendencies is the strength of "horizontal" monitoring,
as all workers now have a very direct and immediate interest in ensuring the
firm's success. Such monitoring would be done as a normal part of one's job
and by those intimately knowledgeable and close to actual workplace operations and thus be very effective. And one would be sinning against one's own
workmates rather than some impersonal, and not necessarily beloved, them.[10]
Additionally, the selection bias involved in choosing workers would tend to
guard against predispositions to shirking.

---

10. Two additional points are relevant here. First, some argue that since all workers do, or
can be made to, suffer from any one worker's shirking, such horizontal monitoring would also
flow effortlessly from individual self-interest in the traditional firm (see Holmstrom 1982). That
position, however, assumes away the inherent adversarial and contested nature of the employment relationship and the importance of concerted and solidaristic action by workers. Doubtlessly, where shared trust and common values prevail, horizontal monitoring will be effective, but
the point is that such conditions are likely to be the hallmark of the LM firm and only occasionally
occur in traditional firms.

Similarly, it is incorrect to presume that functional hierarchy cannot happily coexist within the LM firm. All that is being changed is that such hierarchies must now be legitimized by those who own shares and work rather than by those who just own shares. Moreover, those who work are likely to have more direct and first-hand knowledge concerning supervisory personnel, and that should result in more informed choice. Where hierarchy is functionally contributory to achieving collective goals, why should the beneficiaries therefrom have any interest in not establishing the correct organizational arrangements?

It is highly likely that, as adumbrated earlier, a strong selectivity factor will be operative for the LM firm, certainly in the beginning stages. The particular ethos of such firms may not appeal to all workers since it implies an unusual and demanding level of commitment and cooperation that many would find difficult to provide. True, most traditional firms strive for this kind of "team spirit," but such behavior coexists uneasily with a dominant cultural conditioning emphasizing unreconstructed individualism, and, in any case, it is not the precondition for those firms' existence as it is for the LM firm. For these reasons, the LM firm will, at least initially, be composed of those workers for whom the experience that work is more than just a job has substantial meaning and attraction. Further, the LM firm will have to be sensitive to the time-dependency of commitment and allow individuals to vary their level and intensity of participation over time to accommodate such experiential learning. Such conditioning and familiarization will create options in the future that may be impractical in the beginning. Learning by doing will be an important force shaping the collective culture of the LM firm.

The mechanics of decision making will undoubtedly be complicated, perhaps more so than in the traditional firm. Partly this will reflect the necessarily delicate pluralistic balancing of competing interests. There is no magic ingredient that can miraculously transform all the diverse pressures that cause division among workers into a unifying force. Indeed, a sophisticated constitutionalism and strong conflict resolution mechanisms, rather than simple winner-take-all majoritarianism, are likely to be necessary ingredients for the success of the LM firm. Checks and balances, voting arrangements with due regard for minority positions, tolerance and the acceptance of compromise, a

---

Second (and related), not all concerns over pacing and monitoring are laid to rest simply by virtue of the LM form. As I suggested in chap. 4, n. 2, problems of optimal tautness exist. The traditional firm's usual dominance over its workers implied a more excessive pace (and greater monitoring) than would occur if transactor disparities were absent. The LM firm, by its implied greater equality and by institutionalizing more open channels for worker expression, should be able thereby to do better in resolving such questions of pace and monitoring. Indeed, the theoretical argument for the superiority of the LM firm relies, in part, on the substitution of zero-cost and voluntary cooperation for resource-costly supervison to accomplish the firm's goals. For an analysis of the implications of firm dominance on this and similar issues, see Bowles and Gintis 1990.

willingness to abrogate the traditional cooperative rule of one person–one vote—all of these will have to prevail.[11] Likewise, various safeguards, similar to the complexities of bond covenants, to protect the legitimate concerns of nonvoting shareholders (e.g. dissolution codicils, subordination provisions, and redemption rights options in response to specified changes in capital structure or lines of activity, or to any other firm action that might drastically affect share values or the division of revenues between shareholders and workers—the implicit contract reaches here, too) might be desirable. It is a long and difficult road to travel from recognizing the need for and positive role of workers' voice to defining the exact mechanisms for such empowerment.

Partly though, complexity is the twin of commitment. The degree of involvement and effort levels are likely to be very sensitive to the extent to which a sense of genuine participation and responsibility is communicated through the governance apparatus. Likewise, non-voting shareholders provide immensely useful market breadth and liquidity for shares as well as an external check on inappropriate firm behavior. If commitment and follow-through are important, then some additional complexity may well be a small price to pay.

An important potential deficiency of the LM firm is the extent to which self-absorption and isolation, a sense of narrow and partisan inwardness, become dominant themes in its life. The danger is certainly there that emphasizing cooperation and commitment within the firm can easily degenerate into indifference and unconcern toward all others. Outsiders and the larger society may not be given much weight in the firm's calculations. At first sight, it may seem odd that presumptively cooperative types behave, by focusing all their energies inwardly, as models of Adam Smith's invisible hand at work. Indeed, one would think that, for the LM firm, ordinary greed would be tempered by a more critical and empathetic concern for the wider consequences of one's actions.

Be that as it may, both capital and product markets need to be working efficiently to ensure that wayward tendencies to do less than one's best, or feather one's own nest at the expense of others, or neglect the wider consequences of one's actions are held in check by the knowledge that such behavior will result in unpleasant outcomes and ultimately others will supplant you. Competition in the product market will perform its traditional function of preventing advantage taking and keeping LM firms on their toes. And, as my discussion of the share market has revealed, tradable shares and sophisticated

---

11. It should be noted that for some, the one person–one vote proviso is a fundamental belief and, indeed, defines the LM firm. Consequently linking differential voting to multiple shareholding and departures from simple majority rule would be seen as inconsistent with those principles. Similarly for others, allowing for fluctuations in share values smacks more of the casino and dishonorable speculation than a financial return to honest and dignified labor. But by sketching a system including such features, at least some idea of the opportunity cost of their absence can be gleaned.

forms of nonvoting equity will be especially helpful in curbing self-dealing excesses and bringing the discipline of the capital market to bear upon the firm's actions. The LM firm must walk a fine line in pursuing the gains inherent in more participative work engagement without, at the same time, neglecting the effect of its actions on the larger society of which it is part.

Closely related to this danger of parochialism, and for which external oversight would also be important, is the possibility of insider favoritism and oligarchic arrangements. This could take various forms: an undue elevation of seniority, or cliques and groups based on outside associations carried over into the firm, or just plain old-fashioned cronyism. As I have argued, to the extent that market forces do not operate quickly and strongly, the negative consequences of such practices will not be speedily corrected. Internal vigilance and safeguards against such deviations would be even more essential for the LM firm because of their corrosive consequences upon its unity and esprit. The LM firm relies heavily on cooperation and teamwork to give it a competitive edge; allowing such deviations would undermine its raison d'être.

The concentration of risk inherent in both the workers' income flow and wealth position being dependent upon the firm's fortunes needs to be addressed, and fortunately the remedy is fairly easy and straightforward. Namely, the options of being able to convert some part of one's shareholdings into a mutual fund or of purchasing annuity insurance for one's portfolio should be continuously open, and thus workers could decide how much of such risk they wanted to bear. Such arrangements, however, could not waive the minimum shareholding requirement. All in all, it is hard to worry too much over wealth position risk when contemporary statistics on wealth ownership reveal just how little wealth, apart from residences and retirement benefits, most ordinary workers possess. In that light, the luxury of having a choice seems positively enthralling.

Limits on the size of firms, hence excessive smallness and fragmentation, and too little vertical integration are factors that might cause trouble for the LM firm and therefore require comment. For one thing, shortcomings in these respects were, in fact, largely the result of income-per-worker maximization, and maximizing aggregate income through differential shareholding has eliminated the constraints upon growth arising when expansion meant that existing workers must receive less and confer an unrequited windfall on new hires. For another, it might be thought that the LM firm is doomed to smallness since, arguably, the sense of closeness and belonging—the team spirit ethos—is likely to become less and less powerful as the firm grows larger and more diversified. Since precisely that identification provides the LM firm's competitive edge, bigness would be self-destructive.

This $1/n$ argument has some force, but ultimately it boils down to an organizational challenge: is it possible to devise organizational arrangements that preserve smallness within bigness? No one can deny the formidability of this problem, but that does not mean there is no solution. Abstractly, it is a matter of decentralizing and smoothly meshing the constituent parts together. How to do this, however, would be very time and place specific, and little is gained through abstract speculation. Clearly some existing very large firms have done very well in such decentralization exercises, and there is no reason to be fearful that the LM firm is somehow constitutionally incapable of creative endeavor in this respect.

Finally, the life-cycle problems of the LM firm are likely to be more significant than the ordinary firm's, again because the level of participation and commitment is a two-edged sword—if it is so relied upon to gain a competitive edge, then anything that diminishes it will have a more potent negative impact. Perhaps the LM firm will be uniquely susceptible to such problems because the enthusiasm and ardor that attend its birth will be notoriously difficult to sustain over time. Success becomes taken for granted, routine and normalcy diminish the sense of pioneering and excitement, entropic forces assert themselves—all of these influences have to be struggled against, continuously and strongly. Here too, significant external shareholdings can provide early-warning signs, as those not intimately involved in day-to-day operation might thereby preserve a greater degree of objectivity and perceptiveness regarding destructive trends. Nor should eternal life be an unquestioned given; winding up an LM firm is not unthinkable. Orderly dissolution procedures should be provided for. Centrifugal forces, in sum, will always be present. For its survival, the LM firm must keep them in check, and where survival is not warranted, it must pave the way for a smooth transition.[12]

Discussing these aspects of the LM firm leads to several insights. For one, there is no such thing as a free ride, all downhill and no rough spots. The LM firm must adopt a posture of constant vigilance against the many dangers it confronts in the normal course of events. Beyond vigilance, constitutional supports and organizational design must be sufficiently foresighted to anticipate these challenges; they should not come as great surprises or as utopias unsuspectingly gone sour. Early warnings, preventive maintenance, continuous renewal, and careful cultivation of that ineffable and intangible team spirit are all required to ensure that the LM firm retains its functional capabilities.

For another, sensitivity to the many interactions between behavior and structure will be of the utmost importance. The LM firm must evolve the right kind of organizational structure and collective culture that will support, rather than erode, morale and esprit factors. As the firm grows over time, familiarity and success can be strengthening factors. But they can also be deadening and induce a dangerous apathy and contentedness. Interactions pose the possibility for either virtuous or vicious spirals, and LM firms must take care to see that the former predominate. The LM firm cannot take the position that all conflicts have been eliminated, but rather must ensure that ever-present ten-

---

12. For a discussion of life-cycle problems, see Miyazaki 1984; Estrin and Perotin 1987.

sions are constructively channeled and resolved. Self and group, insiders and outsiders, present and future, risk and safety, stability and expansion, majoritarianism and constitutionalism, a quiet life and dynamism—each of these polarities will subject the LM firm to its special pull, and each must be constantly balanced against the other. Little wonder that a firm's internal organization, which must somehow respond to these diverse opposed forces, will greatly depend upon their precise specification and reconciliation.

Perhaps the LM firm, on this reading, is just a way of making the implicit contract explicit. It pursues the implications of informal agreements to their logical end. Not in the sense of merely formalizing implicit arrangements, but more fundamentally by establishing the structure through which the basic message of implicit contracting can be implemented. Standing alone, implicit contracting is anchored in the shifting sands of the parties sustaining their joint commitments only as long as each one's self-interest is served by the others' fulfilling their obligations. True, custom, time, history, and the buildup of trust can certainly be supportive, but the implicit contract can nevertheless be very fragile and needs all the help it can get. Toward that end, the LM firm adds some essential ingredients; it provides the institutional stiffening, an intellectual rationale, the mechanisms for dispute adjudication, and the modalities for rededication to and renewal of a communal ethos. Self-interest is thus embedded in a sturdy support system, and that is likely to prove necessary for long life and continuity.

CHAPTER 8

The Firm and Work Reorganization

A commonplace observation concerning the behavior of corporate leaders is that, on commemorative occasions, at ceremonial events, and even in the normal course of public discourse, laudatory sentiments extolling their workers' virtues and vital contributions to the firm's success are effusively expressed. Such congratulatory rituals may seem, especially to a cynic, merely empty gestures—customary rites and polite conventions, not to be taken too seriously. Yet whatever their actual merits, the evolution of implicit contract doctrine infuses such ritualistic expressions with real and substantive content.[1] Although no one so far has resurrected the labor theory of value, emphasizing the potentially immense contributions of ordinary workers and establishing proper incentives for their achievement mark a distinct and welcome contribution to the theory of the firm.

Ceremonial observance thus speaks economic truth. But recognizing workers' functional importance has not been accompanied by much change in organizational status or by great enhancement of their authority or rewards; implicit contract notions have so far had limited organizational or distributional impact. This chapter deals directly with that apparent inconsistency: should not the recognition of functional importance lead to substantial rearrangements in the pattern of rewards and authority within the firm?

It will prove useful to review the argument so far. In chapter 3, I showed that external labor markets generate certain anomalous outcomes and do not inexorably allocate workers to their best employments nor ensure their best performance on the job. In chapter 4, I demonstrated that, although intended in many ways to compensate for external labor market deficiencies, internal labor markets do not, in fact, invariably and automatically do so; they even present some further puzzles and complexities to incorporate within a theory of the firm. In chapters 5 and 6, I argued that the emergence and subsequent refinement of IC+ doctrine could best be viewed as a further response to such developments, superior to NC+. And in chapter 7, I explored the common ground shared by implicit contracting and labor management approaches.

---

1. It should also be noted that the notion of a firm having not only shareholders as sole claimants, but also numerous other "stakeholders," seems to be evolving in a similar fashion as a vague expression of plural interests in the firm's fortunes, reflecting the firm's diverse impact on a wide variety of different groups affected by its decisions. Here, too, ritualistic recognition is more evident than practical implementation.

Through analyzing the basis for alternative organizational arrangements, extended implicit contracting notions seek to remedy the deficiencies of both external and internal labor markets by devising an appropriate efficient-markets paradigm within which to locate the theory of the firm. Indeed, the evolution of implicit contract notions themselves, from being based upon simple swaps arising from presumptive comparative advantage to reflecting, ultimately, the far-reaching consequences of associational continuity, was itself progressively compelled by the search for more profound and adequate explanations of firm behavior.

In the process, however, it was noted that an inherent, but insufficiently recognized, tension develops between accepting expanded worker responsibility and contributions and maintaining a governance structure in which traditional executive authority and the scope of decision-making responsibilities are left relatively undisturbed. If the worker counts for so much more, how can the organization of the firm remain unchanged? Was there not something missing to accompany this recognition of the workers' augmented functional importance? Both the common sense of implicit contract insights into the operation of the firm and the increasing readiness of firms to experiment with new forms of work organization support the expectation of significant change. IC+ seems to point toward restructuring the firm to enlarge the workers' role and reorder the pattern of authority and reward sharing. Despite such signs and experimental ferment, actual organizational reform embodying those shifts has not proceeded very far. That needs to be explained.

Whither the Reorganization of the Firm?

Although the logical terminus of the evolution of implicit contract doctrine should be this direct march toward the greater sharing of reward and authority, contradictory trends are evident: as firms seek to unlock the potential productivity gains from a more committed workforce through vigorous and diverse experimentation, they strongly resist movement in directions seeming to endanger their authority and control. Specific actions toward restructuring work arrangements have been cautious and wary, and firms tightly control such experimentation. Accordingly, despite the extensive efforts to reform work, reflecting the search for that productivity pot of gold, hypersensitivity to the loss of managerial prerogative greatly inhibits creating new forms of work organization that conform to the logic of implicit contract doctrine.[2]

The implicit contract literature has, so far, failed to confront the underlying issues defining these limits to modifying work organization. Several different considerations are relevant. First, firms' ambivalence concerning or-

---

2. A senior AFL-CIO official, T. R. Donohue, expresses this sense of inherent contradiction very well: "the institutions on the employer side . . . don't seem to show the flexibility that the constituents of those institutions preach . . ." (U.S. Department of Labor 1989, 14).

ganizational change has been insufficiently appreciated; devolving authority, however essential as an incentive mechanism, creates great anxieties over where such a process will ultimately end. Little attention has been paid to the aspect of contested terrain, the permanent state of relational tension, existing between workers and management. Too often the presumption is that the wage, rather than control and authority, is the chief battleground, the only thing that matters. But as implicit contracting doctrine itself is coming to realize, what is ultimately at stake is who is calling the shots, the scope of management's presumptive right to manage, or, more crudely, who is boss.

As I have mentioned, implicit contracting raises fundamental property rights issues—which current managers assume are closed and have no desire to disturb—because functionally enlarging the workers' role cannot be divorced from the subsequent, directly entailed questions regarding the distribution of authority and rewards. Further, in a conflictual context, firms believe that perhaps the appetite might grow by what it feeds upon. Concessions will be taken as signs of weakness, only whetting the appetite for more. For managers, even contemplating the idea that fundamental power relationships can be adjusted tilts the balance in a threatening direction; once such subversive ideas are broached, a Pandora's box is opened with presumptive consequences that can only undermine managers' position. For reasons such as these, firms treat reorganization schemes very cautiously. Although aware of the productivity and profitability imperatives pushing them to seek ways of tapping their workers' energies and talents, they are also sensitive to the dangers of adversely changing the status quo.[3]

The fact that implicit contracting has been limited is not surprising. True, it reflects the normal search by profit-maximizing firms to gain a competitive edge, and it is strongly supported by the theoretical insights emphasizing the augmented importance of workers. What needs to be explained, though, is why firms are not compelled by the logic of maximization and the play of competitive forces to move more fully and quickly to change their authority and incentive structure. After all, if workers are truly the source of the firm's success, holding its fate in their hands, then surely the locus of power and authority needs to be shifted to reflect that reality. But managers willingly rushing to make such concessions are hardly ubiquitous; diminishing one's authority is not usually viewed as an urgent priority by those so endowed.

One result is an observed ambivalence in some firms' approach to the issues posed by implicit contracting doctrine. Alternatively, as discussed in previous chapters, other firms vigorously reassert traditional organizational

---

3. Although it should be clear from the context of decision making, let me emphasize that I use the term *firm* as a convenient and conventional representation of managerial authority. I am aware that, within the managerial sphere, there may be dissonance and competing groups. Although such division may be relevant for some issues, omitting its consideration is a useful simplification in light of the focus of this book.

arrangements and managerial prerogatives, making no concessions to implicit contracting considerations. The ambivalent firm, too, is fearful of the consequences of forthrightly accepting IC+, but tempted by prospects of sizable gains. It opts for controlled change in an attempt to capture the best of both worlds. The incentive structure designed to accommodate workers' enhanced functional roles is constrained, not seriously affecting the internal balance of power within the firm. Surprisingly, perhaps, firms have some scope for wriggling out of this apparent dilemma; many things can be done to strengthen worker participation without unduly jeopardizing the essentials of managerial control. Such leeway explains the prolific and ingenious—but at all times jealously guarding managerial authority—schemes for employee involvement in recent years, and the increasingly intense search for new ways to safely tap the workers' potential.

Can such creative expedients suffice? If further evolution of implicit contracting is inexorable, if halfway houses are not viable, will not the constraint of power maintenance have to ultimately give way? No one can provide definitive answers to such questions, but posing them at least tests the widely prevalent belief that somehow market forces always operate to make good arrangements drive out bad. Those holding advantages, even if potentially vulnerable, are usually positioned to erect formidable barriers in their defense.

If managers are so wary of undermining their position, why are workers not eagerly jumping on the bandwagon and getting behind various plans for reshaping work organization to their advantage? Several reasons are apparent. Perhaps most important is that workers, under existing property rights dispensations, are rarely in a position to initiate or insist upon such changes. They can propose, but they know that others dispose. In addition, the novelty and unfamiliarity of such ideas inhibit their spread, even among prospective beneficiaries. They seem beyond the pale of feasibility, outside the usual universe of discourse, too different from prevailing arrangements. In any case, as I discussed in chapter 7, there are some very difficult technical problems in coordinating group and individual interests, in mediating potential conflicts among differently situated work groups over fundamental goals (as, for instance, in allocating the firm's income between present payoff and prospective growth), and, in general, in devising organizational forms and representational structures that command sustained and overwhelming worker approval. Establishing appropriate governing arrangements is not easy, and much learning by doing will be necessary.

In principle, solutions based on apportioning transferrable claims or shares that reflect individual contributions to workers can be equitably devised; in practice, ensuring active markets for such shares and mediating conflicting objectives among workers will be difficult tasks. Fundamental group-versus-individual tensions will erupt again and again, putting the established arrangements to a severe test. Perhaps more important, the self-interest of specific worker groups can diverge from that of their fellows and the wider society. For instance, in the case of a declining industry where wisdom might suggest reallocating resources to other pursuits, the affected workers might have strong job-preservation drives. Finally, far-reaching institutional changes such as those under discussion do not usually take place without first finding resonant support in the larger society. A readiness factor, a zeitgeist phenomenon, a widely held belief that the time has come to implement and go ahead with a new idea is usually a precondition for the serious launching of such initiatives.

It is thus one thing to argue generally about the theoretical possibility of tapping the work force's potential; it is quite something else to devise mechanisms for achieving such ends. No one yet has produced and implemented a demonstrably foolproof blueprint for achieving enormous productivity gains through work reorganization. Hence, the emphasis on experimentation, as both a strategy for learning and de facto description. I have already detailed some of the major stumbling blocks, and their possible resolution, to more participative job redesign; here I merely observe that it makes good sense to feel one's way tentatively and hesitantly in the absence of specific blueprints. Trial and error will be the inescapable path for arriving at more productive forms of work organization.

Finally, it is necessary to recognize that, even if firms were more forthcoming in sharing power and workers were to seek such changes more aggressively, both powerful externalities, that uncouple private gain from social advantage, and pervasive uncertainties, that induce great caution, would be inhibiting. Such deterrents take several forms. An adversarial milieu itself stifles certain kinds of innovative change. Narrow self-interest would certainly prevent firms from risking their present dominance in work arrangements for gains, however desirable, that subsequently might prove to be their undoing. A satisfactory bird in the hand is likely to be worth a lot more than several splendid possibilities in the bush. In a conflictual context, moreover, all actions usually have great symbolic significance and frequently are but one round in an ongoing contest; strategic behavior, in other words, dominates the process. For instance, actions that may seem highly desirable on the surface will be aborted because of fears of future adverse consequences. Furthermore, as subordinate parties, initiatives by workers are inhibited both by their vulnerability to victimization and by the inability to ensure that the fruits of struggle will be fully harvested by those who wage it. The process of organizational reform is thus beset by both great uncertainties and externalities so that, even if firms and workers were more eagerly interested in work reform, the path to its achievement would still be steep and difficult.

But steep and difficult is not the same as unlikely or undesirable. No matter how severe the obstacles or how hard it is to overcome them, changes in our underlying economic environment are pushing toward work reorganization. First, the rising skill and education of the work force as well as its increasing cultural sophistication compel new approaches. Workers increasingly become both more capable of performing complex and challenging tasks and more insistent that their higher level attainments be put to practical use. Work must continually change in the face of such startling transformations in the human beings involved in its performance.

Second, technological developments, on balance, also lead to new possibilities for enlarging work responsibilities and tasks. Despite countercurrents, it seems clear that routine tasks are more likely to be taken over by the machine than higher-order work requirements. Inevitably, the nature of jobs will shift toward greater reliance on judgmental decisions and informed reactions to unforeseen contingencies, both of which, in turn, call for precisely those types of effort variability and human capital inputs that form the basis of the case for enhanced worker importance.

True, the pace of such advance is still an open question. For one thing, as a recent symposium emphasized (Piore 1986; Shaiken, Herzenberg, and Kuhn 1986), the incentive structure guiding decision-makers' choices concerning job design matters very much; nothing happens automatically. Eliciting high levels of performance from workers is certainly devoutly wished, but it also requires, as previous chapters have spelled out, concrete and specific changes in work organization. For another, the difficult issue of optimum decentralization is engaged. On the one hand, the initiatives and flexibility of peripheral experimentation should be encouraged, but on the other hand, particularistic commitment and narrow fixation must be guarded against. Partially, this is a matter of the technical division of labor between the center and periphery in assigning decision responsibility. Partially, questions relating to authority and control, now and in the future, must again be confronted. The process of gaining greater knowledge and functional autonomy cannot be divorced from challenges to current hegemonial jurisdictions.

Another very relevant factor is that such technological development in an age of highly sophisticated electronic communication will enormously improve managerial sensing and monitoring capabilities. Rather than reshaping the division of labor between human and nonhuman inputs, technology can tempt managers to use such capabilities to more tightly control their work force. How vigorously firms would pursue that option remains an open question.

Finally, it is abundantly evident that the pace of economic change itself has greatly accelerated, and that has profound implications for work design. Drastic reductions in transport and communication costs, more integrated world markets, rapidly changing preference and spending patterns—these and their consequences dramatically foreshorten economic time-horizons; in an economic sense, the world shrinks and the future comes more quickly. The idea that a worker could look forward to an extended career of doing essentially similar tasks now seems on the verge of being anachronistic. Worker reallocation, great shifts in the importance of different activities and skills, and premiums on flexibility are likely to be the motifs of the future. More than ever, this will require a work force sensitive to the fiercely blowing winds of change and readily adaptable to the transformational imperatives ahead. The natural resiliency and adaptability of workers must be cultivated and strengthened; rote methods of work and techniques that fail to engender initiative and responsiveness to changing circumstances will not be suitable for workers in the future. Moreover, firms tend to be more concerned with here-and-now conditions rather than brood about likely possible future states of the world. Yet their responses greatly condition the shape of that future. Such intertemporal externalities suggest corrective social intervention.

Indeed, the question of social intervention can be cast more broadly. If firms are unduly alarmist, overweighting what they might lose and systematically undervaluing potential gains, and if workers, too, are trapped into immobility by knowledge deficiencies and situationally determined risk aversion, then society loses because desirable actions are thereby aborted. Additionally, conflicts over control and power can be attenuated and softened, to a great extent, and need not always take an all-or-nothing form. In many cases, all would gain as cooperation makes possible the realization of hitherto unattainable states; work reorganization need not be a zero-sum game. Nor should it be too difficult to devise indemnification schemes whereby unfortunate outcomes can be underwritten out of the gains generally accruing from more cooperative participation. Market forces are unlikely, within reasonable time periods, to overcome the many such inherent externalities inhibiting efforts to reorganize work, thus opening the way for constructive social intervention.[4] That option will little mollify those for whom externalities remain as bare theoretical possibilities of no practical importance, nor those who believe the visible hand of social intervention must inevitably strangle initiative and enterprise. The former position seems a particularly inappropriate theoretical stance to adopt when such extensive substantive change is under discussion, and the latter suggests caution rather than inactivity.[5]

Counterarguments and Rebuttals

So far, I have pointed, first, to a fundamental contradiction between the augmented evaluation of worker contributions and the failure to move very far in realigning the underlying disposition of authority and rewards to conform to that reality, and then, further, to the powerful forces both inhibiting and pushing forward such realignment. The latter set of forces, in my judgment,

---

4. For a comparable argument, see Levine and Tyson 1990.

5. For a stimulating analysis of the impact of new technology on labor-management relations and work design, see Walton and McKersie 1989. They discuss two alternative approaches: mutual compliance/adversarial and mutual commitment/cooperation, that are broadly consistent with NC+ and IC+, respectively. Their position in favor of the latter reflects many of the considerations addressed in the text.

will be ultimately ascendant. But not every one would accept this position. Some would believe the arguments invalid and do not support an inference that IC+ is the wave of the future. These counterarguments fall into two major categories: one concerning the validity of IC+ itself and the other questioning the urgency of transformational imperatives.

On the Validity of IC+

Consider first the argument about the validity of IC+. It can be summarized along three lines: (*a*) The basis for implicit contracts is overdrawn and over-dramatized. No such motivational or organizational legitimacy crisis exists; workers, by and large, still respond to normal pecuniary incentives and have no burning desire to stretch their authority and responsibility to areas traditionally reserved for managers. Matters are thus not as you say, and your proposed remedies are correspondingly inapposite; (*b*) Even if your view were more acceptable, whatever needs to be done is surely, in fact, being done. Profit maximization would compel firms to respond appropriately, and by your own testimony, they are busily engaged in such extensive reorganization. They are addressing the problems you raise in their own way—even using, where desirable, your remedies; (*c*) In any case, whatever the truth about the extent of implicit contracts or appropriate remedies, nothing in principle and little in practice prevents the changes you suggest; and if they were so necessary and correct, they would sweep the field, overwhelming all obstacles. The obvious fact that they have not done so permits the inference that either conditions or remedies, or both, are not as you say.

Each of these counterarguments contains a grain of truth, but each individually and all collectively are not of sufficient weight to undermine the general argument. Indeed, (*a*) and (*b*) contradict each other, since one cannot assert that no problem exists, and in the next breath claim that it had already been resolved. Similarly, argument (*c*) has some logical inference difficulties, since I have already shown why movement might be considerably slowed and delayed and, hence, not to attain some specific goals at some precise moment does not imply their never being reached. But more pointed and telling objections can be raised against each of the counterarguments.

With regard to the first, I am not saying that some variant of implicit contracting is required for all jobs to reach high-level work performance. Some jobs may be precisely delimited, well defined, and able to be monitored at nominal cost, so that dependence upon worker effort and initiative will not be critical. But most jobs can never be completely robotized, and individuals are not stamped out by a cookie cutter; the majority of jobs, and the trend over time, will not coincide with this interpretation of task and job content. For instance, as is well known, the growth of the service sector has been the overwhelming source of additional jobs, and, to the extent that such jobs are characterized by extensive human contacts, it is hard to imagine, except for the likes of, say, vending machines and ATM's, their being robotized. More-over, since higher relative earnings tend to be positively associated with the possibility of inherently greater performance variability, weighting jobs by their relative earnings would magnify the importance of such variability. And the fact of interdependence among workers within job teams could also imply greater performance variability, since each member would have to work at full speed for the group to realize its potential. Similarly, although certainly sur-veillance and monitoring techniques will reflect improvements in sensoring and information-transmission technology, the brave new world of the future is unlikely to be the equivalent of a self-measuring, self-enforcing piece-rate system—the secular decline in the importance of piece-rate arrangements speaks to this point.

Likewise, my argument does not insist that all workers be embryonic Leonardos, striving to be universal geniuses of the workshop and the office; worker preferences will remain diverse, and some will always prefer thor-oughly routine and familiar work sequences. At the same time, it must not be overlooked that workers are culturally conditioned, and expectations can be self-fulfilling in these respects. If work has been predominantly characterized by robot-like repetition, time and the promotion of alternatives are needed to change ingrained expectations. Finally, does the implied view of work and workers betray an innate attachment to Taylorism in the sense of erecting a wall between conception and execution?

More crudely, are we meeting a "can the animals run the zoo" argu-ment, whereby it is presumed that the lower orders lack the intrinsic capabilities to achieve high-level performance requiring initiative and intel-ligent choice? Or is this argument confusing the true proposition that mer-itorious performance is often properly rewarded with the false one that the current system invariably ensures that each level of merit finds its exactly right and just place in the scheme of things? That some individuals do receive justified recognition and reward for achievement does not prove that all indi-viduals have an equal chance to fully exploit their talents. What the ultimate capabilities of a highly motivated work force may be, and what heights can be reached through unleashing its skills and talents, are not matters easily judged, but even the most cursory examination of economic history would reveal the tremendous impetus to growth when human beings become so energized.

Another way of summarizing these issues is to present them as an over-arching problem of system design. At the core of these arguments over work organization lie profoundly different premises concerning the fundamental nature of the forces that shape it. As I similarly pointed out in chapter 6, should work organization be designed such that: (1) good-intentioned persons can generate the most benefits or evil-intentioned persons do the least harm; (2) hopes or fears should dominate as motivators; (3) the focus should be on encouraging workers to "turn on" and put out or on preventing them from "turning off" and shirking; (4) inducing high levels of performance or extract-ing the contractual pound of flesh is most emphasized; (5) securing coopera-tion and building trust are most highly valued or guarding against the infinite varieties of moral hazard has a superordinate claim; (6) linkages, sharing, coordination, and networking, or solitary individuals acting on their own, constitute its core; and (7) the possibility of gain or the avoidance of loss should be stressed?

Framing positions as such polar opposites is certainly caricature, but it illuminates why work organization can assume such varied and sharply differ-ent forms. Although the premises outlined are not put forward as necessarily either/or imperatives, nor is the possibility precluded of combining them without necessarily forcing formal consistency on the set so chosen, yet when taken together they do have a kind of litmus test quality. They define funda-mentally different worldviews, and systems of work organization framed in their image would surely reflect that disparity.

The second argument, as Panglossian and comforting as it may be, has much less force than seems apparent on the surface. True, firms have both the specialized and locally comprehensive knowledge and the most direct and vital interest to rectify what is not proceeding according to expectation and calculation. Further, an outside critic must always worry about not having both insider knowledge and a direct stake. Presumably professionalism is a defense against those charges, safeguarding the integrity of the critical pro-cess. Moreover, for many specific cases, because the evidence concerning the best forms of work organization is bound to be controversial at best, and inconclusive at worst, a wide range of opinion will prevail; one should prop-erly be tentative concerning questions of absolute and inevitable superiority of this or that form of work organization over some challenger. One need have no qualms whatsoever, though, about asserting that those who benefit most from the status quo will have the utmost confidence in its superiority and desirability and will be very careful about disturbing it. Similarly, much scope exists for cosmetically altering work arrangements without greatly affecting the underlying structure of power within an organization, and simultaneously convincing important others, including workers, that great and significant shifts have occurred. Although the incentives, capabilities, and possibilities for some movement in the direction of more participative work arrangements can logically be expected, and indeed observed, the question still remains of whether firms can actually pursue such changes wherever they may lead.

Two broad consideration, both previously discussed, stand in the way. First, it is axiomatic that power sharing never comes easily; authority is usually closely held and zealously guarded. Strongly buttressed by a ruling ideology that stresses both the rights inherent in and accruing to private property and the belief that social arrangements are sufficiently flexible to permit individual mobility and institutional innovation to flourish, managers are unlikely to accept the idea that devolving authority may yield superior outcomes. Their immediate self-interest as well as ideological preconception makes them hostile to forms of work organization that might diminish their powers.

Second, the processes of struggle and conflict, the inherent adversarial positions of management and workers, are well understood by all parties. Not only are firms extremely sensitive to power challenges, but they are also well aware of the potential collective strength of their workers as an organized force. Hence, as emphasized previously, the importance of strategic bargaining, whereby all actions and specific work reorganization proposals, however desirable in and of themselves, will be strained through the filter of how they affect the balance between contending forces, now and in the future. Even very small clouds can cast very large shadows in such sensitive environments. In short, firms will preclude certain work reorganization options, and, having done so, the remaining alternatives may be inadequate. Within the set of possibilities so constrained, firms may not be able to fashion the most desirable work arrangements.[6]

The third challenge, that nothing stands in the way of firms implementing whatever reforms are worthwhile and, consequently, their absence vitiates my argument, is a salutory reminder that the best proof of any pudding is always the eating. All would-be reformers and academic dreamers hear, in due course, this variant of the "if-you're-so-smart-why-aren't-you-rich" argument. Ultimately, this is a compelling contention—but only after a reasonable time has gone by and if the presumption of barrier-free entry is correct. In both instances, doubts arise. Even in the absence of barriers, work reorganization clearly involves considerable experimentation and learning, and the adaptation process, entailing much behavioral change, cannot be an overnight phenomenon. Similarly, for reasons already indicated, freedom to reshape work organization is significantly constrained. In the normal course of things, then, this process will be extended and proceed unevenly; the absence of immediate success is no proof of ultimate failure. We are witnessing, rather, the early stages of a long-drawn-out adjustment in which the possibilities associated with emergent participatory work organizations are being more thoroughly explored. Certainly their mushrooming growth, the rich variety of organizational forms, and the wide interest these experiments have engendered are positive indications. Success, of course, is not preordained, but neither should failure be presumed. A decade or two hence will be the proper time for a more definitive judgment.

On Transformational Imperatives

With regard to the transformational imperative argument, some suggest that the greater the frequency and necessity for making severe and far-reaching

---

6. For a salutory reminder concerning the importance and relevance of concerted activity by workers in affecting forms of work organization, rather than making the outcome the automatic byproduct of rational decision making and efficient markets, see Ulman 1990.

changes, the less this process can be entrusted to those for whom it would imply painful and distasteful adjustment. Workers' short-run preservationist tendencies, they argue, would be too powerful to let them respond to the insistent demands of distant and dimly understood forces. Would they be sufficiently visionary, to their perhaps considerable immediate cost, to remold their jobs and concomitant skills? Have we not had enough experience with similar situations to be aware of how reluctant and resistant workers are to make such changes? No one need berate them for that because an unwillingness to gamble on the future is perfectly understandable. But out of such a cabined and cribbed world view, what possibility is there for extracting the longer run vision needed for economic transformations? Putting workers in charge of their own destinies would be, in this view, shortsighted.

The fundamental misconception of this argument lies in not recognizing that the transformational imperative is not a once-and-for-all change, but a continuous and ceaseless requirement. Precisely because workers will have to change their work activities more frequently and adjustment will be a continuous process, they will have to internalize awareness of this necessity and be prepared for it. Change must be propelled from within as a natural response in an environment where survival itself, not just optimal outcomes, will depend upon the quality of such responses. Informed behavior, compared to being blindly led, can be a more potent transformational mechanism and accomplish the necessary shifts in resource use more smoothly. Although in circumstances where each party seeks to impose adjustment burdens on others, hanging tough and resistance are proper strategies, such behavior is not an innate part of a worker's genetic makeup; rather, it reflects strategic positioning within particular institutional circumstances. If workers find it in their interest to be supple and flexible with regard to changing work organization, they will doubtlessly pursue such ends.

Indeed, if implicit contract notions are accepted, firms have little choice. They are greatly dependent upon their workers' initiatives and full-fledged cooperation, and they can neither compel nor induce such actions through either sanctions or pecuniary reward alone. Furthermore, a rough relational parity is likely to be the proper basis for all dealings. Trust flowers best when parties are roughly equal in stature and power, and augmented trust can be profoundly important in leading to a mutually satisfactory and socially constructive adjustment process. If workers are suspicious and disbelieving when firms plead poverty in wage negotiations, imagine the skepticism that would greet a firm's protestations that far-reaching adjustments in work organization are needed. Perhaps the worst possible case may occur all too often: firms will have used the market compulsion argument so frequently that they will not be believed when it is, in fact, true; resistance will be such a natural response by workers that cooperation will be impossible when it is truly required. Only where mutual trust has been nurtured and prevails will such negative interactions be avoided.

Society also loses when the stronger party, usually the firm, imposes a solution that takes little account of longer term joint interests or of the costs borne by the weaker party; that only sets the stage, when positions might later be reversed, for retribution in kind. Moreover, adjustments involving large-scale resource reallocation are never easy. A belief that somehow market processes themselves ensure orderly and not-too-painful change can work against taking measures that would moderate an otherwise very rough passage. Ironically, presuming a smooth, automatic adjustment, when in fact it will be costly and difficult, makes it even worse; being prepared for tough choices, by cushioning undue hardship and facilitating shifts in resource use, makes them less painful. Harsh and income-reducing adjustments may be necessary, but they are a last, not first, resort, and implicit contracts can create a milieu where more cooperative, creative, and less costly options are manifest.

Relational parity is also conducive to greater freedom of expression and participation, since vulnerable supplicants would shrink from assuming responsibility and be little inclined to fully contribute. Responding to transformational imperatives, however, is likely to require new ideas and approaches, and participation by all as equals will yield more and better proposals. After all, firm-specific human capital skills are composed as much of generalized problem-solving capabilities in a familiar context as they are of greater specialized knowledge concerning a specific process or product. Furthermore, broad-based participation generates a higher level of commitment and followthrough, and that can be critically important. Finally, here too in one way or another, society must bear the huge social costs incurred when firms make no effort to find creative solutions that rechannel obsolete high-level skills and talents into new and more currently demanded pursuits. Firms can, of course, take key and more mobile personnel and adjust by setting up shop elsewhere. However privately profitable that might be, it makes no allowance for the potential output society loses as those left behind move to an inferior next-best employment. The adage "use it or lose it" applies to firm-specific human capital.

Pertinent Considerations

What kind of resolution is possible, then, in this familiar conflict between forces generating and resisting change, between reorganizing work along emerging functional lines and maintaining present arrangements? Is collision inevitable? Can such conflicts be softened and tempered by public policies channeling differences into more creative paths that are at least acceptable, if not completely satisfactory, to all parties? Are such paths feasible when the major participants seem unwilling or unable to be the designated agents of the requisite transformation, where the outlines of the future are so hazy, and where inhibiting externalities are so important? In these circumstances, is slower change desirable, experimentation inevitable, and society's interpretation of its stake in the outcome a major factor? Can outcomes be influenced by the opportunities for cooperative and consensual actions, or will the more evident play of opposed and conflicting interests be dominant?

Specifically, several very diverse and broad considerations are likely to affect the resolution of these questions. First, by their own actions, firms have shown great agility in responding to worker pressures for improving jobs. They have walked a fine line between satisfying such demands and not relinquishing what are viewed as essential elements of control. At the same time, they are beset by nagging fears about whether such steps are irreversible and whether each step encourages and increases the demand for further movement. Symbols are important, and firms and workers proceed more reluctantly when they fear that there is no turning back. For this reason, a carefully crafted safe-return option, allowing all parties a justified recourse to move back toward a previous position if greatly dissatisfied, might prove useful.

A second issue concerns whether this pattern of internal evolution, of step-by-step change within existing firms that adds up to perceptible and irrevocable redefinition, will be the major way of transformation, or whether de novo formation of firms committed to participatory principles will set an irresistible example that inspires emulation. Although the dynamics of change can hardly be predicted, it should be noted that neither of these options is preclusive. Indeed, they should be highly interactive, with the experience of de novo firms influencing the pace at which existing firms will move and the examples of ongoing organizational reform incorporated in new endeavors. As such processes unwind, clearer indications of relative importance will be apparent.

A third factor in evaluating the dynamics of change is the difficulty in distinguishing, as a practical matter, true and fundamental change from artfully doctored expedients designed to give the semblance, but lacking the real substance, of far-reaching adjustment. As mentioned before, firms have great license to change appearances and surface manifestations without truly changing basic relationships. There is great scope for manipulative and cosmetic strategies, and a high noise-to-signal ratio is likely. Attention must accordingly be focused on substantive aspects, and not the inevitable accompanying barrage of public relations' glitz and glitter.

Fourth, what if firms disdain the politer forms of struggle and, rather than camouflaging their positions, decide to play economic hardball? What if, in other words, capital goes on strike? Firms can, after all, pursue many options—relocation, shutdown, strike breaking, coopting the workers' leadership, guerrilla warfare against visible advocates of greater worker participation, litigational paralysis—that would make few concessions to the niceties of implicit contracting, or to public pressures for more cooperative approaches. Alternatively, in an era of multinational enterprise, easy capital mobility, and multiplant operation, will firms not simply flee to more hospitable climes at the first instance of what seems, to them, unreasonable worker encroachment? In sum, the large firm, in one way or another, is likely to have many alternatives besides having to come to terms with the work organization requirements of a skilled and talented work force, and the important question is whether those alternatives will be costlier, privately or socially, in other significant respects.

A fifth factor relates to the general environment within which the work reform process takes place. How level is the playing field? Do more economically efficient organizational arrangements have a free and unfettered chance to demonstrate their capabilities, or are the scales systematically rigged against forms of economic organization that radically and seriously challenge reigning arrangements? In situations where externalities assume major importance, will markets perform well even if they were otherwise benevolently neutral with regard to alternative organizational arrangements? Pat answers to such questions do not exist, but at least such interrogatories underline the importance of context and milieu in discussing the possibilities for organizational change. Too often, a natural Darwinian process of inevitable selective adaptation is presumed instead of realizing that the milieu within which such evolutionary patterns develop is itself the product of human endeavor. What has been initially wrought can also be reshaped through human intervention.

A sixth characteristic is that a mix of organizational forms, rather than complete and overall dominance by any one, is likely to occur. Further, various hybrids, combining in different proportions the attributes of their purer counterparts, will emerge. Partly, this will reflect the ongoing importance of experimentation, given the great amount of uncertainty. Partly, it will be the result of experience and evidence contributing to the refinement and reshaping of initially rough conceptions. And partly, it will be an echo of the underlying diversity in our economic universe. The factors determining the relative efficiency of alternative organizational forms are indeed manifold and consistent with a wide range of institutional expression. What does well in one situation will be matched by other arrangements better suited to different circumstances. Circumstantial variety will be sufficiently abundant to allow many flowers to blossom; situational specificity will play an important role in determining the appropriate organizational form.

Finally, major organizational change often occurs in response to extraordinary circumstances or crises.[7] This has both positive and negative implica-

7. See Mitchell, Lewin, and Lawler 1990. They argue, from a historical survey of various schemes for incentive pay systems, that the introduction and subsequent development of such pay systems are very much influenced by the ebb and flow of exigent circumstance rather than reflective of any monotonic trend. This kind of economic historian's perspective should also prevent any rush to judgment concerning the future of IC+ and supports taking a decade-to-decade, rather than year-to-year, view. As Ehrenberg wryly commented: ". . . the historical motivation for the adoption of these [pay] policies seems to the casual observer to be different from what current day analytical labor economists hypothesize" (1990, 88).

tions. A crisis can bring people together and compel, as the basis for advancing one's own interest, a recognition of the benefits of cooperation and joint action. But adversity is not the usually hoped-for starting point for adventurous change. A failing firm, say, may offer opportunities for experimenting with new forms of work organization and induce a sense of joint sacrifice for the common good, but it also establishes very hard initial conditions. To the extent that work reorganization is likely to be born in adversity, judgments concerning validity or success must allow for that. It will be difficult to do so, and thus the specter of sui generis will hang over the evaluations of many such cases. Normal circumstances, whatever they may be, will not usually be the relevant background conditions.

Although the general thrust of these considerations may tend to inhibit work reorganization along extended implicit contract lines, some meliorative factors should also be noted. First, as usually occurs with efforts to introduce institutional novelty, consciousness raising, cultural reorientation, and continuing public education are part and parcel of the process whereby new ideas can take hold. Room must be made in the public arena by conditioning people for such change. Widening individuals' horizons and expanding the sense of what is possible perform the essential function of readying the public mind for new ideas. Too often, because new forms of work organization seem impossibly visionary and unattainable, even those who might thereby benefit may find them unattractive. But as a more conscious awareness of their real possibility becomes diffused, attitudes can rapidly change. The interrelationships between awareness and subsequent activism must be kept in mind.

Second, and similarly, the critical impact of longer run considerations and externalities suggests the need for public scrutiny and intervention where required. Notoriously and naturally, private transactors tend to consider only more immediate interests and consequences, but, as we have seen, work organization issues are better viewed against a broader backdrop.

Third, as a direct reaction to the excesses and Prisoner's Dilemma aspects of countervailing strategic behavior, the positive contribution of greater trust will be more and more appreciated. Interacting behavior is an integral part of any work organization problem; implicit contracts rest on the belief that the parties will not take short-run advantage of each other for fear of breaching and undermining the implied long-term agreement. The extension of implicit contracts to cover a wider and nontraditional area must be accompanied by deeper commitment and trust among the parties, and only if the rewards are sufficiently attractive, or the alternatives sufficiently disastrous, will such behavior be forthcoming. That cooperative activity might bring mutual gains is not a very earth-shaking idea, but, in the historical context of hostility and conflict, time and effort are needed to build sufficient trust for realizing those possibilities. Admittedly, increasing trust and inherent adversarial positions make a very odd couple, but that is not reason enough to disavow the possibility of their enduring, if uneasy, coexistence or even the eventual dominance of trust.

Finally, it should again be emphasized that work reorganization is not the unfolding of a master plan, the realization of an impeccably exact blueprint detailing all the steps for reaching well-defined objectives. Rather, work reorganization is an idea, an approach seeking ways to mobilize human ingenuity and creativity through establishing on-the-job conditions conducive to their development. What such conditions might be in particular embodiments depends very much on specific circumstances. It would certainly be surprising if there were one best form of work organization, mechanically applicable to all situations. Instead, substantial variety and hybrids are likely to emerge, as creating job conditions best suited to this pattern of circumstantial variety proceeds in the normal trial-and-error fashion. Easy resolution, simple answers, smooth adjustment—these are unlikely to be much in evidence, but the potential size of the payoff should exercise a magnetic attraction to persist in exploring IC+ alternatives.[8]

Summary and Conclusions

The contrast between the increased functional responsibilities and importance of workers and the limited realignment of formal authority and power in the workplace has been drawn, perhaps too pointedly, to underscore the case for measures lessening this inherent tension. True, in practice and perhaps for long periods, numerous practical expedients can moderate its intensity. Yet this inherent tension is impossible to ignore and likely, moreover, to be exacerbated by fundamental economic trends. But if the problem seems clear, the solution does not. If it were only a minor squabble over the trappings of authority, a functionalist response whereby authority flows from function might be indicated. As worker contributions would become increasingly recognized in defining the firm's success, the requisite realignment of authority and power would soon follow. But things are not that simple. Devising institutional forms for empowering workers does not come easily, even in the unlikely event that firms might smile benignly on such a shift. Nor do sophisticated dies lie ready at hand to stamp out ideal work arrangements at the press of a button, even if deep misgivings about power sharing were overcome.

Persuasive theoretical arguments and stubborn practical difficulties are not, however, a strange combination. More often than not, that reflects the

---

8. For a more extended discussion of work reorganization possibilities, see Rozen 1983, chap. 6. For a useful review of the evolution of work reorganization and job redesign notions and some case studies evaluating the factors affecting their diffusion within firms, see Yorks and Whitsett 1989. For a review focusing more specifically on recent trends in the concurrent introduction of new kinds of both work organization and technology, or "synchronous innovation," see Ettlie 1988.

institutional obstacles to change and the extent to which the real world departs from our theoretical constructs. So it will probably be with these work organization issues. The logic behind the increased role for workers does not appear to be in danger of being undone by a superior paradigm; IC+ can hold its ground against NC+. Eventually, functioning markets do allow more productive forms to drive out inferior ones. And not only will workers be pressing their direct interests, but the resounding third-party advantages and social gains that follow from realizing the productivity potential of a "turned-on" work force will lead to incessant public pressures. Likewise, the process of vetting the infinite variety of proposed new work arrangements will reveal ever more promising variants. Again, one does not foresee a lockstep march toward some predetermined and fixed goal, but inexorable pressure toward still only dimly visible forms of work organization that can best unleash the initiative and creativity of more and more workers. That, in my view, is the ultimate meaning of the implicit contracting approach to organizational choice. When all is said and done, at stake is how best to allow human ingenuity its free rein and induce its most effective performance. If the fundamental ideas behind implicit contracting are correct, fostering the creation of work arrangements for achieving those goals should have a high priority.

CHAPTER 9

Whither Organizational Choice?

A concluding chapter not only offers an opportunity to summarize complex arguments, but also to highlight their logical connections, draw the various individual threads together, collect and display whatever insights need further elaboration, and, in general, put things in perspective. The clearest characterization of this work is to call it an extended venture into the economics of organizational choice and its determinants. It began with an inquiry into various anomalies, from the standpoint of traditional theory, present in the functioning of labor markets. It then explored the internal organization of the firm in response to both such anomalies and the increasingly recognized complexities of workers' relationship to their firms. Next, three possible organizational arrangements—implicit contracting plus, neoclassical plus, and labor-managed firms—were examined, in the light of labor market anomaly and the complexity of the firm's internal arrangements, as alternative approaches to the problem of organizational choice. Finally, some general issues relating to the future organization of the firm were discussed.

Perhaps the most logical regrouping of the argument's various strands would be as follows: an underlying vision of the nature of workers, jobs, and their milieu is the starting point in defining an organizational possibility set. Differences in these elements, how forcefully they push in particular directions, how much variability in outcome they allow, how different combinations can be reconciled with each other—these basic conceptions of reality dominate subsequent discussion in the sense that choosing particular positions with regard to these elements exerts an enormous influence on ultimate work arrangements. Next, the influence on outcomes of three intervening variables must be considered: (1) how powerful a disciplining and persuasive force is exercised by the *market* in compelling particular arrangements and choices; (2) what kind of influence can be exerted by *trust and cooperation* among firm members, and what is the likelihood that such attitudes may flourish; and (3) how do positional *power* differences affect organizational behavior and outcomes? Once the imprint of those various factors can be adequately traced, the choice among competing organizational forms becomes clearer to see and easier to explain, and prediction is more solidly grounded.

Underlying Structure

Having outlined the logic, it remains to spell out the details. Unsurprisingly, the vision of reality underlying the analysis is a major dividing line, both methodologically and with regard to its factual content. The methodological aspects concern the spareness and universality of our primitives. One-dimensional agents operating within a well-defined environment, responding to explicit incentives and closely regulated by contract, constitute one kind of package; a more highly complicated world, in which tasks, workers, and contractual relations cannot be so easily specified, offers a different vision. The former permits greater precision and exact answers; the latter makes everything more dependent upon process rather than ineluctably coming to virtually predetermined conclusions. Some might argue that scientific progress is associated with the narrow focus of the former approach. At issue, however, is not the generally accepted argument that what matters is predictive accuracy rather than the relevancy of assumptions, but, more fundamentally, what are the relative advantages of different degrees of abstraction and stylized presumption? Whatever gains flow from specificity and greater tractability associated with more narrow assumptions, more is lost through irrelevance and inapplicability. Even more important, perhaps, nothing is really at risk by starting with a more general and richly complicated approach. The simpler view can always be extracted if that should prove useful, since the more general case will always contain the simpler cases nested within. Besides, path dependency is strongly at work; presuppositions concerning initial conditions imply predisposition toward specific ultimate conclusions.

The practical consequences of such methodological differences, as previous chapters have revealed, show up in many ways: suppositions of routine and well-defined tasks and workers with limited capabilities and an insatiable taste for shirking fit nicely with the presumption that hierarchy and close supervision are the natural order of the universe; stable patterns of demand and technological fixity justify centralizing decision making; informational uncertainty and complexity and rapid innovative activity cry out for more decentralization; assuming completely free and voluntary exchange among equally empowered agents will generate different outcomes than if choice is more summarily constrained and agents are differentially empowered; and so on. To summarize and simplify, such associations suggest a pattern of organizational comparative advantage whereby specific endowments predispose toward organizational forms best suited for those conditions. Prior specification of basic and underlying attributes irresistibly shrinks the degrees of freedom attached to organizational choice. Such presumptions, it should be recognized, impart a particular spin to the consequent analysis and its conclusions as well as limit the scope for universal generalization.

Some minimize the influence of such comparative advantage considerations, however, and argue that the conventional framework, having served so well in the past, should not be discarded for new and major revisions. Others similarly reject the implied greater importance of peer and group influence in the general belief that the individual must remain the basic unit of analysis, and that bringing group-individual interactions to the foreground somehow contaminates an otherwise methodologically sound procedure. Sometimes such views are vigorously and openly argued and reflect critical judgment; more often they are unexamined presumptions or simply unjustified filial devotion to current orthodoxy. Usually, the issue is not the usefulness of stylized facts in general but choosing those most specifically relevant. Certainly, tradition has its virtues; we all stand on the shoulders of others in the upward climb of science. But ultimately the proof of the pudding must be the eating, and explanatory cogency takes precedence over conformity with past standard practice. In sum, wherever it may lead, analysis must be sensitive to both what kinds of logical follow-ons are entailed by particular specifications and why those specifications should be chosen.

Intervening Variables

Controversy over the respective roles allotted to (*a*) market forces, *b*) cooperative and trustful relationships, and *c*) power conflicts and adversarial processes in determining organizational arrangements are related to, but distinct from, questions concerning initial foundations. Although disagreements are often ones of degree more than kind, small variations can have exceedingly large consequences. First, the role of the market. How compelling is the market as a force determining organizational outcomes? If no wiggle room exists, if all structure and actions are closely and completely predetermined by market forces, then there is little further to discuss. Outcomes will inevitably reflect the powerful play of such pressures; individual actions count for naught, except as they are simply the expression of what must be. But clearly much of the new theory of the firm is an attempt, based upon more complicated circumstances and expanded behavioral options, to open up more space for observed outcome variability. As an additional difficulty, disagreement about how strictly contracts can be enforced and the relative importance of tight contractual specification or looser relational arrangements will lead to corresponding differences about relying on monitoring and enforcement or on more highly motivating workers as implementing strategies. Markets certainly matter, but so do other things too. As the recent Report by the MIT Commission on Industrial Productivity expressed its reservations about relying solely on the market, ". . . there is no efficient market in which organizational forms and attitudinal complexes compete with one another" (Dertouzas et al. 1989, 38–39).

For some, these differences may seem to boil down to a clearly delineated choice between viewing the market as slightly imperfect, but on the whole generating a predictable outcome, or as evidencing such fatal and serious lapses that no outcomes can be precluded. However appealing such two-sided reductionism might be, some further considerations suggest withholding judgment, especially with regard to market omnipotence. For one, the fact that job design is largely an employer responsibility and tightly held prerogative might suggest that, when push comes to shove, firms will take full advantage of this position of strength to achieve their ends. True, powers to initiate job design, and first-mover capabilities generally, confer tremendous leverage; but firms can become trapped, too, by their prior commitments, and worker resistance to undesired forms of work organization can be a source of built-in and continuing conflict over time. Ultimate outcomes thus become less predetermined. For another, it should not be thought that time is necessarily on the side of the market, that powerful market forces require only sufficient time to make their influence felt. Simply put, the reason for this is that the strength and play of market forces are themselves determined by still other factors at work in the economy and society, and time and events can influence those, and thus indirectly market forces too, in profound and unpredictable ways. The upshot is that no simple resolution, neatly defining for all seasons the precise writ of the market in determining optimal organizational structures, is possible; its role and importance will vary.

The role of trust in defining organizational choice is even more conjectural. In a world of explicit quid pro quos and easy monitoring, trust would have little bearing. All relationships and reciprocal obligations would be spelled out in excruciating, feudal detail, and compliance would be automatic. But relational contracting and the subtleties and intricacies of the de facto interconnected web of mutual dependency lead to different patterns of behavior. Now the success of organizational arrangements depends upon the willingness of parties to empathize, to accept and understand each other's position, to keep their word, to be honest and cooperative, and to put forth their best efforts. Such behavior, it should be noted, is less related to individual probity and morality and more to considerations of system equity and legitimacy. Trust is not something inherent in an individual's psychological makeup, but is built up over time as organizational conditions of openness and fair and equitable treatment encourage individuals to increasingly rely upon each other. Trust grows in organizations where such conditions obtain and is stunted by their absence. Once relational contracting is accepted, then sustaining motivation for high-level performance becomes an all-encompassing focus of firm activity and shapes desired organizational structure. In turn, the precondition for reaching desired performance levels is likely to be an overriding and pervasive sense that organizational arrangements are just and equitable.

Perhaps an incredulous skeptic, at this point, may rightfully ask if the discussion doesn't refer to some utopian rather than real world. Who would argue for partiality and inequity, anyway? Surely, taking people as they are in organizations as they actually function, the stumbling block is that the presumptive fairness conditions are not easily specified, but rather endlessly disputed. Conflict, opposition, disagreement, differential perception, and interpersonal tension are the human condition. Yes, but perfection is not at issue. Trust can withstand difference and disagreement, as long as good will prevails; trust can absorb differential outcomes, as long as the process producing them is deemed generally fair; trust can weather adversity, as long as it is equitably shared; and trust can abide perceptual differences, as long as they are honestly held. Indeed, organizational arrangements must be robustly designed to be precisely supportive in these ways and to function as system shock absorbers responding to inevitable differences and runs of good and bad fortune.

Perfection will never be attained, but pragmatically more trust can greatly improve outcomes, and, moreover, trust feeds upon itself. In any case, what choice is there? All firms preach the virtues of cooperation and trust within the organization. What matters is whether practice follows precept, and where or when it does not is unlikely to remain a mystery to those affected. In any case, trust is certainly not a free good; the glitz and glitter of public relations campaigns to create its aura without the actual substance of trust's sustaining elements do not usually lead to its augmentation. Here, as elsewhere, there is no substitute for the real thing.

Finally, the issue of power must be faced. Power rests uneasy not only on the heads of monarchs, but also as an explanatory variable in the hands of economists. A central feature of most economists' conception of an exchange economy is the notion that all transactions are wholly voluntary, and occur between willing and uncoerced parties. No one has a gun at the head of another; the option of no-trade is always very live; other alternatives have been thoroughly canvassed, on a cost-effective basis, and discarded; what you see is what you should get. The idea of voluntary exchange among relative equals is, mildly exaggerating, virtually genetically imprinted in our minds as economists. That exchange may involve subtle and obscured elements of pressure and even coercion, and that transactors may bring grossly disproportionate strengths to bear on the terms of exchange, are merely complicating afterthoughts.

But why should such a limiting, two-valued behavioral logic be so readily accepted? Why should a virtually either/or, completely free or completely coerced approach be so dominant? I have already shown the complexity and multidimensionality attached to motivational concerns. There is a world of difference, generally ignored by economists, between an acceptance that is enthusiastically based on complete satisfaction and one that is resentful and grudging, a for-the-moment accession until something better comes along (previously expressed in the distinction between choosing and settling). Outwardly, either acceptance looks the same, a purchase is a purchase; but inwardly, and more important in regard to future behavioral implications, the differences are immense. Assuming voluntary exchange among equals eliminates, ex hypothesi however, the possibility of distinguishing between choose or settle, and accordingly the need to probe for varying degrees of acceptance by transactors, as might be found by closer scrutiny of the underlying nature of their relationship. All transactions are majestically elevated to the equally lofty plane of voluntary exchange among equals—or else they would not occur.

But power disparities denied and unexplored ill serve the search for a more adequate explanation of what determines organizational choice. Where exchange involves dominance by one party and is, thus, more imposed than freely agreed, will not the possibility of realizing its full productive potential be thwarted by the continuing effort of the adversely affected party to redress both circumstance and outcome? And can trust ever truly flower in the context of dependency and domination? Will not organizational choice be based, in fact, on the reality of contested exchange among unequals rather than on fictional presumptions concerning transactor equality and completely uncoerced exchange? Power is difficult to measure and operationalize, and certainly involves some fuzzy relationships, but that is no reason to disregard its influence in determining organizational choice.[1]

Likewise, the implications of strategic behavior within such a conflictual context need more spelling out. Insufficient attention, in my view, has been paid to the interdependence between path and goal. Strategy and conflict tend to be viewed too mechanically and formally, without taking full account of the rich set of possible interactions. Too often, behavioral patterns are set as if they are independent of the process taking place, when that process has a formative effect on choice and behavior. Recall the "Lucas Critique." A string of choose decisions has very different behavioral implications than a series of settle decisions. Alternatively, and especially in situations of continuing and deep conflicts, allowing more scope for successive rounds of action and response to influence the choice process will generate the previously stressed conditionality and outcome variability. Put somewhat differently, process endogeneity, in the sense of outcomes being conditioned by the pattern of interactions occurring between conflicting parties, implies outcome variability. We may instinctively bridle at the inconclusivity of "it all depends," but tentativeness, rather than crisp and certain answers, seems to fit the circumstances better.

In sum, once the presumption that market forces control all behavior in a completely deterministic pattern no longer strictly holds, then organizational choice becomes a more open proposition.[2] Moreover, looser linkages, greater

---

1. For a salutory reminder of the implications of concerted activity by workers, see Ulman 1990. Ulman has also argued that not only voice and exit can shape work organization, "muscle" cannot be ignored either.

2. It is instructive to trace the evolution of the "on what" it is that "it all depends": from the structural certainties of objective market circumstances, to the equilibrium surmises of the inter-

conditionality, and substantial variability all weigh heavily on the side of motivational rather than contractual approaches. Once the market allows this greater degree of wiggle room, then trust and cooperation become more important and the adversarial process and its disequilibrating features must be recognized. The nature and extent of market influence now must be spelled out in more defined and specific ways, trust and cooperation become the determinants of firm efficiency and survival, and questions of the distribution of relative power among the firm's members figure importantly in explaining forms of organization.

No longer is it possible to maintain that a strict hierarchical, command-and-obey structure is ideal and will do for all circumstances. Organizational arrangements now become shaped by specified intervening variables. And internal consistency considerations, moreover, suggest that the various components of such organizational arrangements must fit together in a coordinated way rather than allowing picking and choosing across individual elements. In other words, both outcome-variability and outcome-sensitivity need to be kept in mind; the former reflects the contextual richness, complexity, and strategic interactions at play in general and the latter the functional dependence on specified circumstantiality. Traditional conceptions of the firm must now be defended rather than assumed as a natural condition, and only after more rigorously and fully specifying the relevant circumstances, can the choice of organizational form become well defined. Naturally, substantial disagreements over the nature of those circumstances will spill over into arguments about desired organizational arrangements. Such arguments will have the merit of being focused on substantive issues, concerning which the parties are specifically obligated to defend their positions.

In this connection, two points are relevant: (*a*) challenges to traditional conceptions of the firm must bear the burden of proof, since few will want to reject that which has served in the past and, as a corollary, much ingenuity will be expended in trying to make new approaches and ideas consistent with those traditional views; and (*b*) situational contingency will be an important factor, and, hence, it would be unlikely for only one kind of firm structure to exist in a profoundly variegated world. Of course this merely reiterates the point that organizational form follows presumptive circumstance.

Free Lunches?

Beyond these general conclusions, the combination of organizational choice and outcome variability raises a very troubling issue for economists: the possibility of (almost) a free lunch. That possibility flows from several sources. First, once the fact of heightened productive powers for workers in

---

subjectivity and reaction functions of strategic games, to, finally, the process endogeneity and inherent outcome variability described in the text.

coordinated team activity is accepted, and once the importance of motivation is conceded, then getting much more output from relatively trivial changes that more highly motivate workers is an inescapable conclusion. After all, the notion of efficiency wages is only slightly changed by allowing workers to respond to organizational considerations too. Second, and related, our previous discussion of the importance of pace and tempo in group activity is closely tied to motivational variability. Where linkages, cooperation, information sharing, and networking aspects matter for the production process, induced rhythmic changes will flow from revising organizational arrangements to affect coordinated work activity. Here, too, organizational choice becomes the crucial issue.

A third factor involves disequilibrium and multiple equilibria ideas. As stressed throughout this book, the richness and complexity of circumstances as well as path-goal interdependence multiply the possible outcomes. We cannot presume that somehow all conceivable trades that might improve well-being are done deals. More strongly, we have identified specific situations where possible betterment is distinctly indicated: settling rather than choosing, one-tailed mismatches and, in general, relatively easy upgrading, authority maintenance at the expense of productive efficiency, inter alia. Beyond that, we know that it is illegitimate, as Dow has explained with regard to transaction cost theory, to expect equilibrium comparative statics' propositions to account for and track the unfolding of historical events.[3] Such attempts remind one of that hoary, and mercifully now very rare, antitrust defense where firms that fixed rigid and uniform prices pointed to the inflexible economic law of one price as proof positive of extensive competition.

The presumption of Pareto optimality as the de facto, or even asymptotically ultimate, outcome is unjustified. Indeed, an even more ironic and devastating inversion of traditional thought lies in the possibility that the very frictions and imperfections, ostensibly inhibiting neoclassical mechanisms from grinding out their inevitable result, may instead be the very instruments for improving outcomes. They provide fixed points to anchor our expectations and regularize our behavior, thus permitting the gains from continuity and patterning. Norms and conventions can as often be helpful instrumentalities as they are sometimes impediments.[4] Nor, finally, can deviations from some *optimum optimorum* be dismissed as merely transients, short-run aberrant

---

3. See Dow (1987, 34–35). For a similar critique, see Jacoby and Mitchell 1990.

4. Compare the position of an economic historian discussing the molding of the post–Civil War work force in the South: "Rather than thinking of kinship, ethnic, and linguistic loyalties as market 'imperfections,' it is more appropriate to consider these forces as part of the way the market functions and expands. The trust among kinfolk is what ensures that reasonably accurate information is passed along concerning job openings, wages, working and living conditions" (Wright 1986, 75). Similarly, consider the arguments for preferring rules over authority, i.e., fixing the growth rate of a monetary aggregate, or the way in which the gold standard or fixed exchange rates seemed to work, as exemplifying this stabilizing (if pragmatically true) role of common presumptions.

phenomena soon to be replaced by their equilibrium counterparts; they persist too long as potential and enticing invitations to free lunches to be so summarily dismissed. Disequilibrium and multiple equilibria notions of the world are not usually what economists carry around in their heads, but that is where new views of how labor markets function and the internal organization of the firm unmistakably lead.

Fourth, the tension between authority maintenance and organizational choice opens another channel for potential betterment. Partially, this reflects the distortions and inefficiencies introduced as the parties duel and struggle for dominance in situations where ill will and hostility predominate. I am aware that organizations are not governed solely by principles of sweetness and light, but where little trust is present, the consequences will move the firm away from optimal positions. And nowhere is this more apparent than when firms respond by deliberately creating arrangements that safeguard and perpetuate authority at the expense of more productive ways of doing things.

The failure to recognize such organizational failings flows from incorrect presumptions by analysts concerning the nature of authority and intraorganizational relationships. Indeed, in this regard, astonishing lapses are exhibited:

1. the automatic assumption of completely voluntary exchange among equals rather than realizing the pervasiveness of contested exchange among unequals;
2. the narrow economistic argument that, even in the face of this or that system rigidity (say, wages), firms are completely free to adjust other elements of the employment contract to achieve their objectives, despite negative reactions and opposition to those moves by workers (and perhaps society generally), and thereby also reach the competitive equilibrium outcome of amounts supplied equaling amounts demanded;[5]

---

5. It should be recalled that by *economistic* or, perhaps better still, *economisticism*, I mean presuming the omnipotence of pure economic forces to somehow grind out, no matter what (but with well-known qualifications for externalities, public goods, and the like), an optimal outcome—a competitive-equilibrium allocation equivalent—that is unmodified in any way by the realities of institutional and social counterpressures; such outcomes, ex hypothesi, cannot be bettered. Although I have indicated my disagreement with that position, it should also be understood, however, that I do not thereby intend to either disparage the importance or power of those economic forces, nor diminish how subtly and pervasively they can operate. Rather, my position is that no complete and exhaustive model of the real world has been, or could be, specified such that the no-betterment condition can never be doubted. The optimality presumption alerts us to the market's virtues and the necessity to understand the reach and strength of its multidimensional adjustment processes; at the same time it can lead us to overlook the market's defects and inadequacies and, above all, the inescapable real-world richness and complexity that generate outcome variability. Like Solow, do not all economists have to be, to a greater or lesser extent, hopelessly eclectic as they strike a balance between these two contending views of the market? Or, to paraphrase E. M. Forster, are not two cheers for the market sufficient?

3. the failure to appreciate the potential for great cost reductions and productivity increases from voluntary cooperation as compared to costly and authoritarian monitoring (inclusive of perverse reactions thereto);
4. the improbable belief that horizontal monitoring easily fits within a top-down management structure;
5. the supposition that the deus ex machina of an external authority, not bound by the constraint against budget breaking, can devise contractual arrangements for teams that will neatly eliminate free riding (Holmstrom 1982; for a critique, see Eswaran and Kotwal 1984);
6. the attribution to workers of such powerful self-aggrandizement drives that individuals will, through such "sleazy" channels as ruthlessly undercutting their mates to improve their relative position (Lazear 1989) and deviously diverting their time and energies toward influencing authorities' decisions in their favor (Milgrom 1988), pursue wasteful instead of output-increasing activities, and to such a degree that a firm's organizational arrangements must be specially designed to curb such unproductive behaviors;
7. the presumption that tournaments that foster competition among workers can be neutrally effort inducing, without regard for who sets, and how, the rules and with no hint of the need for any joint determination (Carmichael 1989); and finally,
8. the equally dubious prominence attached to concern for reputation as the guarantor for the firm's promise keeping, with inadequate recognition of the interpretive ambiguities and contextual complexities thereby raised.

All of these positions concerning authority structure and intraorganization relationships seem seriously deficient, for the diverse reasons specified or implied, as valid representations of what actually prevails inside the firm and are thus an unhelpful basis for determining desirable patterns of work organization. As previously stressed in this book, it is one thing to presume, with congenial assumptions, that somehow individual choice leads to best outcomes; it is a very different matter, adopting more critical underlying views, to also believe that actual outcomes exemplify the reification of optimality. Unless the internal workings of the firm are thoroughly dissected, that trap is easily fallen into, the status quo is too quickly rationalized and accepted, and the possibilities for actual betterment will be neglected. Economists need to be more open to distinctions between behavioral man and economic man, and between an all-pervading and relatively harmonious closed equilibrium system and the more varied range of outcomes generated by the influence of chance, novelty, relational disparities, and inherent conflict.

Perhaps the most painless way to present the free lunch argument would be to subsume it within a general innovational framework in which organizational change would be on a par with the introduction of new technology.

Relatedly, several economists have explained organizational variation along comparative advantage lines based upon seemingly critical attributes of firm structure. Oi (1983) has suggested that large firms hire better workers and pay them more in order to economize on scarce managerial talent that can be put to better uses than having to supervise workers. Williamson (1980) views organizational evolution as simply a matter of continuous minimization of always significant transaction costs. Hashimoto (1990) argues that because the costs of joint consultation and consensual modalities are lower in Japan, largely for reasons of cultural homogeneity, Japanese firms can invest more in cooperative and participatory employment relationships. Hutchens (1989) has stressed that task simplicity and monitoring ease may be very relevant for explaining career wage structures and incentives: where tasks and monitoring permit the equivalent of piece-work assessment, the lifetime wage structure does not need to focus on shirking prevention.[6] It is thus not a very large leap from recognizing that organizational choice can be strongly influenced by this or that firm attribute to asking the question of how changes in organizational arrangements can generate better outcomes, and are they, in fact, occurring? Again, if others feel more comfortable speaking in terms of organizational innovation, rather than free lunches, I see no great harm done.

In tune, then, with the tenor of these organizational choice considerations, a central theme of this book has been that the nature of work organization is closely tied to outcome variability. That general argument is strengthened by taking account of the importance of motivational and other factors influencing the tempo and pace of economic behavior, by recognizing the persistence and pervasiveness of disequilibrium and likelihood of multiple equilibria, by understanding that organizational blockage and power maintenance play upon each other, and by being aware that organizational innovation can be a powerful force for betterment. To some, such inherent outcome variability is anathema, implying unbridled indeterminacy; a more moderate view would simply hold that not all hope for causal relations has to be abandoned when complexity is given its proper due. The world must be accepted for what it is and not be oversimplified to fit into predetermined categories.

It should be noted, however, that, especially when viewed from the firm's perspective, some additional practical considerations might cause organizational innovation to proceed slowly and hesitantly. For one thing, such far-reaching change is not lightly entered into; firms would naturally adopt a wait-and-see attitude about the transitory or permanent character of any disturbance. For another, I have previously mentioned mind-sets as a factor, and there is little doubt that the firm's current decision makers would require a great deal of convincing to believe in, let alone undertake, such power sharing. Certainly in this latter connection, the existence of seemingly more congenial alternatives would be tempting: the possibility for flight to locations

---

6. See my discussion in chap. 6 for some additional relevant examples.

where pressures for organizational change were absent, the establishment of various kinds of core-periphery or subcontracting arrangements to distinguish between a favored few and all others, or even toughing it out in an old-fashioned and knock-down labor-management war. In the face of such heady temptations, little wonder that organizational innovation is resisted.

Finally, discussing alternative organizational arrangements and stressing their circumstantial conditionality is different than unequivocally predicting dominant organizational forms. Our purpose has been the former—to enlarge the possibility set, not prejudge outcomes. Yet this very process inherently raises the question of what determines which alternative will prevail in what circumstances. Certainly, it is hard not to believe that IC+ does not seem to have the future on its side. Informed action and an awareness of why changes need to be made should dominate blind obedience, since firms organized so that all can contribute to the fullest measure of their capabilities should outperform, on the average, firms organized in other ways. But however much such insights may ring true, they still must be more abundantly demonstrated to overcome both justifiable skepticism and inertial commitment to traditional approaches.

In this connection, a point that both Newbery and Stiglitz (1987) and Weitzman and Kruse (1990) make in similar contexts seems worth repeating. For the former it is used to justify, in the context of a formal and consistent implicit contract model, the existence of involuntary unemployment:

> There are no simple explanations of involuntary unemployment. Earlier Keynesian models, and the subsequent fixed price literature, made a contribution in identifying the importance of wage rigidities for unemployment. Wage rigidities, however, are not sufficient by themselves to generate unemployment. Standard implicit contract theory provided an explanation of wage rigidities, but it did not explain unemployment. This paper has asked whether natural restrictions on the set of feasible contracts will lead to unemployment. We have shown how plausible versions of the restrictions implied by limitations on information, enforcement, and complexity, *taken one at a time,* do not lead to unemployment. But in fact, all of these limitations are present at the same time. Under these circumstances, implicit contracts can then provide an explanation of unemployment. (1987, 427; italics added)

Taking a position on the relationship between profit sharing and productivity that is substantially identical with mine on the more general issue of implicit contracting, Weitzman and Kruse make the same point:

> The purpose of this paper is to bring together the partial strands of eclectic evidence from a wide variety of fields and perspectives. . . . Although we try to be reasonably comprehensive, detached, and objec-

tive in this survey, the possible link between profit sharing and productivity is ultimately not the sort of proposition that lends itself to crisp proof or disproof. We cannot honestly give decisive answers and must end up instead with the traditional plea for more research. And more research is generally needed in this area. Yet, without denying all that, we think it is also fair to conclude that total agnosticism is not warranted. The weight of the evidence leans toward a positive link. From many different sources there emerges a moderately consistent pattern of *weak support* for the proposition that profit sharing improves productivity. *Any one piece of evidence can be legitimately challenged because no single piece is conclusive. But taken as a whole, the many different parts add up to a fairly coherent picture of a weak positive link between profit sharing and productivity.* (1990, 95–96; last two sentences, italics added)

Although each of the factors discussed may not individually be sufficiently powerful to overturn traditional presumptions concerning appropriate organizational arrangements, their cumulative effect does make the argument more persuasive, since they all move in the same direction. The preponderance of evidence may not be the equivalent of certainty, but it should not lightly be rejected.

In view of the fact that the possibilities for relatively free lunches shake the very foundations of economic thought, perhaps some final words on that theme are appropriate. How serious a heresy is it for organizational choice and outcome variability to promise such great betterment at such an apparently ridiculously low cost? And what is left of maximizing behavior and rationality if such gains lie so readily at hand, but little movement toward their attainment is observed? At one level, it is instructive to remember that this is an ancient quarrel, especially in this area of economics; the battle between the old and new labor economics is still alive and well (see Reder 1989; Jacoby 1990; Jacoby and Mitchell 1990; Ulman 1990). It is similarly revealing to trace the evolutionary development of the idea of organizational choice: from being ignored and denied relevancy to its acceptance as the outcome of maximizing behavior based on presumptive firm characteristics to a questioning of how such predetermined conclusions can emerge from a complex and multidimensional environment to, finally, the kinds of arguments made in this book. Such movement clearly indicates that the last word on this issue remains to be written.

The belief that, because agents are motivated to do the best they possibly can for themselves, there exist no possibilities for improvement over current arrangements is misconceived. It is not lèse-majesté, but common sense, to recognize that the actual economy is not always at, or even necessarily close to, some grand Walrasian equilibrium. Free lunches do exist in the sense that the relatively small resource costs associated with organizational change can lead to substantial gains in economic well-being, but no inexorable pressures are irresistibly working to automatically, swiftly, and inevitably force such change. It does not diminish economics, in my view, to present a picture of such richness and complexity, and hence more open-ended possibilities, even if that implies departures from a previously orderly and precise world— eventually that view of the real world will change accordingly. Economics and economisticism must part company.[7]

Some Policy Objectives

Admittedly, these theoretical musings do not yield definitive and neat conclusions. At the practical level, however, many profound issues of vital social concern become more explicable, and even more tractable, once they are linked to how work is organized:

1. achieving full employment without severe inflationary dangers;
2. overcoming our productivity doldrums;
3. responding better to an increasingly globalized economy and urgent transformational imperatives;
4. coping with greater diversity and heterogeneity in the workforce and heightened sociocultural tensions;
5. mitigating the impact of both externalities and short-run opportunistic behavior by firms that cause private actions to diverge from social optimality;
6. more fully tapping the productive potential of an increasingly capable work force; and
7. meeting the urgent social stability requirement to expand opportunities for those who, for one reason or another, have so far benefited much less from economic growth—for all of these diverse concerns, work reorganization can be an essential ingredient in their successful resolution.

Given their magnitude and complexity, however, it would be foolhardy to presume that work reorganization alone is a wonder drug that can cure any ailment. Certainly other measures, each focused on the more specific aspects

---

7. Perhaps it might be helpful to frame the presumption of equilibrium, and therefore the impossibility of improvement, within the classical type I/type II error scheme of hypothesis-testing. Since outcomes cannot presumptively be bettered, a type I error (false positive) would be to accept an outcome when it should be rejected; a type II error (false negative) would be to reject a change when it should be accepted. Thus the belief in inevitable optimality can cause two kinds of problems: accepting outcomes when improvement is possible or mistakenly rejecting potential improvements. The former would be characterized by an intensive search for plausible conditions that could justify an observed outcome as optimal, and the latter by equally ingenious rationalizations proving the inappropriateness of any departure therefrom or the invalidity of any proffered change.

of the particular issue, will also be needed, and the relative contribution of work reorganization will be greater in some than others; judgment will be on a case-by-case basis. Moreover, work reorganization itself, as noted previously, is not completely unconstrained, since it does not take place in a vacuum. For instance, if our educational system is not doing its job, then that will be a limiting factor. Finally, the time-dependency of the severity of these various issues must be taken into account. Although work reorganization is not a quick fix and will be most effective when applied steadily and persistently, nevertheless, like other policies, it too is subject to the rapidly changing priorities that flow from the twists and turns of current events. In sum, both its limitations and capabilities must be kept in mind.

The issues themselves can be logically grouped into five distinct, but in many ways interrelated, goals—(1) full employment, (2) low inflation, (3) high levels of productivity growth, (4) a smoothly functioning resource reallocation mechanism, and (5) distributional equity—that stand out as having both major economic policy significance and strong work organization connections.[8] The first two goals, full employment and the absence of inflation, can be taken together. It is safe to say that, especially in view of the early 1991 recession and the uncertainties it brings, those goals will remain a continuing focus of economic policy. True, some may question whether any major response is required, believing that such problems have been greatly meliorated in the light of our seven-year, peace-time expansion, with a relatively stable inflation rate and an unemployment rate below 6 percent for more than three years. This would be especially true if they also believed that the recession will be mild and short. Others may even view the recession as a hoped-for "soft landing" and a lovely pause that refreshes, and counsel complete restraint on the premise that natural resiliency and self-cure will quickly work their magic.

But like Sherlock Holmes' famous dog that didn't bark, appearances are not always what they seem. To be sure, there are some positive signs: wage

---

8. A word of caution is indicated here; this section is presented with great trepidation. Crystal balls are always cloudy, and I lay no claim to prescience. I am trying to explore, in a preliminary and sketchy way, the interactions between some current economic problems and trends and the potential for improvement that work reorganization might bring. Actual economic conditions can quickly change. In particular, April 1991 circumstances—the aftermath of the war in the Persian Gulf and great instability in the Middle East, the continuing turbulence in Eastern Europe and the Soviet Union, exacerbated Third World crises, and a domestic recession whose ultimate severity cannot be foretold—do not create a propitious political and economic climate for getting a clear glimpse of the future. Accordingly, this section's assessment is based on the assumption that developments in the present international trouble spots will be sufficiently limited to have only a modest macroeconomic impact. Should those (or other) situations worsen and turn into or trigger something of more major proportions, then the economic consequences would be correspondingly greater and the analysis would have to take that into account. Similarly, if the current economic recession turns into a deeper and more prolonged downturn, then that, too, will change the policy parameters.

pressures have been very moderate and the Great American Job Machine has performed admirably—about 19 million new jobs from the trough of the 1981–82 recession (1982,IV) to the peak of the first half of 1990; bothersome employment cost increases have been strongly influenced not by runaway wage gains, but by other factors such as productivity growth deceleration and our inability to stem soaring medical outlays; inventories have not ballooned and export growth has been impressive; and structural adjustments to the combined impact of the energy shocks and our changing international position are going forward.

Yet forebodings predominate: productivity lags; the quality and compositional distribution of jobs raise nagging doubts; the expansion bypassed some significant sectors and groups in the economy, and, thereby, distributional outcomes have been very uneven; despite much talk and some progress, the twin deficits and inadequate domestic savings stubbornly persist; the rate of inflation may be stable, but its level still remains too high; excessive financial leverage and a battered and fragile financial structure are a clear and present danger to economic health; and the international economy continues to be perilously balanced. Above all, no one can predict the evolution of the current recesssion; the potential threat of a protracted and more severe downturn must be kept in mind. These uncertainties and doubts about the future should dampen celebration of past success. In short, it would be unwise to proclaim the "end of business cycles" and unconditional victory over inflation.

The third issue, the productivity growth slowdown, remains a mystery, despite the oceans of words pouring out to explain it. Sure, the usual suspects—low savings, lagging investment, prematurely obsolescent capital, pollution control, greater uncertainty and shorter term time-horizons, labor force demography, work ethic shortcomings, even measurement errors and conceptual flaws—are rounded up, but in the end much is left unexplained. Even the considerable sectoral variation in productivity is little understood, including sharp differences between the manufacturing and the service sectors. Indeed, one of the strongest arguments for looking at work organization is the belief that answers to our productivity puzzles have deep microeconomic roots.

The fourth issue focuses on reallocative efficiency. Changes in patterns of economic activity and shifts in relative sectoral importance are the normal accompaniment of economic growth and an evolving world economy. In periods of boom and expansion, such changes can take place with minimum disruption; expanding sectors are magnets attracting resources by offering better terms. In periods of slow growth or if competitive weakness compels retrenchment or when rapid technological change occurs, however, the ability to smoothly alter patterns of economic activity can be seriously impaired. All of these latter conditions seem to currently prevail: the pace of technological change has accelerated, a new international division of labor is being worked out, a more integrated world economy and a consequently greater intensity of competition is apparent, patterns of comparative advantage are rapidly shifting, and the global enterprise is becoming a more important organizational structure for both responding to and shaping such far-reaching developments. Hence, all national economies now operate under the lash of transformational imperatives to a degree unknown in the past. Despite the tendency for domestic industries to seek protective shelter from these "gales of creative destruction," the ultimate Darwinian resolution is not in doubt; economic trophies will always be captured by the most flexible and adaptable national economies.

Finally, a fifth issue turns on matters of distributional equity with regard to both the persistence of a significant underclass problem and the greater frequency of dislocation stemming from transformational imperatives. Partly this reflects the inherent problems of an emergent hourglass society in which both ends of the income distribution seem to be enlarged at the expense of the middle group. To switch metaphors, the evolving structure of jobs is consistent with moving toward, in a great many social dimensions, a two-pyramid society joined at their apexes rather than bases. Partly, the transformational imperatives themselves imply a future with more frequent and wrenching job changes for all workers. Given the presumption that favored groups in fact cannot, and morally should not, completely insulate themselves from the misfortune of others, more vigorous efforts are needed to spread the benefits of economic change more widely and share its burdens more equitably. Pervasive social pathology and intense feelings of exclusion afflicting some parts of an interdependent society create uneasy and unstable conditions for all. The social ills of modern life—crime, drugs, juvenile delinquency, family instability, and a generalized sense of anomie—do not necessarily flow directly, and certainly not solely, from economic circumstances, but their mitigation would surely be hastened by an expansion of widespread economic opportunity. The 1980s have been, in these respects, largely a decade of marking time and inadequately confronting the social pathologies of our era; the future is likely to be worse if such complacency continues.

Trends in Work Organization and Labor Markets

Work organization and labor market developments will play an important role in resolving the issues I have outlined. To understand these processes more fully, the impact of trends in labor market supply, demand, and organization must be analyzed. With regard to supply, the dominant motif is increasing heterogeneity. In the last decade of this century, about 80–85 percent of the incremental work force will be women, minorities, and immigrants; the shift toward a more highly trained, skilled, and educated, and thereby differentiated, work force will continue but, at the same time, a substantial number of drop-outs and marginal workers will also persist and require special arrangements; likewise, aspirations will continue, perhaps more rapidly, to soar; and work force growth rates, assuming no sharp increase in immigration, will slacken. The work force will thus be more varied and differentiated, more generally capable, more demanding, and will grow less rapidly. On the whole, these supply parameters move in the right direction for a future where more rapid adjustment and greater flexibility will be necessary. But they are also distinctly more challenging, even threatening, to traditional organizational arrangements, and thus doubts arise about whether such opportunities can be exploited.

On the demand side, the twin forces of globalization and faster technological change will call the tune. This implies that the structure of jobs will be changing more quickly, as both shifting patterns of comparative advantage and advancing technology operate within a more compressed time dimension. Additionally, certainly globalization and probably technological change will lead to an increase in more complex and higher skill jobs and fewer simple and low-skill jobs. And the mixed bag of service jobs will continue to grow more rapidly than other kinds. The great unknowns on the demand side are the sensitivity and flexibility of firms in redesigning jobs to match concurrent work force changes.

Indeed, how these supply and demand forces will play out through accommodating changes in work organization is a complicated question. More talented workers with higher aspiration levels, but more varied and diverse in their racial, ethnic, and gender composition, suggests that work arrangements must change to both realize the potential gains and accommodate the greater variety. As I discussed in some detail in chapter 8, many jobs will have to be correspondingly more customized and flexible. Perhaps the most severe challenge will be to develop more cooperative and decentralized work arrangements to allow freer scope for more highly developed talents.

Similarly, greater strain will be placed on matching mechanisms, reflecting both the greater frequency of job change as well as the shifting composition of jobs. Although, broadly speaking, the kinds of jobs that workers want and are capable of performing will match well with the attributes of jobs firms will be offering, there are clouds on the horizon. Both sides of the market will have to adjust to the faster pace of change, and firms will have to be more flexible in providing work arrangements that allow more room for individual freedom and initiative. Additionally, special attention must be paid to the two previously mentioned specific groups who will probably be most adversely affected by these changes: displaced workers and, especially, those whose job skills, for one reason or another, do not keep pace and who would therefore become increasingly disadvantaged; and those constituting that vast underclass whom society, and especially our educational system, has found it inordinately difficult to adequately prepare for modern life, and who will become increasingly unqualified as a more technologically complex economy evolves. The caveats suggest that private action alone may be insufficient, and more extensive and active labor market training and education policies will be required.[9]

Economic Problems and Work Organization: Interactions

What are the implications of these work organization and labor market issues for our persistent economic worries? In general, the problems of maintaining high employment levels and avoiding inflation are exacerbated by greater job-change frequency and shifts in the compositional structure of jobs; roughly, the more numerous and difficult the matches, the higher the frictional unemployment and the more pressure on wages and, hence, prices. Improvements in the matching process, through reorganizing work and quickening worker adaptability, will thus become more and more useful.

Work organization reform can also be instrumental in other ways. It can maintain job-worker fits over time by ensuring that jobs change sufficiently in response to evolving worker capabilities and requirements, and vice versa. It should also lead to very welcome augmented, and hence inflation-dampening, productivity gains from improved matches. Work reorganization can likewise reduce wage pressures as a natural concomitant of greater worker satisfaction with other job attributes and with the quality of worklife in general. Further, more satisfied workers are likely to show greater restraint and willingness to cooperate with income policy approaches. It seems clear by now that our macroeconomic problems need to be resolved at the microlevel, and these desirable consequences of work reorganization promise substantial improvement. Despite progress in reaching lower unemployment rates and a relatively stable, but still too high, rate of inflation, nervousness about the persistence, and concern over the fragility, of these accomplishments indicate that work reorganization's contributions will be needed. Recession, moreover, certainly exacerbates such anxieties.

With regard to productivity, work reorganization makes great improvements possible and, indeed, such gains are at the very core of the case for it. In addition, the generalized requirement to do better in all areas can be usefully distinguished from the specific imperatives implied by changing international comparative advantage. The latter suggests that work reorganization may figure prominently in both (*a*) special efforts to revivify weakened and struggling export and import-competing industries whose underlying competitive capabilities are still generally judged formidable; and (*b*) generally facilitating, at the same time and in harmony with the natural comparative

---

9. For a consensus statement reflecting growing public concern over labor market issues and our economic future, see Commission on Workforce Quality and Labor Market Efficiency 1989.

advantage of a technologically advanced society, the shift to new and more highly valued activities in an evolving international division of labor. The more generalized requirement implies a more uniform and across-the-board emphasis on raising the overall level of human performance. These two approaches are obviously interrelated, but each emphasizes different elements and controversy over priorities and timing is likely. In such circumstances, predetermined strategy should yield to creative improvisation on an adjust-as-you-go basis. Here too, a microlevel emphasis is apparent, and, likewise, sustaining high levels of motivation will be a central focus. Although private efforts along these lines will shoulder the major responsibility, public policies can be very supportive and helpful.

Responding to transformational imperatives through improving the real-locative process is closely tied to productivity improvement. A better educated and more highly skilled workforce is much more adaptable and re-deployable. Resource reallocation does not, however, have to depend upon knowing the future and picking winners; rather, improving the adjustment mechanism, especially by providing more flexible internal work arrangements to more easily and correctly match jobs and workers, allows quick response to whatever happens.

As I have indicated, the importance of smoother and quicker adjustment can hardly be overstressed, given trends in the world economy. But here, private responses may unfortunately diverge, for understandable reasons, from socially optimal ones. In an adversarial situation, both firms and workers have a strong interest in maintaining familiar and known positions, rather than venturing into unknown areas where the impact upon the strategic balance between them cannot be foreseen. If there is a probability of being adversely affected by otherwise generally beneficial proposals for change, each has a strategic concern not to initiate, and indeed to resist, any such proposals. Each worries that any gain for the other will automatically become its loss; each may display an almost suicidal intent to avoid a short-run setback even if that makes a terminal loss ultimately more likely. As long as trust is absent, feasible options are closely circumscribed and society ends up losing.

Further, work reorganization, to be successful, often requires accommodating and supportive legal and institutional changes, and these are not always provided on a timely and sufficient basis. And to make matters even more difficult, public policies embodying good programs and intentions always run the danger of being subverted to less praiseworthy ends by the political process. That is certainly nothing new, but in a more competitive world economy, reallocative pressures multiply, and program deficiencies will cause greater harm. Thus, where private actions can be unhelpful and public policies distorted, work reorganization will not be easy. But in view of the obstacles to private actions, public measures that address broad and overall issues like educational inadequacies, resource immobilities, and the need to build a climate for trust and cooperation will, despite their possible deficiencies, be necessary.

Finally, distributional issues need to be faced. Both in fact and certainly in popular perception, the specter of an hourglass society is becoming frighteningly apparent. Although many in the work force benefit from, and are well positioned to take further advantage of, an evolving world economy, substantial numbers can fall distinctly behind in the process of economic transformation. Partly, the problems of an underclass persist: many are caught in a vicious circle of reinforcing poverty exacerbated by little chance of escape— low income, discrimination, poor schooling, unstable families, and inadequate opportunities combine to create an interacting social pathology. It becomes clearer each day that our society cannot endure these widening gaps within our midst without seriously compromising our most valued ideals. Partly, the other side of the coin of more flexible patterns of work organization is the harsh consequences for those specific workers on whom the greatest adjustment burdens are placed and/or who have the most difficulty in rapidly adjusting to changing circumstances. There is a silver lining, though, from conjoining these two concerns; a program that responds to the middle-class need for greater worker flexibility and deployability will also be useful for dealing with poverty and under-class problems. A general and universal program to make human resources more deployable in response to more rapidly changing circumstances will be much easier to sustain (and finance) politically, and, at the same time, it can also serve the needs of a low-income clientele without thereby stigmatizing them.

What Is Being, and Needs to Be, Done?

It would indeed be strange if the forces shaping our economic future were, in fact, so dominant, and yet no reaction could be induced. Initially, therefore, I will trace private firms' responses and note their deficiencies. Subsequently, I will discuss the scope for more active work reorganization and labor market policies.

Three interrelated reaction strategies of private sector firms can be distinguished: first, the mean-lean firm, operating through cost reduction, downsizing, and restructuring; second, the global firm, forsaking any national allegiance concerning resource allocation and operating as a supranational entity; and third, a core-periphery strategy, narrowing the firm's range of commitment to include only a small group of employees and relying more on outsourcing, subcontracting, temporaries, and greater turnover, thereby shifting more of the adjustment burden onto the external market. There is nothing mutually exclusive about these options, and it would not be strange to find all three used by any given firm.

Although each of these may be a perfectly rational and maximizing private response by firms and, indeed, contains strong positive elements, judged by more embracing and wider social considerations, they are likely to prove deficient; here too, private and social rationality can diverge. Restructuring and cost cutting can certainly restore a firm's competitive edge. But if the motivation for corporate reorganization lies in accepting a more vulnerable and exposed financial structure in a grab for quick short-run gains rather than in attaining more streamlined and efficient use of the firm's resources, then the firm's future is severely at risk. And if cost cutting is done in ways that impair worker cooperation and trust, abrogating the implicit contract and alienating a large part of the work force, then on balance more harm than good could be done.

Similarly, if firms become increasingly globalized, ready to shift production facilities across countries almost overnight in response to the vagaries of exchange rates, political climates, concessionary deals, and the like, then what helps them may leave the domestic economy with some expensive adjustment burdens. International (like intranational) mobility can yield obvious gains, but a wise public policy will ensure that the calculations of private parties take into full account all the costs and benefits flowing from those moves. Private gains accompanied by even greater social costs are no bargain. And although under more uncertain conditions, a core-periphery strategy might make private sense in limiting a firm's commitments, again that may simply shift the costs of uncertainty elsewhere on a zero-sum basis, rather than providing true insurance or, where possible, more creatively addressing and reducing the sources of uncertainty.

Analytically, two related factors cause private responses to be socially less than optimal: the importance of externalities and the tendency toward myopic decision making. Externalities arise because there is no reason for a firm to take into account the costs and benefits to others. The mean-lean firm's legacy of dispirited and alienated workers and, if a deep recession occurs, debt-loaded and heavily leveraged capital structures; the global firm's flight to brighter overseas havens idling domestic resources whose alternative employment opportunities may be extremely exiguous; and a core-periphery strategy leaving large numbers of workers unable to build their lives and work efforts around a reasonable degree of job security—all these create the potential for very real and very substantial costs as a direct consequence of actions based solely on private rationality. Although the great difficulties in devising offsetting remedies for such externalities are well known to economists, it would also not be prudent to presume that such severe costs would be borne with equanimity by those so adversely affected.

Likewise, as heretical as it may sound to our economist brethren, these private responses by firms seem to be more a grasping at targets of opportunity and a quick fix than a considered and far-sighted strategy. One suspects that these are not altogether preferred choices, but rather reflect either what the presently ordained rules of the game unwisely dictate or the presumed paucity of other options. Conveniently, creating different rules and better options should lead to more socially desirable behavior. That opens the door to enhancing the opportunities and potential for internal firm flexibility in patterns of work organization, such as offering various forms of public support to firms providing greater job security as the logical trade-off for greater worker adaptability and cooperative reallocation.

A vigorous work reorganization policy, based on the general acceptance of my arguments and backed by political will, can operate in several dimensions. On the job, it would stimulate and reinforce the efforts of firms to develop the skills and flexibility of their workers. Wage subsidies and tax credits for skill development programs, joint private-public and union-management training ventures, statutory support for participative arrangements, expert advice and assistance for small firms lacking the ability to mount such efforts—all such and similar programs would signal the seriousness of a national commitment to raise the productivity and resiliency of our work force. Off the job, it would entail an expanded commitment to human capital development for all and the creation of training and educational programs of universal application and availability rather than having reduced and inadequate versions of such activities merely functioning as a makeshift safety net for the less fortunate. It would enhance geographical and occupational mobility, especially for various categories of workers whose mobility is, for one reason or another (e.g., age, literacy, language competence, discrimination), more severely constrained.

Many elements of this kind of work reorganization policy have, in fact, been tried, and the results have not been uniformly favorable. That experience provides warnings and cautions. Such measures can adversely affect particular regions, occupations, and industries. For instance, areas and sectors dependent upon less-skilled and low-wage labor will be less than thrilled about the reduction in their normal pool of workers. Similarly, those in industries in which the newly trained are entering may have visions of a fixed pie and smaller slices. And, as alluded to earlier, such programs can easily fall prey to all those seeking to privately gain therefrom, and in any case usually confront a "political feasibility tax" with benefits distributed according to the principle that each jurisdictional entity must at least get some prize. Such difficulties, however, need not be fatal flaws. Indeed, the very successful West German apprenticeship programs and Swedish active labor market policies are indicative of the potential for improvement.[10] Obstacles should be viewed as challenges to overcome rather than as reasons for never beginning. In sum, the purpose of expanding organizational choice would be to establish conditions and incentives for firms to respond to the evolving international division of labor and changing economic environment in ways that are both privately and socially optimal, and to institute public programs that reinforce those necessary changes. We dare not do any less.

---

10. For an excellent appraisal of the German and Swedish arrangements, see Osterman 1988.

Bibliography

Addison, John T., and Barry T. Hirsch. 1989. "Union Effects on Productivity, Profits, and Growth: Has the Long Run Arrived?" *Journal of Labor Economics* 7 (January): 72–105.

Akerlof, George A. 1982. "Labor Contracts as Partial Gift Exchange." *Quarterly Journal of Economics* 97 (November): 543–69.

———. 1984. "Gift Exchange and Efficiency-Wage Theory: Four Views." *American Economic Review* 74 (May): 79–83.

Akerlof, George A., Andrew K. Rose, and Janet L. Yellen. 1988. "Job Switching and Job Satisfaction in the U.S. Labor Market." *Brookings Papers on Economic Activity* 2:495–582.

Alchian, Armen A., and Harold Demsetz. 1972. "Production, Information Costs, and Economic Organization." *American Economic Review* 62 (December): 777–95.

Alchian, Armen A., and Susan Woodward. 1988. "The Firm Is Dead; Long Live the Firm: A Review of Oliver E. Williamson's *The Economic Institutions of Capitalism.*" *Journal of Economic Literature* 26 (March): 65–79.

Allen, Steven G. 1981. "Compensation, Safety, and Absenteeism: Evidence from the Paper Industry." *Industrial and Labor Relations Review* 34 (January): 207–18.

Annable, James E., Jr. 1984. *The Price of Industrial Labor.* Lexington, Mass.: Lexington Books.

Aoki, Masahiko. 1980. "A Model of the Firm as a Stockholder-Employee Cooperative Game." *American Economic Review* 70 (September): 600–610.

———. 1988a. "A New Paradigm of Work Organization: The Japanese Experience." In *Wider Working Papers*, WP 36, 1–68. Helsinki: World Institute for Development Economics Research.

———. 1988b. *Information, Incentives, and Bargaining in the Japanese Economy.* Cambridge: Cambridge University Press.

———. 1990. "Toward an Economic Model of the Japanese Firm." *Journal of Economic Literature* 28 (March): 1–27.

———, ed. 1984. *The Economic Analysis of the Japanese Firm.* Amsterdam: Elsevier Science Publishers.

Arnott, Richard J., and Joseph E. Stiglitz. 1985. "Labor Turnover, Wage Structure, and Moral Hazard: The Inefficiency of Competitive Markets." *Journal of Labor Economics* 3 (October): 434–62.

Ashenfelter, Orly. 1982. "A Review Symposium." *Industrial Relations* 21 (Winter): 73–77.

Ashenfelter, Orly, and Richard Layard, eds. 1986. *Handbook of Labor Economics*, vol. 2. Amsterdam: North-Holland.

Askildsen, Jan Erik, Norman J. Ireland, and Peter J. Law. 1988. "Some Consequences of Differential Shareholders among Members in a Labor-Managed and Labor-Owned Firm." In Jones and Svejnar 1988, 65–81.

Barron, John M., John Bishop, and William C. Dunkleberg. 1985. "Employer Search: The Interviewing and Hiring of New Employees." *Review of Economics and Statistics* 67 (February): 43–52.

Barzelay, Michael, and Lee R. Thomas III. 1986. "Is Capitalism Necessary?" *Journal of Economic Behavior and Organization* 7 (September): 225–33.

Becker, Gary S. 1975. *The Economic Approach to Human Behavior*. Chicago: University of Chicago Press.

Best, Fred. 1978. "Preferences on Worklife Scheduling and Work-Leisure Trade-offs." *Monthly Labor Review* 101 (June): 31–37.

Bishop, John. 1987. "The Recognition and Reward of Employee Performance." *Journal of Labor Economics* 5 (October): S36–S56.

Blinder, Alan S., ed. 1990. *Paying for Productivity*. Washington, D.C.: Brookings Institution.

Bonin, John P., and Louis Putterman. 1987. *Economics of Cooperation and the Labor-Managed Economy*. Chur, Switzerland: Harwood Academic Publishers.

Bowles, Samuel. 1985. "The Production Process in a Competitive Economy: Walrasian, Neo-Hobbesian, and Marxian Models." *American Economic Review* 75 (March): 16–36.

Bowles, Samuel, and Herbert Gintis. 1988. "Contested Exchange: Political Economy and Modern Economic Theory." *American Economic Review* 78 (May): 145–50.

————. 1990. "Contested Exchange: New Microfoundations for the Political Economy of Capitalism" and "Reply to Our Critics." *Politics and Society* 18 (June): 165–222, 293–315.

Brown, Charles. 1980. "Equalizing Differences in the Labor Market." *Quarterly Journal of Economics* 94 (February): 113–34.

Brown, Charles, and James Medoff. 1989. "The Employer Size Wage Effect." National Bureau of Economic Research. Working Paper no. 2870.

Brown, William, and Peter Nolan. 1988. "Wages and Labor Productivity." *British Journal of Industrial Relations* 26 (November): 339–62.

Burtless, Gary, ed. 1990. *A Future of Lousy Jobs*. Washington, D.C.: Brookings Institution.

Carmichael, H. Lorne. 1989. "Self-Enforcing Contracts, Shirking, and Life-Cycle Incentives." *Journal of Economic Perspectives* 3 (Fall): 65–83.

————. 1990. "Efficiency Wage Models of Unemployment: A Survey." *Economic Inquiry* 28 (April): 269–95.

Coase, Ronald. 1937. "The Nature of the Firm." *Economica* 4 (November): 386–405.

Commission on Workforce Quality and Labor Market Efficiency. 1989. *Investing in People*. Washington, D.C.: U.S. Government Printing Office.

Conte, Michael A., and Jan Svejnar. 1990. "The Performance Effects of Employee Ownership Plans." In Blinder 1990, 143–72.

Davis, Steve J., and John Haltiwanger. 1991. "Wage Dispersion between and within U.S. Manufacturing Plants." Mimeo.

Dertouzas, Michael C., Richard K. Lester, Robert M. Solow, and the MIT Commission on Industrial Productivity. 1989. *Made in America*. Cambridge, Mass.: MIT Press.

Dickens, William T., and Lawrence F. Katz. 1987. "Inter-Industry Wage Differences and Theories of Wage Determination." National Bureau of Economic Research. Working Paper no. 2271.

Dickens, William T., Lawrence F. Katz, Kevin Lang, and Lawrence Summers. 1989. "Employee Crime and the Monitoring Puzzle." *Journal of Labor Economics* 7 (July): 331–47.

Dickens, William T., and Kevin Lang. 1985. "A Test of Dual Labor Market Theory." *American Economic Review* 75 (June): 792–805.

Dow, Gregory K. 1987. "The Function of Authority in Transaction Cost Economics." *Journal of Economic Behavior and Organization* 8 (March): 13–38.

Dubin, Robert, ed. 1976. *Handbook of Work, Organization, and Society.* Chicago: Rand McNally.

Duncan, Greg J., and Frank P. Stafford. 1980. "Do Union Members Receive Compensating Wage Differentials?" *American Economic Review* 70 (June): 355–71.

Dunn, L. F. 1977. "Quantifying Nonpecuniary Returns." *Journal of Human Resources* 12 (Summer): 347–59.

Edwards, Paul K. 1990. "The Politics of Conflict and Consent: How the Labor Contract Really Works." *Journal of Economic Behavior and Organization* 13 (January): 41–61.

Edwards, Paul K., and Hugh Scullion 1982. *The Social Organization of Industrial Conflict.* Oxford: Blackwell.

Edwards, Richard C. 1979. *Contested Terrain: The Transformation of the Workplace in the Twentieth Century.* New York: Basic Books.

Ehrenberg, Ronald G. 1990. "Comment." In Blinder 1990, 89–94.

Ehrenberg, Ronald G., and Robert S. Smith. 1982. *Modern Labor Economics.* Glenview, Ill.: Scott, Foresman.

Estrin, Saul, and Virginie Perotin. 1987. "Producer Cooperatives: The British Experience." *International Review of Applied Economics.* 1:152–75.

Eswaran, Mukesh, and Ashok Kotwal. 1984. "The Moral Hazard of Budget Breaking." *Rand Journal of Economics* 15 (Winter): 578–81.

Ettlie, John E. 1988. *Taking Charge of Manufacturing.* San Francisco: Jossey-Bass.

Flanagan, Robert J. 1984. "Implicit Contracts, Explicit Contracts, and Wages." *American Economic Review* 74 (May): 345–49.

———. 1990. "The Economics of Unions and Collective Bargaining." *Industrial Relations* 29 (Spring): 300–315.

Fogel, Walter. 1979. "Occupational Earnings: Market and Institutional Influence." *Industrial and Labor Relations* Review 33 (October): 24–35.

Fox, Alan. 1974. *Beyond Contract: Work, Power, and Trust Relations.* London: Faber and Faber.

Frank, Robert H. 1984. "Are Workers Paid Their Marginal Product?" *American Economic Review* 74 (September): 549–71.

———. 1985. *Chooosing the Right Pond.* New York: Oxford University Press.

Frantz, Roger S. 1988. *X-Efficiency: Theory, Evidence, and Applications.* Boston: Kluwer Academic Press.

Freeman, Richard B., and James Medoff. 1979. "The Two Faces of Unionism." *Public Interest* 57 (Fall): 69–93.

———. 1984. *What Do Unions Do?* New York: Basic Books.

Gibbons, Robert, and Lawrence Katz. 1989. "Does Unmeasured Ability Explain Inter-Industry Wage Differences?" Harvard Institute of Economic Research Discussion Paper no. 1464.

Gordon, David M., Richard Edwards, and Michael Reich. 1982. *Segmented Work and Divided Workers.* New York: Cambridge University Press.

Green, Francis. 1988. "Neo-Classical and Marxian Conceptions of Production." *Cambridge Journal of Economics* 12 (September): 299–312.

Greene, William H. 1986. "Frontier Production Functions: Comment." *Econometric Reviews* 4:335–38.

Greenwald, Bruce C., and Joseph E. Stiglitz. 1988. "Examining Alternative Macroeconomic Theories." *Brookings Papers on Economic Activity* 1:207–60.

Groschen, Erica L. 1988. "Sources of Wage Dispersion: The Contribution of Interemployer Wage Differentials within Industry." Federal Reserve Bank of Cleveland, Working Paper no. 8802.

Grout, Paul A., and Ian Jewitt. 1988. "Employee Buy-Outs: Some Theoretical Issues." *International Journal of Industrial Organization* 6 (March): 33–46.

Hall, Robert E. 1980. "Employment Fluctuations and Wage Rigidity." *Brookings Papers on Economic Activity* 1:91–123.

———. 1988. "Comments." *Brookings Papers on Economic Activity* 2:587–91.

Hall, Robert E., and Edward P. Lazear. 1984. "The Excess Sensitivity of Layoffs and Quits to Demand." *Journal of Labor Economics* 2 (April): 233–57.

Hashimoto, Masanori. 1981. "Firm-Specific Capital as a Shared Investment." *American Economic Review* 71 (June): 475–82.

———. 1990. "Employment and Wage Systems in Japan and Their Implications for Productivity." In Blinder 1990, 245–94.

Hashimoto, Masanori, and Ben T. Yu. 1980. "Specific Capital, Employment Contracts, and Wage Rigidity." *Bell Journal of Economics* 11 (Autumn): 536–49.

Helwege, Jean. 1989. "Sectoral Shifts and Interindustry Wage Differentials." Federal Reserve Board. Finance and Economics Discussion Series no. 102.

Hodgson, Geoffrey M. 1982. "Theoretical and Policy Implications of Variable Productivity." *Cambridge Journal of Economics* 6 (September): 213–26.

Holmstrom, Bengt. 1982. "Moral Hazard in Teams." *Bell Journal of Economics* 13 (Autumn): 324–40.

Hutchens, Robert M. 1989. "Seniority, Wages, and Productivity: A Turbulent Decade." *Journal of Economic Perspectives* 3 (Fall): 49–64.

Jacoby, Sanford M. 1990. "The New Institutionalism: What Can It Learn from the Old?" *Industrial Relations* 29 (Spring): 316–40.

Jacoby, Sanford M., and Daniel J. B. Mitchell. 1990. "Sticky Stories: Economic Explanations of Employment and Wage Rigidity." *American Economic Review*, 80 (May): 33–37.

Jensen, Michael C., and W. H. Meckling. 1979. "Rights and Production Functions: An Application to Labor-Managed Firms and Codetermination." *Journal of Business,* 52 (October): 469–506.

Jones, Derek C., and Jan Svejnar, eds. 1982. *Participatory and Self-Managed Firms.* Lexington, Mass.: D. C. Heath.

———. 1988. *Advances in the Economic Analysis of Participatory and Labor-Managed Firms.* Vol. 3. Greenwich, Conn.: JAI Press.

Kahn, Laurence M. 1989. Review of Leibenstein 1987. *Industrial and Labor Relations Review,* 42 (April): 472–73.

Kanemoto, Yoshitsugu, and W. Bentley MacLeod. 1988. "The Theory of Contracts and Labor Practices in Japan and the United States." Institute of Socioeconomic Planning. Discussion Paper Series, no. 363. University of Tsukaba, Japan.

Katz, Lawrence, and Lawrence Summers. 1989. "Industry Rents: Evidence and Implications," *Brookings Papers on Economic Activity.* 1: 209–75.

Kaufman, Bruce E., ed. 1988. *How Labor Markets Work: Reflections on Theory and Practice.* Lexington, Mass.: Lexington Books.

Keynes, John Maynard. 1936. *The General Theory of Employment, Interest, and Money.* New York: Harcourt, Brace.

Klein, Lisl. 1976. *New Forms of Work Organization.* Cambridge: Cambridge University Press.

Kletzer, Lori. 1989. "Returns to Seniority after Permanent Job Loss." *American Economic Review* 79 (June): 536–43.

Kochan, Thomas, Robert B. McKersie, and Peter Cappelli. 1984. "Strategic Choice and Industrial Relations Theory." *Industrial Relations* 23 (Winter): 16–39.

Krueger, Alan, and Lawrence Summers. 1988. "Efficiency Wages and the Interindustry Wage Structure." *Econometrica* 56 (March): 259–93.

Kruse, Douglas L. 1990. "The Economic Implications of Employment Rights and Practices in the United States." *Journal of Comparative Economics* 14 (June): 221–53.

Lang, Kevin, and Jonathan S. Leonard. 1987. *Unemployment and the Structure of Labor Markets.* New York: Basil Blackwell

Lang, Kevin, Jonathan S. Leonard, and David M. Lilien. 1987. "Labor Market Structure, Wages, and Unemployment." In Lang and Leonard: 1–16.

Layard, Richard, and Stephen Nickell. 1989. "The Thatcher Miracle?" Centre for Labour Economics, London School of Economics. Discussion Paper no. 343: 1–42.

Lazear, Edward P. 1981. "Agency, Earnings Profiles, Productivity, and Hours Restriction." *American Economic Review* 71 (September): 606–20.

———. 1989. "Pay Equality and Industrial Politics." *Journal of Political Economy* 97 (June): 561–80.

Leibenstein, Harvey. 1966. "Allocative Efficiency vs. X-Efficiency." *American Economic Review* 56 (June): 392–415.

———. 1976. *Beyond Economic Man.* Cambridge, Mass.: Harvard University Press.

———. 1987. *Inside the Firm.* Cambridge, Mass.: Harvard University Press.

Leonard, Jonathan S. 1987. "Carrots and Sticks: Pay, Supervision, and Turnover." *Journal of Labor Economics* 5 (October): S136–52.

Levine, David I., and Laura D'Andrea Tyson. 1990. "Participation, Productivity, and the Firm's Environment." In Blinder 1990, 183–237.

Levy, Frank. 1988. "Incomes, Families, and Living Standards." In Litan, Lawrence, and Schultze 1988, 108–53.

Litan, Robert E., Robert Z. Lawrence, and Charles L. Schultze, eds. 1988. *American Living Standards: Threats and Challenges.* Washington, D.C.: Brookings Institution.

Lucas, Robert E. B. 1977. "Hedonic Wage Equations and Psychic Wages in the Returns to Schooling." *American Economic Review* 67 (September): 549–58.

Lupton, Thomas. 1976. "Shop Floor Behavior." In Dubin 1976, 171–203.

MacLeod, W. Bentley. 1988. "Equity, Efficiency, and Incentives in Cooperative Teams." In Jones and Svejnar 1988, 3–23.

MacLeod, W. Bentley, and James M. Malcomson. 1989. "Implicit Contracts, Incentive Compatibility, and Involuntary Unemployment." *Econometrica* 57 (March): 447–80.

McCloskey, Donald. 1990. "Their Blackboard, Right or Wrong: A Comment on Contested Exchange." *Politics and Society* 18 (June): 223–32.

Marglin, Stephen. 1974. "What Do Bosses Do? The Origins and Functions of Hierarchy in Capitalist Production." *Review of Radical Political Economy* 6 (Summer): 33–60.

Marsden, David W. 1986. *The End of Economic Man?* New York: St. Martin's Press.

Meade, James E. 1972. "The Theory of the Labor-Managed Firm and Profit-Sharing." *Economic Journal* 82 (March): 402–28.

Metcalf, David. 1989. "Water Notes Dry Up: The Impact of the Donovan Reform Proposals and Thatcherism at Work on Labor Productivity in British Manufacturing Industry." *British Journal of Industrial Relations* 27 (March): 1–31.

Milgrom, Paul R. 1988. "Employment Contracts, Influence Actvities, and Efficient Organization Design." *Journal of Political Economy* 96 (February): 42–60.

Milgrom, Paul R., and John Roberts. 1988. "Economic Theories of the Firm: Past, Present, and Future." *Canadian Journal of Economics* 21 (August): 444–59.

Mitchell, Daniel J. B. 1982. "Gain Sharing: An Anti-Inflation Reform." *Challenge* 25 (July-Aug.): 18–25.

———. 1989. "Wage Pressures and Labor Shortages: The 1960s and 1980s." *Brookings Papers on Economic Activity* 2:191–231.

Mitchell, Daniel J., and Mahmood A. Zaidi, guest eds. 1990a. "A Symposium: The Economics of Human Resource Management." *Industrial Relations* 29 (Spring): 155–359.

———. 1990b. "Symposium Introduction." *Industrial Relations* 29 (Spring): 155–63.

———. 1990c. "Macroeconomic Conditions and HRM-IR Practices." *Industrial Relations* 29 (Spring): 164–88.

Mitchell, Daniel J., David Lewin, and Edward E.Lawler III. 1990. "Alternative Pay Systems, Firm Performance, and Productivity." In Blinder 1990, 15–88.

Miyazaki, Hajime. 1984. "On Success and Dissolution of the Labor-Managed Firm in the Capitalist Environment." *Journal of Political Economy* 92 (October): 909-931.

Mortenson, Dale T. 1978. "Specific Capital and Labor Turnover." *Bell Journal of Economics* 9 (Autumn): 972–90.

———. 1986. "Job Search and Labor Market Analysis." In Ashenfelter and Layard 1986, 849–919.

Nalbantian, Haig. R., ed. 1987. *Incentives, Cooperation, and Risk Sharing*. Totowa, N.J.: Rowman and Littlefield.

Nelson, Richard, and Sidney Winter. 1982. *An Evolutionary Theory of Economic Change*. Cambridge, Mass.: Harvard University Press.

Newbery, David M., and Joseph E. Stiglitz. 1987. "Wage Rigidity, Implicit Contracts, Unemployment and Economic Efficiency." *Economic Journal* 97 (June): 416–30.

Newell, A, and J. Symons. 1989. "The Passing of the Golden Age." Centre for Labour Economics, London School of Economics. Discussion Paper no. 347:1–36.

Nolan, Peter, and William Brown. 1983. "Competition and Workplace Wage Determination." *Oxford Bulletin of Economics and Statistics*, 45 (August): 269–87.

Nordhaus, William D. 1984. "Reflections on the Current State of Macroeconomic Theory." *American Economic Review* 74 (May): 419–21.

Noyelle, Thierry. 1987. *Beyond Industrial Dualism: Market and Job Segmentation in the New Economy*. Boulder, Colo.: Westview Press.

Oi, Walter Y. 1983. "The Fixed Employment Costs of Specialized Labor." In Triplett 1983, 63–116.

Okun, Arthur M. 1981. *Prices and Quantities: A Macroeconomic Analysis*. Washington, D.C.: Brookings Institution.

Osterman, Paul. 1988. *Employment Futures*. New York: Oxford University Press.

———. 1989. "New Technology and the Organization of Work: A Review of the Issues." In U.S. Department of Labor 1989, 5–13.

Osterman, Paul, ed. 1984. *Internal Labor Markets*. Cambridge, Mass.: MIT Press.

Parsons, Donald O. 1986. "The Employment Relationship: Job Attachment, Work Effort, and the Nature of Contracts." In Ashenfelter and Layard 1986, 789–848.

Pemberton, James. 1985. "A Model of Wage and Employment Dynamics with Endogenous Preferences." *Oxford Economic Papers* 37 (September): 448–65.

Pencavel, John. 1987. Review of Marsden 1986, *Journal of Economic Literature* 25 (Dec.): 1897–98.

Perry, George L. 1980. "Inflation in Theory and Practice." *Brookings Papers on Economic Activity* 1:207–41.

———. 1983. "What Have We Learned About Inflation?" *Brookings Papers on Economic Activity* 2:587–602.

Phillimore, John. 1989. "Flexible Specialization, Work Organization, and Skills." *New Technology, Work, and Employment* 4 (Autumn): 79–91.

Piore, Michael J. 1980. "The Technological Foundations of Dualism." In Piore and Berger 1980, 55-81.

———. 1986. "Perspectives on Labor Market Flexibility." *Industrial Relations* 25 (Spring): 146–66.

———. 1989. "Corporate Reform in American Manufacturing and the Challenge to Economic Theory." MIT Department of Economics. Working Paper no. 533.

Piore, Michael J., and Suzanne Berger. 1980. *Dualism and Discontinuity in Industrial Societies*. Cambridge: Cambridge University Press.

Pryor, Frederic L. 1983. "The Economics of Production Cooperatives: A Readers Guide." *Annals of Public and Cooperative Economy* 54 (April–June): 133–72.

Putterman, Louis. 1984. "On Some Recent Explanations Why Capital Hires Labor," *Economic Inquiry* 22 (April): 171–87.

———. 1986a. "The Economic Nature of the Firm: Overview." In Putterman 1986b, 1–43.

———. 1987. "Corporate Governance and Risk-Bearing." *Journal of Institutional and Theoretical Economics* 143 (September): 422–34.

Putterman, Louis, ed. 1986b. *The Economic Nature of the Firm: A Reader*. Cambridge: Cambridge University Press.

Reder, Melvin W. 1989. *Industrial and Labor Relations Review* 42 (April): 456–59.

Robertson, Dennis H. 1952. *Utility and All That*. London: George Allen and Unwin.

Robinson, Joan. 1951. "The Pure Theory of International Trade." *Collected Economic Papers.* 1:182–205. Oxford: Basil Blackwell.

Rosenberg, Sam. 1989. "From Segmentation to Flexibility." *Labour and Society* 14 (October): 363–407.

Rozen, Marvin E. 1982. "Job Quality, Labor Market Disequilibrium, and Some Macroeconomic Implications." *Journal of Economic Issues* 16 (September): 731–57.

———. 1983. *The Economics of Work Reorganization.* New York: Praeger.

———. 1985. "Maximizing Behavior: Reconciling Neoclassical and X-Efficiency Approaches." *Journal of Economic Issues* 19 (September): 661–85.

Samuelson, Paul A. 1989. "Robert Solow: An Affectionate Portrait." *Journal of Economic Perspectives* 3 (Summer): 91–8.

Schiller, Bradley R., and Randall D. Weiss. 1981. "Pensions and Wages: A Test for Equalizing Differences." *Review of Economics and Statistics* 62 (November) 529–38.

Schlicht, Ekkehart, and Carl C. von Weizsacker. 1977. "Risk Financing in Labour-Managed Economies: The Commitment Problem." *Zeitschrift für die Gesammelten Staatswissenschaften,* Special Issue, 53–66.

Schmidt, Peter. 1986. "Frontier Production Functions" and "Reply." *Econometric Reviews* 4:289–328, 353–55.

Schultze, Charles L. 1977. *The Public Use of Private Interest.* Washington, D.C.: Brookings Institution.

———. 1985. "Microeconomic Efficiency and Nominal Wage Stickiness." *American Economic Review* 75 (March): 1–15.

Scitovsky, Tibor. 1976. *The Joyless Economy.* New York: Oxford University Press.

———. 1980. "Can Capitalism Survive? An Old Question in a New Setting." *American Economic Review* 70 (May): 1–9.

Sertel, Murat R., Ed. 1982. *Workers and Incentives.* New York: North Holland.

Shaiken, Harley, Stephen Herzenberg, and Sarah Kuhn. 1986. "The Work Process under More Flexible Production." *Industrial Relations,* 25 (Spring): 167–83.

Shapiro, Carl, and Joseph E. Stiglitz. 1984. "Equilibrium Unemployment as a Worker Discipline Device." *American Economic Review,* 74 (June): 433–44.

Smith, Robert S. 1979. "Compensating Wage Differentials and Public Policy: A Review." *Industrial and Labor Relations Review,* 32 (April): 339–52.

Solow, Robert M. 1980. "On Theories of Unemployment." *American Economic Review* 70 (March): 1–11.

Stephen, Frank H. 1984. *The Economic Analysis of Producers' Cooperatives.* New York: St. Martin's Press.

Stiglitz, Joseph E. 1975. "Incentives, Risk, and Information: Notes Toward a Theory of Hierarchy." *Bell Journal of Economics,* 6 (Autumn): 552–79.

———. 1987. "The Causes and Consequences of the Dependence of Quality on Price." *Journal of Economic Literature,* 25 (March): 1–48.

Strauss, George. 1975. "Organization Development." In Dubin 1976, 617–85.

Thurow, Lester C. 1975. *Generating Inequality.* New York: Basic Books.

Triplett, Jack E. 1983. *The Measurement of Labor Cost.* Chicago: University of Chicago Press.

Turnbull, Peter J. 1988. "The Economic Theory of Trade Union Behavior: A Critique." *British Journal of Industrial Relations* 26 (March): 99–118.

Ulman, Lloyd. 1990. "Labor Market Analysis and Concerted Behavior." *Industrial Relations* 29 (Spring): 281–99.

U.S. Department of Labor. Bureau of Labor-Management Relations and Cooperative Programs. 1989. *The Challenge of New Technology to Labor-Management Relations.* BLMR 135. Washington, D.C.: Bureau of Labor-Management Relations and Cooperative Programs.

Vanek, Jaroslav. 1970. *The General Theory of Labor-Managed Market Economies.* Ithaca, N.Y.: Cornell University Press.

Viscusi, W. Kip. 1979. *Employment Hazards: An Investigation of Market Performance.* Cambridge, Mass.: Harvard University Press.

Walton, Richard E., and Robert B. McKersie. 1989. "Managing New Technology and Labor Relations: An Opportunity for Mutual Influence." In U.S. Department of Labor 1989, 33–43.

Ward, Benjamin. 1957. "The Firm in Illyria: Market Syndicalism." *American Economic Review* 68 (October): 566–89.

Weiermair, Klaus, and Mark Perlman, eds. 1990. *Studies in Economic Rationality.* Ann Arbor: University of Michigan Press.

Weitzman, Martin L., and Douglas L. Kruse. 1990. "Profit Sharing and Productivity." In Blinder 1990, 95–140.

Williamson, Oliver E. 1979. "Transaction-Cost Economics: The Governance of Contractual Relations." *Journal of Law and Economics* 22 (October): 233–62.

———. 1980. "The Organization of Work: A Comparative Institutional Assessment." *Journal of Economic Behavior and Organization* 1 (March): 5–38.

———. 1985. *The Economic Institutions of Capitalism: Firms, Markets, Relational Contracting.* New York: Free Press.

Williamson, Oliver E., Michael L. Wachter, and Jeffrey E. Harris. 1975. "Understanding the Employment Relation: The Analysis of Idiosyncratic Exchange." *Bell Journal of Economics* 6 (Spring): 250–78.

Willis, Robert J. 1986. "Wage Determinants: A Survey and Reinterpretation of Human Capital Earnings Functions." In Ashenfelter and Layard 1986, 525–602.

Wolfstetter, Elmar, Murray Brown, and Georg Meran. 1984. "Optimal Employment and Risk Sharing in Illyria: The Labor-Managed Firm Reconsidered." *Zeitschrift für die Gesammelten Staatswissenschaften* 140 (December): 655–68.

Wright, Gavin. 1986. *Old South, New South.* New York: Basic Books.

Yarbrough, Beth V., and Robert M. Yarbrough. 1988. "The Transactional Structure of the Firm." *Journal of Economic Behavior and Organization* 10 (July): 1–28.

Yellen, Janet L. 1984. "Efficiency Wage Models of Unemployment." *American Economic Review* 74 (May): 200–05.

Yorks, Lyle, and David A. Whitsett. 1989. *Scenarios of Change: Advocacy and the Diffusion of Job Redesign in Organizations.* New York: Praeger.

Index

Wage determination: and compensating differentials, 18, 23–36, 51; and equal pay for equal workers, 17, 18, 36–37, 51; and wage-productivity links, 17, 18, 20–22, 51
Wage differentials, 39, 51
Wage norms, 37, 58
Wage-productivity links, 2, 17, 18, 20–22, 45, 46, 51, 52, 97–98n.13, 103
Wages, multifunctionality of, 18–19, 20–22, 38
Weitzman, Martin L., 174
West Germany, 185
Williamson, Oliver E., 58–59, 75, 173
Women, in the work force, 32
Woodward, Susan, 92
Worker heterogeneity, 19, 23, 24, 25–28, 30–36, 52, 53, 176
Worker homogeneity, 24, 28
Workers: collective action by, 50, 51, 52, 59, 60, 61, 66, 72, 122–23n, 126; overqualification of, 18, 41, 42–43, 51; quality of, 28–29, 51, 96–97, 149–50, 182; sources of heterogeneity among, 31–32. *See also* Job-worker matching; Motivation of workers; Participation of workers; Productivity of workers; Worker heterogeneity
Worker selection, 26–27, 51
Work organization, ubiquity of changes in, 41
Work pacing, 45, 46, 49, 61n, 68, 125, 170, 173
Workplace uniformity and standardization, 32–33, 53
Work reorganization: impact of, 81; and job-worker matching, 41, 47, 80; problems in, 53, 145–62, 176–83
Work rhythms, 42, 45, 61n, 68
Work tempo, 42, 45, 49, 61n, 68, 125, 170, 173

X-efficiency, 12n, 58

Yellen, Janet L., 44–46
Yugoslavia, 129

Zaidi, Mahmood A., 43, 111